On Augustine

On Augustine

Rowan Williams

BLOOMSBURY
LONDON · OXFORD · NEW YORK · NEW DELHI · SYDNEY

Bloomsbury Continuum
An imprint of Bloomsbury Publishing Plc

50 Bedford Square   1385 Broadway
London   New York
WC1B 3DP   NY 10018
UK   USA

www.bloomsbury.com

Bloomsbury, Continuum and the Diana logo are trademarks of Bloomsbury Publishing Plc

First published 2016

© Rowan Williams, 2016

Rowan Williams has asserted his right under the Copyright, Designs and Patents Act, 1988, to be identified as Author of this work.

All rights reserved. No part of this publication may be reproduced or transmitted in any form or by any means, electronic or mechanical, including photocopying, recording, or any information storage or retrieval system, without prior permission in writing from the publishers.

No responsibility for loss caused to any individual or organization acting on or refraining from action as a result of the material in this publication can be accepted by Bloomsbury or the author.

British Library Cataloguing-in-Publication Data
A catalogue record for this book is available from the British Library.

Library of Congress Cataloguing-in-Publication data has been applied for.

ISBN: HB: 978-1-4729-2527-5
ePDF: 978-1-4729-2529-9
ePub: 978-1-4729-2528-2

2 4 6 8 10 9 7 5 3 1

Printed and bound in Great Britain by CPI Group (UK) Ltd, Croydon CR0 4YY

To find out more about our authors and books visit www.bloomsbury.com. Here you will find extracts, author interviews, details of forthcoming events and the option to sign up for our newsletters.

Contents

Introduction vii

Abbreviations and Note on Translations xi

1. 'A Question to Myself' Time and Self-Awareness in the *Confessions* 1

2. The Soul in Paraphrase: Augustine as Interpreter of the Psalms 25

3. Language, Reality and Desire: The Nature of Christian Formation 41

4. 'Good For Nothing'? Augustine on Creation 59

5. Insubstantial Evil 79

6. Politics and the Soul: Reading the *City of God* 107

7. Augustine on Christ and the Trinity: An Overview 131

8. Wisdom in Person: Augustine's Christology 141

9. The Paradoxes of Self-Knowledge in Augustine's Trinitarian Thought 155

10. *Sapientia*: Wisdom and the Trinitarian Relations 171

11. Augustinian Love 191

God in Search: A Sermon 207

Index 212

Introduction

The chapters that follow were written over a long period, more than twenty-five years in fact. Many of them started life simply as part of my own attempts to make sense of Augustine's arguments as I taught various texts of his to undergraduate classes. I can't say that I began with any overarching theory about how to read Augustine. But – as these essays will show – certain themes emerged as holding together aspects of Augustine's thinking, and so the reader will find some overlap, even repetition, in the discussions here. What has been intriguing is to see how Augustinian scholarship overall has moved in the last quarter of a century towards a fuller appreciation of Augustine as someone who reflects carefully on a central tension in the human condition – between the fact that we have to begin all our thinking and praying in full awareness of our limited, embodied condition and the fact that we are summoned by our creator to go beyond limited and specific desire, reaching out to an endless abundance of life. These essays reflect a small part of that shift in emphasis within the scholarly world – a shift that has not gone without some criticism but which has undoubtedly refreshed everyone's reading of the saint. It has made it harder to repeat the clichés about Augustine's alleged responsibility for Western Christianity's supposed obsession with the evils of bodily existence or sexuality, or its detachment from the world of public ethics, its authoritarian ecclesiastical systems, or its excessively philosophical understanding of God's unity, or whatever else is seen as the root of all theological evils. Textbooks still recycle some of this, alas, as do popular works of religious history. But the case for the defence is now grounded in a formidable range of learned monographs in most of the main European languages; and it is not likely that we shall ever go back uncritically to the earlier paradigms.

In pursuing these readings of Augustine over the years, I have been helped and stimulated more than I can readily say by many colleagues and students.

Apart from the immense encouragement of older scholars who had done so much of the groundwork for a new approach to Augustine – especially Gerald Bonner, Henry Chadwick and Robert Markus – I owe a great debt to a number of younger researchers, some of whom I had the privilege of supervising for part of their studies. Among this younger generation, Lewis Ayres, Michel Barnes, Robert Dodaro and Carol Harrison have been particularly important in educating me further. More recently, I have benefited from the work of writers like Luigi Gioia, Michael Hanby, Roland Kany, Charles Mathewes, Edward Morgan, Lydia Schumacher, Susannah Ticciati and, of course Miles Hollingworth, whose brilliant synthesis of 2013, *Saint Augustine of Hippo*, draws so many threads of research and interpretation together. In addition to this, I must express my gratitude to other participants in various conferences on the saint – in Dublin, Lancaster, Toronto and Marquette University – and in seminar groups and master classes at successive Oxford Patristics Conferences, where several of the ideas in these chapters had their first airing. The 'new look' in Augustinian studies has made some impact in the wider world of philosophical theology, and the studies collected here have been enriched by conversation with John Milbank, Catherine Pickstock and Graham Ward. My thanks are also due to many friends in the Order of Saint Augustine, in Ireland, the UK and the United States, for generous hospitality and warm support. For several years I had the delight of sharing with the Revd Anthony Meredith SJ the teaching of an Augustine special subject paper in the Oxford Honours School of Theology; his patient, acute and precise interpretations of the texts were a constant stimulus (and reproach) to a less exact mind. And finally, Robin Baird-Smith's enthusiasm for assembling these essays into a book has been a stimulus to get back to work on them; several exasperated researchers over the years have lamented that many of these pieces were proving inaccessible because they had been published in rather out-of-the-way places, and they have Robin to thank for persuading me to pull them together. As always, my gratitude for his support is very great.

Not all of these essays are designed as full-blown academic studies and none of them is primarily concerned with strictly historical or chronological issues. Chapters 1, 2, 7 and 8 were written for a less specialized readership, and Chapters 4, 5 and 11 focus less on the detailed analysis of Augustinian texts than on their use in contemporary debates on various subjects. I am also aware that these essays include no extended discussion of the major controversies of Augustine's episcopal career, the struggles with Donatism and Pelagianism, though these are touched on in passing. This is largely the result of which texts I happened to be teaching, but also of an interest in the fundamental categories of Augustine's work (the nature of human identity or finite selfhood in its relation to God, the character of Trinitarian divine love and its embodiment in Christ) – from which I believe the specific doctrinal concerns about grace and the limits of the Church derive. I hope that the themes outlined in these essays will help to make better sense of certain aspects of Augustine's engagement in these particular controversies; but I recognize that the absence of any treatment of these significant dimensions of Augustine's concerns means that this book has no claim to be a comprehensive approach to the saint's works.

As I have indicated, research on Augustine has flourished abundantly in the last few decades. Rather than rewriting all these pieces so as to take account of more recent work, I have decided to add some brief extra material after some chapters or groups of chapters so as to give some indication of the sort of direction taken by scholarship and interpretation in the years since the original delivery or publication of the essays. These new sections do not aim to provide an exhaustive bibliography, but they should at least sketch in some of the ways in which the field continues to develop.

It will be obvious that I believe Augustine to be a thinker supremely worth engaging with – not only as a specifically Christian mind but as someone whose understanding of subjectivity itself, of what it is to be a speaking and thinking person, is of abiding interest. He grasps, as few if any pre-modern writers did, the way in which the shaping of a sense of self is a narrative business: our memory is central to whatever we mean by the life of 'spirit', conscious appropriation of who we are, and so even if we are seeking a perspective on ourselves and the world that is not bound to the changing life of a material environment, we cannot avoid coming to terms with how the passage of time is inscribed in our knowing (of ourselves and of our world). We cannot develop a practice that will simply allow us to leave time and the body behind and it is something of this absorption in time and the body which makes sense of Augustine's suspicion of both the search for the 'perfect' Church and the idealizing of a contextless free will – that is, his suspicion of what might underlie Donatism and Pelagianism. In an intellectual culture deeply confused about the self, its reality and continuity, Augustine offers some searching and constructive questions about what we know, don't know, can't know and can't doubt in our awareness of ourselves as thinking beings. And for him this is inextricably bound in with how he reads his own story – as one in which the embodied Word of God speaks to and engages with him in the actualities of history, drawing him into a relation with the divine that is in itself eternal and limitless and always rooted in what is learned within a community of material others here and now. He deserves all the lavish attention he has received over the centuries; my hope is that these reflections may prompt some beyond the community of Christian belief and belonging to read him afresh as a thinker who illustrates beyond any doubt that Christian theology can be a vehicle for the most serious reflection on the nature of our humanity: its varieties of self-enslavement, its obscurity to itself, its emergence in relatedness and reciprocity.

Rowan Williams
Cambridge, Lent 2015

Abbreviations and Note on Translations

Abbreviations

civ.	*De civitate Dei (On the City of God)*
conf.	*Confessiones (Confessions)*
div.qu.	*De diversis quaestionibus (On 83 Diverse Questions)*
doctr. chr.	*De doctrina Christiana (On Christian Teaching)*
en.Ps.	*Enarrationes in Psalmos (Discourses on the Psalms)*
ep.	*Epistulae (Letters)*
Gn. adv. Man.	*De Genesi adversus Manichaeos (A Commentary on Genesis against the Manichaeans)*
Gn.litt.	*De Genesi ad litteram (A Literal Commentary on Genesis)*
serm.	*Sermones (Sermons)*
trin.	*De Trinitate (On the Trinity).*

A note on translations

All of Augustine's works are available in English translation, though a number still exist only in rather cumbersome nineteenth century versions. New City Press is producing a new set of translations, *The Works of St Augustine, a Translation for the 21ˢᵗ Century*; these can be strongly recommended. They include an excellent five volume version of the *Enarrationes in Psalmos* (Expositions of the Psalms), and a new version of *De doctrina Christiana* (*Teaching Christianity*). The Oxford World's Classics series also includes a version of this work (*On Christian Teaching*), as well as a translation of the *Confessions* by one of the greatest modern Augustinian expositors, Henry

Chadwick. R.S.Pine-Coffin's Penguin Classics translation of the work has stood the test of time well; but the version by Maria Boulding OSB, published by Ignatius Press, is probably the best and most readable modern version. The Penguin Classics *City of God* by Henry Bettenson (revised in 2003 by G.R.Evans) is the most accessible version of this text. Older translations of the *De trinitate* have been conveniently republished by Veritatis Splendor Publications (2012) and Aeterna Press (2014), but the New City Press version when complete will be the most serviceable for the modern reader.

General studies and biographies

There are countless general introductions to Augustine, but the following are the most outstanding recent surveys:

Peter Brown, *Augustine of Hippo*, 2nd edition, Berkeley CA, University of California Press 2000.

Henry Chadwick, *Augustine: A Very Short Introduction*, Oxford University Press 2001.

Miles Hollingworth, *Saint Augustine of Hippo. An Intellectual Biography*, Oxford University Press 2013.

Robin Lane Fox, *Augustine: Conversions and Confessions*, London, Allen Lane 2015.

James J. O'Donnell, *Augustine, Sinner and Saint*, London, Profile Books 2005.

Philip Rigby, *The Theology of Augustine's Confessions*, Cambridge, Cambridge University Press 2015.

1

'A Question to Myself'
Time and Self-Awareness in the Confessions

I am singing a familiar song: a simple activity, you might think, but, once you start examining it, something rather odd and complex. As the noises come out of my mouth and larynx, my imagination is somehow 'calling up' the words and phrases to come, but without actually presenting them for inspection. From one point of view, you might say that it's like squeezing something from one container into another through a narrow aperture: the future, the next bit of the song, is passing through the present moment into the past. But that can't be quite right: the song is in my memory, in my past, already. What is slipping through the present moment is my continuing performance of a song I have once learned. But that can't be quite right either: the performance doesn't exist as a complete entity, there's nothing that exists ahead of me to move from the area in front of me to the area behind me. And what is going on when I can't remember the next line: is it 'there' or not? Yes, because I learned it once; no, because it is not sitting somewhere waiting to be inspected.

When he reflects on how we should define 'time', Augustine uses a similar example:[1] as I sing a psalm, I have implicitly in mind a whole process which gradually slips from future anticipation into memory. I experience what

---

[1] *conf.* XI. xxviii/38–xxxi/41. Compare the long discussions of memory in X.viii/12–xix, 28.

he calls 'distension', a pulling out of present awareness in memory and expectation; yet it is not that there are objects called 'past' and 'future' which change their volume. What changes is the character of my attention, slipping from recollection to anticipation and vice versa. And what Augustine in effect does is to put a question against the way in which we constantly make it harder for ourselves to think clearly about being an intelligence working in *time* by imagining it in *spatial* terms: the observer turns the light of attention on an observed object. But the shift in attention which Augustine is reflecting upon cannot work like that.

As soon as we try to think about our own acts of thinking, the spatial model is useless. The most ordinary activity of making sense – uttering a connected and intelligible sentence – is in fact quite a strange business: the syllables of a word, the words of a sentence, have to 'vanish' for the sequence to build up and do what it is meant to do. There is no meaning without this passage into *absence* because we cannot accumulate sounds without succession in language. What I am now saying, in any possible present moment, has to disappear, to fall silent and be displaced; even if I think I am repeating something, I shall have displaced one utterance by another, pushed what has just been said into silence and absence, rather than simply retrieving something that is the same. And when I do seek to retrieve what has already been said, I face problems once again: my memory is not a territory, a space, that I can survey at a glance.

My present consciousness is bordered by drifts of sequences, half-grasped or half-recollected connections, neither wholly present nor wholly absent. Understanding myself, understanding what I am saying, involves not only speaking out what I clearly see but listening for those 'drifts', gently interrogating them. All of which leaves tantalizingly unclear just what and where the 'I' is that is doing the interrogating: it is not and cannot be a thing that stands apart from another thing called 'memory': in a crucial sense (as Augustine says explicitly)[2], memory is what I am. The puzzle is that so much of what I am is absent from conscious awareness. To acknowledge the role of memory is to recognize that 'I' am not a simple history to be unveiled and displayed for inspection, nor a self-transparent reasoning subject. To be an

---

[2] Ibid. X.ix/15, xi/18 and especially xvii/26.

intelligence in time is to be inescapably unfinished, consistently in search. I am never just 'there'. *Je est un autre*, 'I am another', might be a summary of much of Augustine's reflection in the *Confessions*.

That is why it is so difficult to read the *Confessions* as an autobiography in either the ancient or the modern sense.[3] Earlier classical and Christian writers had produced narratives of part or all of their lives: Augustine's distinctiveness is the refusal to present a narrative that in any sense claims clarity or finality. Its pivot is at one level obviously his decision to seek baptism, recorded in Book VIII; but in another way the pivotal discussion comes in Book X, where he lays out very fully the unresolved nature of his present feelings and reflects on the whole issue of memory – a reflection followed (to the modern reader's surprise) by three further books dealing with time and creation. Those who have found the unity of the whole work elusive have missed the fact that he is not recording an edifying and coherent life but performing two different tasks. As he says in Book X, he is exposing his continuing confusions and irresolutions as an encouragement to others: you don't have to have made a good story of your life in order to be a faithful Christian. And he is praying.

Purely formally, the whole of the *Confessions* is a prayer; to work out who I am, I need to be speaking to and listening to God. He exploits fully the multiple meanings of the word *confessio* itself: it means any sort of acknowledgement (of sin or of spiritual conviction, for example); but it also means, in the Latin of Augustine's Bible, acknowledging God in prayer and praise.[4]

The agenda of the work is declared at the very beginning, when Augustine, in effect, poses the question of how human beings are capable of this strange activity which is the 'confession' of God. It seems to be utterly natural to us, given that we are (in one of the most frequently quoted phrases of the book[5]) 'restless until [we] rest' in God; yet how can it make sense to invoke or address a reality beyond the scope of any human mind, a reality unknowable but everywhere present?

---

[3]On this, see Charles Mathewes, 'Book One: The Presumptuousness of Autobiography and the Paradoxes of Beginning', in the excellent *Reader's Companion to Augustine's Confessions*, ed. Kim Paffenroth and Robert Peter Kennedy (Louisville, KY: Westminster John Knox Press, 2003), pp. 7–23.
[4]See Pierre Courcelle, *Recherches sur les 'Confessions' de saint Augustin* (Paris: Boccard, 1950), pp.13ff.
[5]I.i/1, a phrase echoing the Neoplatonic conviction that the soul rests only in the One.

The self-exploration that follows can be read as a defence of the possibility of invoking God by seeking to lay bare something of the relation between finite being and an unfathomably gracious creator, and also by arguing that the questioning self itself is also unknowable and uncontainable. It is not that there is a problem with the finite subject addressing the infinite God, moving from the known to the unknown; it is more that, once we have recognized how obscure we are to ourselves we somehow see that only in relation to the infinity of God can we get any purchase on the sort of beings we are – moving through time and 'growing into' ourselves in the encounter with an inexhaustible other. But this in turn requires a whole picture of what finite and time-bound existence is; hence the speculative concluding books of the work.

Augustine is writing against the backdrop of a classical (especially Stoic) tradition much preoccupied with the cultivation and defence of the free exercise of rational choice; interested in how we deploy our mental resources effectively in making clear and defensible decisions.

Although much of his earliest work is still marked by this tradition, the *Confessions* take his thought in a radically different direction. As Charles Mathewes says, 'Augustine wants us to see our lives as much less intelligible than we usually think they are.'[6] He is fascinated by the ways in which will or desire runs ahead of reasoning and by the impossibilities of summoning all the resources of the mind for making clear decisions; by the role of apparent accident in prompting the will to major self-determinations; by the unreasonable jealousies of babies, by the phenomenon we describe by saying 'It's on the tip of my tongue', by the emotional ambiguities of music and the confusion of feeling in the bereaved.

All these are dealt with in the *Confessions* as they are in no other comparable work of the ancient world.

The book itself reproduces the kind of self-awareness I have already characterized as a 'drift of sequences': vivid episodes, elaborated, reflected on, interrupted by sudden, almost violent outbursts of philosophical bewilderment. If there is a narrative coherence to be sought, it is not in the narrator's control (however controlled in a purely literary sense the text may

---

[6]Art. cit., p. 9.

in fact be); as Mathewes insists, there cannot be a Christian self-portrayal that is wholly under the writer's control in any simple way, and Augustine is consistently dramatizing this sense that the root of the matter, the 'beginning', is always elsewhere.

The coherence is given by the divine listener/observer, the God who 'reads' what is being written; and if that is the case, what is written is not finally defined by what is available for human inspection and will naturally avoid attempts at final formulation. I am not there for myself but for God; I can't make the links that will make sense of my life. To know myself truthfully is to know a speaking subject trying, in word and imagination, to come to terms with absence – the absence of God as an object, the absence of final and satisfying objects in the light of the always locally absent but universally pervasive God, the absence of a finished self. I know myself as an act of questioning, a lack and a search, perpetually unsatisfied in this life, yet not frustrated. The self's native climate comes to be seen as a sort of eros without the anxiety to possess.

Is Augustine the first major thinker to understand the self's meaning as involved with loss? Book IV of the *Confessions* (iv/7–x/14) provides an analysis of mourning and melancholia that might well arouse echoes of Freud in the modern ear. He describes how, after the death of an intimate friend, he comes to hate the places associated with him because of the friend's absence: they no longer announce his imminence, 'saying, "Here he comes!"'.[7] Augustine feels that he wants to die himself, yet knows that the misery of his life is preferable to death and that toying with the fantasy of dying to be with his friend is bit of self-indulgent drama. In other moods, he fears death all the more because when he is dead there will be nothing of his friend left. Tears become a consolation of sorts: attachment to the dead friend is translated into attachment to unhappiness itself.

Finally, Augustine leaves the site of his bereavement to avoid his memories. In retrospect, his judgement is that he had failed to love his friend *humaniter*, humanly;[8] he had loved another mortal as though that human other were both immortal and the one necessary object that would complete his own selfhood. He

---

[7] IV/9.
[8] IV.vii/12.

had not taken in the finite otherness of the friend. In the vocabulary of Kleinian theory (which, even more than Freud, resonates with Augustine's account of his growing up), he has failed to move on from the paranoid-schizoid stage (the other is unconditionally there for me, there is no life for me or the other independent of this relation in which my needs are met) to the depressive position (loss is unavoidable but also liveable). We have to grow into 'the capacity to bear the loss of the external presence but nonetheless retain that presence internally in the face of absence, of doubt and uncertainty, of loss of trust, and even of fear of betrayal by the loved one'.[9] It is a theme that will preoccupy Augustine for the rest of his life (we shall see in later chapters some of the ways in which it returns in different contexts): our great temptation is 'inhuman' love, loving the finite for what it cannot be, loving people or things for the magical symbiotic relation they have to my sense of myself, my security and self-identity.

It is in this context, significantly, that Augustine notes the centrality of absence or loss in the simple activity of uttering a sentence: time passes, clinging to any object is clinging to pain and dismembering my soul and thus dismantling language.[10] Melancholic attachment, paranoid-schizoid grief, is a refusal to *speak*, to let time pass so that representation and meaning can happen – not consolation, not explanation, but a position in the world that can be owned and communicated. The paradox, familiar to Augustine and recovered by Hegel, is that this occupying of a position, this adult owning of where I am through speech or thought, can occur only when I have discovered that I am not 'there', that I am not a determinate, fully self-present substance whose needs and desires can be catalogued and negotiated with finality. The depressive position or Hegel's unhappy consciousness or Augustine's therapies of desire are none of them meant to be comprehensive pictures of the self's maturity; but they set out the necessary conditions for anything that could be called maturation, in that they wean us away from the belief that we can take for granted a substantial selfhood there for inspection prior to the processes of mourning that mark our growth.

---

[9] Margot Waddell, *Inside Lives: Psychoanalysis and the Growth of the Personality* (London: Duckworth, 1998), p. 172.
[10] IV.x/15.

But if we say that Augustine's originality lies in defining the self as incomplete and temporal, formed in loss and absence, is there any sense in which this is in his work a specifically religious understanding? And if so, does the theological framing of his account of selfhood end up subverting it? A major modern discussion of Hegel claims that 'God is the idea in which unhappy consciousness projects both its longing for the parent as substance and the overestimation one accords that source precisely when one feels it slipping away'.[11] This needs some spelling out.

The devotional reaching out to another self, but one that is infinite and unchangeable, recognizes the endless character of desire but reassures us that this 'inner' endlessness in the other is also an infinite good will and thus an infinitely desirable reality. The possibility of unending or uncontrolled lack and longing that goes with the recognition of the self's insubstantiality and its creation in and through mourning is in itself frightening; but the fear can be allayed by projecting an infinite attention that meets us at every point of lack, even if we say that it never becomes an object that merely completes the desirous self and removes that self from the risks of time. But: this in turn leaves us with a self whose true character is never at our disposal, a self that is defined by its relation to the fictive otherness of God. We are never 'just' ourselves, which means that that religious devotion leads to self-alienation and self-abasement. Pleasure becomes suspect because it represents the self-coincidence and self-content that religious discourse declares impossible or inadmissible. Given Augustine's well-rehearsed difficulties over sexuality, do we not have to say that the superficially modern or even postmodern self evoked in the *Confessions* collapses back into the crudely self-alienated subjectivity of a faith that uses thinking about God to *prevent* thinking about itself or owning itself? Doesn't theology freeze the unhappy consciousness and leave no dialectical liberation possible?

This is a serious and interesting challenge. I shall not attempt here to discuss at length what Augustine says and does not say about sexuality. It is undeniable that it is one of the recurring preoccupations of the *Confessions* (though not as

---

[11] Walter Davis, *Inwardness and Existence: Subjectivity in/and Hegel, Heidegger, Marx and Freud* (Madison, WI: University of Wisconsin Press, 1989), p. 62.

obsessively as some think); yet it is not simply treated as an index of self-alienation, as something that characterises the body over against the mind or will. Augustine can certainly use such language at times. But he is at least as concerned to see sexual desire as problematic because it is specially liable to become a case of 'inhuman' love. For a variety of reasons, personal and philosophical, Augustine regularly associates sexual desire with fantasy, acquisitiveness and the search for avoidance of loss. And this may make us pause before simply accepting the kind of critique I have just outlined. Augustine is not so much preoccupied with criticizing pleasure as self-content as with challenging a *premature* and limited account of self-content, a reduction of the joy for which we are destined by identifying it with a passing temporal state. Pleasure here is something we talk about; something that belongs with the succession of states of feeling, the alternations of presence and absence, the variety and instability of the world that language represents; the joy we are made for, union with God, is never going to be 'speakable' in that way, never a past or passing moment of self-coincidence.

This is why Augustine must be taken seriously in his repeated denials that God can be thought of as an object that, so to speak, 'outbids' competing objects in gratifying desire. Book X.vi/9 asks what it is that the writer loves in loving God; and the answer is that it is no kind of sense-impression – though he labours, here and elsewhere, the analogy between the delight of encounter with God and the delights of the senses. God is 'the life of my soul's life'; and, as the life of the soul, God must be sought in the soul's characteristic activity, and so, above all, in the memory – not as a remembered object of perception, but in the remembrance of 'joy' or the remembrance of the desire for joy in the truth (X.xxi/30–xxiii/33).

This takes some unpacking. Augustine is not claiming that everyone has a natural recollection of delight in God, simply that we are all aware of states of attunement to reality which we value and seek to recover. We desire to be truthful; we cannot intelligibly say that we desire to be deceived. The state of not being deceived is what we long for and intermittently experience; and if we know what this means, we know what it means to love God, even if only in the most inchoate way. But we have already seen in the *Confessions* that the knowledge of the truth is always a knowledge of our incompletion; thus we *cannot* know God as a simple desired object that satisfies us. The openness to God's reality implied in any openness to truth entails an openness to hear what we are not prepared to hear, what challenges our own account of what we desire (X.xxvi/37). There is a gradual and in significant ways painful process of reconceiving desire or configuring it afresh in the light of what is actually encountered. Rather than declaring a straightforward schism between unreformed desire, sensual pleasure and the state of contact with God, Augustine leaves us with an unsettled, always questionable appropriation of pleasure, of desire gratified. What is 'invested' in pleasure? he asks; what weight is given to it in the self's construction of itself? What are the inducements that prompt us to stop with the moment of gratification and to resist loss? In this context, God is, at the very least, the unsettling absence that will pervade sensual pleasure, the meaning that is not said or embodied in any of the meanings of the material world as attempt to digest or mould it.

But that cannot be all. God is not an immense projected object of desire, a definite answer to determinate but humanly unanswerable questions or longings; but neither is God an empty principle of critical instability, a marginal postmodernist gap. God is that which exceeds desire and description; but to speak of encounter with God as a reality wholly prior to and independent of us, we can't avoid borrowing the language of desire and sensuality. The attempt to speak *to* God, the attempt which Augustine undertakes in the *Confessions*, is an attempt to expose the incurable incompleteness of the speaking and remembering subject, in the hope of receiving a unity constructed not by human words and human power (a unity which doesn't therefore need to be *defended* by the anxious and violent deployment of words and power) but by the divine act of seeing and hearing (or reading). It is indeed an act of omnipresent divine attention; but its accessibility does not mean that it is ever capable of being appropriated, moulded to existing and uncriticized or unthought desire, owned in human representation. Because of the sheer investment of the human self in this exposed speaking, the emotional tenor of what is said about God will have about it something of the passions that relate to sensual experience. But because what is in view is the coincidence of the mind not with itself as a settled substance but with the truth of its dependence and incapacity, the experience of God in this life can never be of straightforward fruition or lasting possession, God as the fantasized completion of the self.

Augustine returns more than once, especially in the great work of his later years on the Trinity, to the theme of self-knowledge as knowledge of the unknowing and unfinished self;[12] so that God is known as both the 'witness' to this unfinishedness, never circumscribed by the agenda the self sets, and as the goal to which the incomplete self looks. God's presence is an 'infinite attention'; but that attention is a perspective radically not at our disposal and not determined by what we think we need. It is a mistake to think of this as self-alienation, however: the real self-alienation, so Augustine effectively suggests, lies in the idea of a finite self-coincidence, a state of satisfied desire in which the awareness of incompletion was set aside – which, in Augustine's framework, would mean a state beyond speech or thought, an escape from the finite and from the loss without which we should not learn how to inhabit our human condition.

This leads on to a further dimension of what is set out in the *Confessions*. The seventh book details some of the intellectual struggles that immediately preceded Augustine's return to Catholic Christianity, and in particular his fascination with Neoplatonism. He describes eloquently (in VII.x.16 and xvi.22, for example) his relative success in following the recommendations of the 'books of the Platonists' (whether Plotinus himself or his disciples) for arriving at a vision of intelligible unity: the last remnants of dualistic myth fall away as he grasps the notion of an eternal light of the mind, an *active* truth empowering the finite intellect. As he comprehends the immaterial nature of God, he sees more clearly the immaterial nature of the soul and so the non-substantial nature of evil[13] (that is, not the insignificance of evil but the fact that it is a modification of a substantial reality, not a subject in itself). Systematic introspection, in the sense of an examination of mental processes as they actually work rather than the examination of inner mental objects, brings him to the apprehension of a bodiless God, a recognition that in turn reinforces the freedom of the soul from bodily constraint. But these perceptions fail to produce a change of habit or imagination.

---

[12] See below, Chapter 9.
[13] See below, Chapter 5.

In one of Augustine's most memorable phrases, they fail to present a reality that is 'not just to be looked at but to be lived in'.[14] The vision of timelessness cannot by itself deliver changes in time: in Augustine's own terms, it cannot produce *caritas*, love, the generous impulsion towards new objects. Insofar as such visions may give you the sense of having achieved a stable perspective, a view from eternity, they encourage pride, the false self-confidence that obscures true vision.[15] Change in the direction of *caritas* is produced only by the effect of God's becoming human in Christ. God assumes the form of an earthly, temporal identity, vulnerable to loss and suffering: it is the centrepiece of God's 'rhetoric' in communicating with us, God's persuasion of us, not in argument but in fleshly life. The weakness of God, the presence of God in a mortal life, undermines whatever we take for strength – especially the sense of intellectual or spiritual strength that comes from a visionary metaphysic of the sort Augustine has been exploring. In the world of faith, meanings are found not by appeal to eternal truth as *content* of the mind's processes but by assimilation to God's own acceptance of the limits of time and body. They are found, in fact, by the communal learning of love in association with the fellowship of Jesus; by Catholic baptism.

Augustine's Christ in the *Confessions* is not primarily a teacher of wisdom imparted from heaven. He does indeed communicate wisdom, *sapientia*,[16] but he does so through enabling participation in the pattern of his own entry into time.[17] Christ unites with human flesh, says Augustine (VII.xviii.24), the wisdom that our weak stomachs would otherwise be unable to digest; but in order to digest it, we must recognize our own earthly condition and accept it. Unless and until we can do this, we are not yet, in his phrase (ibid.), sufficiently humble to acknowledge the humble Jesus as God. It is the divine weakness in Jesus' life that challenges us to conversion; when we 'throw ourselves down' upon the weak God, prostrate at our feet, we learn the wisdom that will draw us up to heaven (ibid.).

---

[14]VII.xx.26.
[15]See, e.g. VII.xviii.24, xx.26–end.
[16]See below, Chapters 8 and 10.
[17]See Jean-Marie Le Blond, *Les conversions de saint Augustin* (Paris: Aubier, 1950), pp. 143–5, on Augustine's move from *Gottesmystik* to *Christusmystik*, from a self-reliant attempt to reach the infinite to an acceptance that the *way* is the incarnate Christ, with no short cut by way of ecstasy.

Without that act of abandonment, throwing ourselves down upon the incarnate one, nothing is learned. The ascent to heaven is first a descent to our earth; as with Christ, so with us. This is the element in Augustine's spiritual narrative that most decisively moves beyond his earlier Platonist aspirations for mystical vision. He has described, as we have noted, his own essays in Platonist introspection and their real but limited success; heavenly wisdom, however, ceases to be simply an object of vision and becomes a continuing temporal experience, a way of moving through time, a following of Christ's way.

Knowing God is bound to the passage of time in a new manner; so that to speak of God and the knowledge of God is always going to be in some way connected with narrative. The question of who or what exactly I am, the nature of self or soul, is to be understood in relation to the story of Christ's acceptance of the weakness of mortality. If my identity is determined by the inaccessible but unfailing attention of God's love, the incarnation of the divine Word in Jesus is a declaration that this divine attention is in touch with us and transforming us through a particular worldly series of events transmitted by human telling, active in the present through the historical body of the Church. So to receive what God gives requires the humility that embraces my present mortal and temporal situation – including the embrace of the concrete historical authority of the Church.

Now to suggest that the Church will tell me who I am is something so deeply alien to (probably) a great part of the contemporary religious consciousness that we need to pause a moment on the question. It will sound like the theocratic ambition with which Augustine is sometimes unjustly charged, the confusion of historical institution with the voice of God that has been the curse of Christian history in the eyes of so many. Augustine emphatically believed that no self-scrutiny in an imagined vacuum would deliver to me any knowledge of myself that could make a difference to how I actually behave. I am changed only when I begin to follow the path of Christ and, by grace, to shape a biography of my own that conforms to the contours of his, embracing mortality and limit in order to receive a life beyond mortality and limit. But this way is made specific and tangible in the community of believers, in the common language and practice of the Church.

Accepting the reality of my limit in this way is, of course, another version of accepting the absence in my self-awareness of any moment of perfect self-coincidence; accepting the particular vulnerability of not being in control of memory, not being in control of what I can see of myself. The abandonment shown in humility, falling down upon the prostrate Christ, the dead Christ, is of a piece with the abandonment that is central to the whole enterprise of the *Confessions*, that is, the repudiation of the 'finished' self. Self-knowledge comes as we walk with Christ; our experiences of passing time, the awareness of loss and absence, become intelligible in a new way as they are set in the context of God's 'loss', God's absence from God in the event of the incarnation.[18]

To learn who I am as a consciousness characterized by loss is bound up with encountering the truth of God in a story of loss. Independent of what the incarnation shows us of God, we could conceive God only as alienated from us and without self-relatedness; in the light of Christ incarnate, God's apparent self-estrangement in accepting mortality becomes an assurance of, not a self-coincidence of plain identity but a self-relatedness within which we may find our own reality or truth as grounded in the threefold interaction of divine life that we call the Trinity. And in *Confessions* XIII.xi/12, Augustine offers a first draft of the sort of argument he develops so fully and creatively in his later work on the Trinity, setting side by side the fluid self-relatedness of our own conscious being (being, knowing and willing, in this particular text) and the self-relatedness of God. Ours is a moving image of the eternal plurality of divine life, showing in its time-bound motion something of the timeless relatedness of God. And in that later work Augustine was able to spell out how in fact our own inner self-relatedness would be directed only to a central void if it were not at the same time a relatedness to the eternal love that works at the heart of finite reality, the life of Father, Son and Spirit.

Since – as Augustine would elaborate in other works – it is only in the Catholic fellowship that we properly share the life of *caritas*,[19] love directed where it should be directed, love that is radically other-oriented, then only in

---

[18] To see how this is worked out in the theology of Christ's abandonment and suffering, we must turn to Augustine's sermons on the Psalms; see below, Chapter 2.
[19] This is a major theme of his polemic against the Donatists.

the Church do I understand myself. It is not that an alien institution tells me from outside who and what I am as a conscious human subject, but that there is no intelligible or defensible account of being a person in time independently of what the Catholic faith declares about the nature of divine life. And that declared vision can be made my own only by participation in the common life of Christ's ecclesial Body.

Augustine's initially 'phenomenological' interest in the instability of our self-knowledge is steadily revealed to be part of an integrally theological vision. I do not know myself; but God knows me. God's knowledge of me is available not as a picture I can grasp or as a piece of information, but in the form of trust in God's love – faith, in other words. Such trust is grounded in and enabled by the history of Christ. And that history reveals a divine life of love which secures an eternal place for me within its pattern. That this is learned and realized in the Church means also that such self-knowledge through humility, trust and discipleship can never be a solitary affair; and again, in the *De Trinitate* and elsewhere, the inseparability of my welfare and my neighbour's is carefully worked out in this perspective.

Augustine is not interested in some of the questions which a modern reader would pose – what kind of human self-understanding is therefore available to those outside the visible Body, what role has a non-theological dialectic in clarifying some sorts of truth about human self-awareness. We should not assume his answers – nor indeed assume that his answers would be the only possible ones. But the point is that insofar as the *Confessions* is a book not about individual self-discovery but about a decision for baptism and a complex unfolding discovery of an unexpected vocation, it should not surprise us that the themes traced in this book fit as they do with his broader concerns about Christology, grace and Trinity. He is both an extraordinary 'phenomenologist' of self-awareness and a theologian of his era; a good reading of his work remains sensitive to both. And those who do not accept the theology will still acknowledge the sheer diagnostic skill of the phenomenology.

But to retreat for a moment from the dense interweavings of theological reference and to return to the actual processes of self-examination enacted in the *Confessions*, it should be clear just how, in the light of all this Christological and Trinitarian structure of belief, it becomes *possible* to turn on oneself the kind of comprehensive exploration and interrogation that Augustine undertakes. No particular version of the self that I can construct is finally and infallibly true; in other words, I do not know what may be relevant to the understanding of the ultimate truth of my identity as God sees it. Therefore I am free to acknowledge the variety, the apparent arbitrariness and oddity of what I happen to remember, and to reflect (as Augustine does in Book X) upon the continuing reality of mixed and obscure motivation.

This does not mean that Augustine is writing some sort of early essay in the stream of consciousness style; the book is composed with immense care. But that care of composition is designed precisely to highlight incidents and encounters that are not of obvious 'public' significance in the unfolding of a life but which pose for the narrator certain sorts of question.

Why this kind of reaction to a bereavement? Why this variety of adolescent delinquency? Above all, in Books VII and VIII, why the delay in accepting the Catholic faith? These are not questions answered in the narrative; they are there to illustrate how self-questioning in the presence of God actually works; how becoming 'questionable' to yourself, noticing and wondering about the seemingly arbitrary aspects of your life, flows into the task of speaking with and to God. The indeterminacy of the self we discover means that there is a sort of licence to be interested in all kinds of areas of experience, at all developmental stages, because we cannot know what they contribute in God's eyes. And this surely must be seen as one of the most innovative aspects of the book.

The point may be made if we compare this with other autobiographical styles, ancient and modern. In her 1998 Saint Augustine Lecture,[20] Frances Young compares Augustine with other ancient self-chroniclers, in the light of Georg Misch's 1907 study of autobiography in antiquity, giving special attention to the long autobiographical poem of Gregory Nazianzen. Autobiography in the ancient world is commonly apologetic, but it is also – in a quite broad sense – typological: the individual tells his story as an enactment of some ideal pattern: for Nazianzen, a biblical pattern, or rather a nest of biblical

---

[20]'The *Confessions* of Saint Augustine: What is the Genre of this Work?', *Augustinian Studies*, 30.1 (1999), pp. 1–16.

patterns. *This* story is offered as a paradigm – not in the sense that it represents outstanding, definitive achievement, a sort of heroism in a vacuum, but because it can properly be read as an instance of a pattern, a 'canon', to which others should conform. So autobiography is a bid for one's own narrative to be accepted as illustrating a normative or classic ideal. Hence, so often, the need for apologia: the untidy and questionable parts of a story must be shown not to be inconsistent with this overall claim. Both I as narrator and any particular reader will be invited into a fuller understanding of our shared convictions; but there is an important sense in which I can't, as the present teller of my story in this mode or set of conventions, misunderstand myself.

Young argues very plausibly that we have regularly overlooked the typological elements in Augustine's story. He does not, like Gregory, appeal much to specific biblical stories, but rather to a sort of generalized scriptural identity, a scriptural 'voice', expressed most fully in the Psalms, which speaks of longing, failure, betrayal, acceptance, travel and homecoming. Augustine is a biblical Everyman. But the gap remains between this and other antique models, and it is a gap rather wider than Young's discussion implies. Augustine's personal apologia in the book, undoubtedly a decisive element, is expressed not in an attempt to correct the way others are reading ambiguous events but in a prior moral disarmament: yes, this history is one of real error and apparent waste of time, in sin and procrastination; the miracle is that I am free to confess it all, to bring it into the light as the history that has brought me *here*, to the place where I now stand in the face of God's mercy as God's minister. My justification is in this present place: how any one incident, whether of grace or betrayal, has contributed to my being here is impenetrably obscure.

So I present my story, not as the paradigm performance of a script but as something suggesting to others that their own chaotic delays and avoidances may yet be woven into a self capable of speaking to and for God. This is spelled out in X.iii/3: how does the reader know when an author is telling the truth? Only by the operation of *caritas*, by which the reader hears what the author is saying as something that is being addressed by *God* to the reader as a means of telling that reader the truth of himself or herself. Reading of Augustine's weakness, the reader may, by grace, be made acquainted with their own weakness, and so become strong in the only way that matters for the Christian, strong in the ability to acknowledge failure and seek aid, strong enough to confess in every sense of the word.

So Augustine's answer to a potential misreading of his life, Augustine's apologia, is a bold turning around of the challenge: self-examination is inevitably caught up in misunderstanding, and it is the more serious the more it claims finality: so don't ask about the author, consider your own location in time and change your own self-deception. Within the charity of the believing community, you will find that the way to understand another Christian is through your own repentance, standing consciously before the same merciful God. *Hypocrite lecteur!* And whatever this amounts to, it cannot be characterized as the sort of conventional apologetic that establishes innocence or integrity against attack. Instead it proposes the drastic notion that loving understanding among believers entails a common acknowledgement of incapacity and hiddenness from oneself, and a common reference to God as the ground of mutual intelligibility. It appeals to a solidarity of interrogative self-awareness.

Augustine has been intriguingly compared with another autobiographer in the studies of Ann Hartle.[21] Rousseau, as Hartle presents him, begins from a confidence in the retrievability of the past. It is not that memory in itself is wholly dependable or comprehensive; but the present consciousness in which memory operates is capable of completing memory's lacunae by *imagination*. This raises an interesting question: if imagination works (as Rousseau believes) according to what is possible, how does the reconstructed story of a life, filled out by imagination, differ from the projected narratives of possible futures that Rousseau occasionally presents? The truth of what is narrated as Rousseau's past doesn't depend on *accurate* retrieval so much as on the present sense of imaginative aptness of 'fit'. 'Rousseau, then, is *not* the sum of the details of his life ... The truth is that *no matter* what the details of one's life, one is 'always the same at all times'.[22] Indeed, it would be possible to say that in this respect

---

[21] *The Modern Self in Rousseau's Confessions: A Reply to Saint Augustine* (Notre Dame, IN: University of Notre Dame Press, 1983); 'Augustine and Rousseau: Narrative and Self-Knowledge in the Two Confessions', in Gareth B. Matthews, ed., *The Augustinian Tradition* (Berkeley/Los Angeles/London: University of California Press, 1999), pp. 263–85.

[22] 'Augustine and Rousseau', p. 278.

Rousseau is less a modern than a postmodern autobiographer: it is the present imaginative exercise of the will that grounds the 'true' self (if that expression has any substantive meaning).

This in turn entails that the self is not necessarily involved in loss (and so not involved in time[23]); understanding oneself does not bring with it the complexities of absence and substitution or displacement. In the light of Augustine's general view of mind and time, the issues discussed at the beginning of this chapter, it is hard to see how Rousseau's approach could provide anything like a coherent account of language itself. If the present conscious self can construct or reconstruct the past imaginatively in a way that is unanswerable, there can be no sense that the past is a matter for shared discourse, no sense that what I have done or been has a life in the reality and perception of others (let alone in the perception of an Augustinian God).

I am always speaking, never spoken of; and my past is thus in no way strange to me, arbitrary or impenetrable. The tenor of a narrative that treats God as the primary reader or auditor, acknowledging the existence of a perspective that remains intrinsically inaccessible, pushes us towards a sense of the past as always strange and liable to provoke questions, even when it is 'my' past. But in that very recognition of strangeness, the past becomes something that can be reflected on in a corporate or a conversational way. Reflection on the self and expression of the self have nothing to do with an ecstatic outpouring of the present imagination; they will entail the time of speaking and of listening, the willingness to bear with silences and gaps, the inescapable absence of myself from myself – which is also the reality of shared language in which what is said is always *to be followed*, to be repeated, replied to, expounded, contradicted.

In this context, Augustine's selfhood is bound to be ironic: I do not simply coincide with what I now say in any sense of being able to make myself fully present in this present; I do not coincide with what I now see in any sense of being able to assure myself that I have nothing left to discover. But this irony is not a safe detachment, a strategy of defence. Acknowledging my ignorance is not adopting some sort of scepticism, but surrendering into God's hands any hope of seeing myself whole. So whatever truth I shall see of who I am will

---

[23] Ibid., p. 266: 'Rousseau claims to see himself from a perspective outside of time.'

depend on my relation to God, a relation of which I am not in control. Thus the irony of admitting that I can't really know much of the truth I'm trying to see or tell is interwoven with the trust, both apprehensive and hopeful, that my entire history is 'received' and held by the act of God, witnessed and drawn together by God's inseparable act of love and knowing.

The irony involved is the irony that is (joyfully) sustained in the kind of prayer that Augustine offers in the discourse of the *Confessions*, the repeated questioning of how God's purpose interacts with the disorder of human act and motivation, and the repeated confessing of God's otherness and majesty, God's transcendence of our agendas. At the very end of the book (XIII. xxxviii/53), Augustine echoes the Platonic question of how anyone (even angel to angel, let alone human to human) can truly teach the truth to another. But his response is not (as it would be for a true Platonist) that we all already possess a truth that needs only to be galvanized into visible life. Instead we are told to ask of God – and thus to look for no single and containable answer but for the resolution of our questioning in a life of continuing praise and penitence.

God alone is simultaneously work and rest, and his completely stable action, both restful and ceaseless, enables us to grasp something of what time and change are (XIII.xxxvii/52). God is what God is and does what God does, integrally, freely, eternally; and it is because God is thus that we live as we do and know what we know. God's active love draws us across the distance between creator and creature: the process of that drawing is time itself, in which we learn and change. Because the gap between creator and creature cannot be conceptualized in any way that suggests ordinary difference or distance, we cannot ever be at rest within this temporal order, settling down with a clear map of where we are in relation to God. Our holiness begins with our acceptance of restlessness, not as a good in itself, and not as a frustrated shifting and turning and wishing for something better, simply the steady acceptance of incompletion and the radical nature of our desire for God's endlessness. In some sense – though he is tantalizingly ambiguous about this at times – Augustine believes we shall be definitively at rest in heaven, though not simply in a condition of stasis; our time will somehow not be as it is now. But meanwhile, we imitate or are assimilated to God's eternal life here and now in our conscious passage through time, not in any escape into an imagined eternity or simultaneity or self-coincidence (or Rousseauesque self-construction from a timeless vantage point). The mental and spiritual exercise that is the *Confessions* is an enacting of its own subject matter: speaking like *this* is true speaking about God: speaking about myself as fallible, incomplete and examining myself with uncertain wonder. This self-interrogation without hope of closure is how I know God, and so how I know myself as well: and God's incarnation is the effective sign that God walks with me in the world of time and acts in the heart of temporal action.

So I turn to my puzzling history, looking not for justification or coherence but precisely for those silences and bafflements that deny me the dangerous luxury of a satisfying self-portrait and draw me away from the self-conscious struggle to be or know myself and towards God, in that act of praise and wonder and bewilderment whose very possibility ought constantly to surprise us. How, Augustine asks, do we speak to let alone about what we do not know? It can happen only if the very utterance of our not-knowing, the Christ-imbued voice of humility, becomes a kind of knowing. And that is the voice Augustine tests and refines throughout the *Confessions*.

We can read the *Confessions* as essentially about how we struggle to be present to ourselves in a full and transparent way yet constantly fail; but also about how this is not a disaster or a tragedy, since we are present to a love which holds together what we cannot unify or sustain by our own resources. The believing self, for Augustine, is a self trustfully accepting its own lack of transparency to itself because it has faith in a reality which addresses and attends to it without interruption – and which can therefore 'interrupt' our own fantasies that we have arrived at full self-understanding. 'If Augustine were to achieve a state where he is fully present to himself, with no possibility of interruption, he will have forgotten God beyond all possibility of recall.'[24] A growing number of studies of Augustine's approach to 'selfhood' have explored this new valuation of 'felt' incompleteness in the saint's thought, correcting earlier models which took Augustine's earliest and most obviously Platonic-influenced writings as definitive. These earlier works – such as the *Soliloquies*

---

[24]James Wetzel, 'The Force of Memory: Reflections on the Interrupted Self,' *Augustinian Studies*, 38.1 (2007), pp. 147–59; quotation from p. 156.

or the *de vera religione* – are more obviously focused on the discovery that we have an immortal and intelligent soul that can be discerned and thought about independently of the body, and on the imperatives for mental and physical life that follow from this.[25] Augustine never retreats from the conviction that we are more than physical and time-bound, but develops it in a highly distinctive way: the soul we discover, the inner self we come to recognize at the end of a process of rigorous intellectual and spiritual purification, is a self still opening out on to two unfathomably elusive horizons: the mystery of the infinite God and the constantly shifting and deceptive content of our human awareness of who we are and have been. The knowing subject cannot contain or master the divine, but neither can it contain or master itself, the 'caverns' of its memory. There can be no final clarity about who we are simply through introspection. Wetzel, quoted earlier, notes how Martha Nussbaum[26] uses this recognition as proof of the ethical danger of Platonism and Platonized Christianity in its refusal to explore the contingencies of actual historical selfhood. But, as Wetzel implies, this rather misses the point: our awareness of the fallibility and self-interest of our scrutiny of ourselves becomes the key to an ethic grounded in communal formation and shared spiritual discernment rather than simply the exploration of an atomized selfhood.

Wetzel's essay stands alongside another study of the Augustinian self, a watershed piece by John Cavadini which has set the agenda for many more recent researchers. This essay, 'The Darkest Enigma: Reconsidering the Self in Augustine's Thought',[27] points out very shrewdly that even to speak of Augustine's view of 'the self' is question-begging: 'we can picture this inner reality, "the self", as a kind of stable, private space, above which God stably hovers as an immaterial light, or at least as a stable interior reality, always ready to be glimpsed by the purified inner vision.'[28] Cavadini is clear that we must be very wary of 'reifying' Augustine's language when what he is most concerned

---

[25] But as a corrective to making the gulf too deep between earlier and later Augustine, see Carol Harrison, *Rethinking Augustine's Earlier Works: An Argument for Continuity* (Oxford: Oxford University Press, 2006).

[26] In her book *The Therapy of Desire* (Princeton, NJ: Princeton University Press, 1994).

[27] *Augustinian Studies*, 38.1 (2007), pp. 119–32.

[28] Ibid., p. 122.

to trace is a *process* of testing, challenging and changing various ways of representing to myself who I am, in the hope of arriving at a less dishonest place. And the least dishonest place is the one where we finally acknowledge that we cannot be truthful without a living participation in God's truth – a place where we are also obliged to see that the boundaries between me and God in Christ have been obscured: 'Where is "the self" that is independent, that is decipherable as a text, without Christ?'[29]

This kind of approach to Augustine is seeking to correct an imbalance still widely found in less specialist literature. Charles Taylor's brilliant and deservedly influential *Sources of the Self: The Making of the Modern Identity*[30] reinforced the older picture of Augustine by emphasizing the novelty of the way in which Augustine establishes *reflexivity* as fundamental in the life of the self, as somehow authoritative in the discovery of truth: 'Augustine shifts the focus from the field of objects known to the activity itself of knowing; God is to be found here.'[31] In consciously adopting a first-person perspective in such a way that seeing myself opens up a kind of seeing of God, Augustine inadvertently opens the door to the typically modern construction of a self whose internal self-awareness or self-interpretation comes to be increasingly beyond challenge; a very ambivalent legacy. Taylor's analysis is by no means wrong or perverse; but it leaves out of account two elements which scholars like Cavadini have restored to the heart of the argument. The first is Augustine's growing preoccupation with the sheer incompleteness of the endeavour of self-knowing. Yes, our recognition of ourselves as reflexive, as capable of first person discourse and thought, is a crucial breakthrough, making it clear (as the *Confessions* spells it out) that neither God nor the self is a kind of *thing*, an object with material boundaries: it is an agency essentially unconfined by matter and space, and this becomes plain only when we 'look within', as Augustine repeatedly encourages us to do, to find something that does not alter in step with our material conditions. *But* this agency is not a self-subsisting reality, first recognizing itself, then moving on to see God reflected in its own

---

[29] Ibid., p. 131.
[30] Cambridge University Press, 1989.
[31] Op. cit., p. 130.

luminosity: its deepest level of self-recognition is when it sees its dependence on the strictly unconditioned and unlimited act of God's gift, and so also sees the ways in which it blocks off its own maturation by refusing dependence, love, worship. As we shall see, the most sophisticated statement of Augustine's understanding in his treatise of the Trinity insists that our self-knowledge is not *as such* in God's image until it becomes a knowledge of our dependence on God's prior action, a knowledge of relatedness. The second qualification that needs to be made to a Taylorian account is simply that Augustine increasingly makes it plain that our self-knowledge is in practice bound up with the common life of the believing community and its disciplines: the turn inwards is – paradoxically – not a turning away from relation with others any more than from relation with the creator. The pattern of common life is what delivers the self from illusory self-contemplation by purifying the nature of the self's love (of itself as of others).

There have been studies of Augustine's model of the self that have sought to bring him back closer to a stress upon privileged and transparent interiority, and to minimize the corporate and relational aspects highlighted by Cavadini and implied in the preceding chapter.[32] But overall the tendency in readings of Augustine has been increasingly in Cavadini's direction.[33] One factor in this has been a growing acknowledgement that we cannot read the *Confessions* in abstraction from the rest of Augustine's work at this period. The *Confessions* reflects very clearly the way in which Augustine's thinking is being shaped

---

[32]See, for example, Philip Cary, *Augustine's Invention of the Inner Self: The Legacy of a Christian Platonist* (Oxford: Oxford University Press, 2000); also the encyclopaedic articles by Wayne Hankey criticizing many aspects of the new approach in Augustinian studies: 'Re-Christianizing Augustine Postmodern Style: Readings by Jacques Derrida, Robert Dodaro, Jean-Luc Marion, Rowan Williams, Lewis Ayres and John Milbank', *Animus*, 2 (1997), pp. 387–415; 'Stephen Menn's Cartesian Augustine: Metaphysically and Ahistorically Modern', *Animus*, 3 (1998), pp. 183–210; 'Between and Beyond Augustine and Descartes: More than a Source of the Self', *Augustinian Studies*, 32.1 (2001), pp. 65–88. I shall return to some of Hankey's points later, but it is enough for now to note that he insists on Augustine's commitment to some sort of fully truthful self-presence in the process of reflexive recognition. The crucial point, however, is what that truthful self-presence sees – a self-contained mental substance or a self always already related and thus imperfect and questing. The whole question of Augustine's relation to Descartes is treated carefully and authoritatively by Michael Hanby, *Augustine and Modernity* (London: Routledge, 2003), chapter 5.

[33]See, for example, Matthew Drever, *Image, Identity, and the Formation of the Augustinian Soul* (New York, NY: Oxford University Press, 2013).

by exegetical concerns; he is not only reading the Bible, he is preaching it as a presbyter and a bishop. And of all the texts with which he is engaging, it is clear from the *Confessions* that the Psalms have a special place. It makes sense, then, to turn from reflecting on the *Confessions* to Augustine the preacher, and to listen to how he reads and interprets the Psalms not only as a writer in the study but as a pastor.

2

The Soul in Paraphrase: Augustine as Interpreter of the Psalms

The very first sentence of Augustine's *Confessions* is a quotation from the Psalms, and for the rest of the work hardly a page goes by without at least one such reference. It would not be an exaggeration to say that the narrative autobiographical voice of the *Confessions* is systematically blended with the voice of the psalmist. Brian Stock observes that the use of the Psalms is central to Augustine's reorientation of 'the ethical direction of his conduct': and, 'As he works toward this objective, words, phrases, and verses from the Psalms are reinterpreted within the narrative of the life that he intends to live.'[1]

Augustine famously describes the impact that the Psalms made in the early days after his conversion: more than once, he uses the language of being 'set on fire' by their words, and he describes how they prompted the expression of his 'most intimate sensations' (*de familiari affectu animi mei* [*conf.* IX.4.8]). Perhaps most strikingly, he can compare the recitation of a familiar Psalm with the history of a human life (*conf.* XI.28.38). The Psalm is a meaningful narrative structure, a history of the soul. And souls only have a history in conversation with God, Augustine argues. Without the divine interlocutor, the

---

[1] B. Stock, *Augustine the Reader: Meditation, Self-Knowledge, and the Ethics of Interpretation* (Cambridge, MA: Harvard University Press, 1996), p. 114.

self is broken and scattered. A perfect knowledge of the self would be like the familiar experience of knowing the whole of a Psalm as you sing it (XI.31.41) – but, for us, such experience is not in the normal run of things. What we can do, it is implied, is to imagine a wholeness of experienced history in our lives as if life itself were a text, as if the remembered story of our conversation with God represented part of an intelligible narrative or a single song.

Any reader of the *Confessions* will be aware that, for Augustine, the reading of the Psalms was more than simply a 'devotional' reading of a holy text, let alone reading to inform or instruct. The psalmist's voice is what releases two fundamentally significant things for the Augustinian believer. It unseals deep places, emotions otherwise buried, and it provides an analogy for the unity or intelligibility of a human life lived in faith. Here is a conversation with God that has a beginning, a middle and an end. And in the course of that conversation, the human speaker is radically changed and enabled to express what is otherwise hidden from him or her. Augustine speaks of what the Psalm he is discussing (Psalm 4, *Cum invocarem*) 'makes of him': the act of recitation becomes an opening to the transforming action of grace (*conf.* IX.4.8).

Unity of the Divine and Human Voice

The Psalm as used in the *Confessions* is thus a kind of digest of the act of faith itself. At the root of this understanding is the assumption that the grace of God changes what we *can* say to God, and so changes what can be said of ourselves. Such a picture, of course, carries with it a number of theological assumptions that need to be drawn out. They are not fully set out in the *Confessions*, but Augustine was already working on them in the early 390s, and they constitute the unifying themes of the *Enarrationes in Psalmos*, the 'Expositions of the Psalms', which he began as a presbyter and continued to deliver from the pulpit during the years of his episcopate. Dating many of these sermons is impossible,[2]

---

[2]Michael Cameron's excellent article on the *Enarrationes* in *Augustine Through the Ages: An Encyclopedia*, ed. A. Fitzgerald, OSA (Grand Rapids, MI: Eerdmans, 1999), pp. 290–306 provides a useful brief overview of the complex chronological issues.

but all commentators on these remarkable texts have agreed that they have a powerful theological unity. My suggestion is simply that this theological unity is illuminated by linking the explicit themes of the *Enarrationes* with the reflections already summarized in the *Confessions* and with some of the wider themes relating to exegesis in other works such as *De doctrina Christiana* (or *Teaching Christianity*).

Briefly, the notion of the Psalm as proposing a structure for telling a unified story of the soul depends on the insight in the *Enarrationes* that the Psalms represent the unifying of the divine and the human voice in Christ. To see Christ as the centre of the task of interpretation presupposes the idea in *De doctrina Christiana* (like the *Confessions*, dating from the late 390s) of Christ as the one who reveals the entire created universe as a 'sign' of God, because he is the supreme *signum* of God's reality. If we approach Christ, and in particular approach his cross, with humility (without which we understand nothing of him), we learn how the humble self-emptying of incarnation and passion open up the full meaning of God as the substantial *res* (thing) to which all signs in their earthly limitedness finally point.

The key passage in the *Enarrationes* is probably in the exposition of Psalm 140, where Augustine identifies two texts fundamental for all Christian hermeneutics – Jesus' question to Paul on the Damascus Road ('Why are you persecuting me?') and the parable of the last judgement in Matthew 25, where Jesus identifies himself with 'the least of the brethren'. Both of these assert the unity of the Head and the Body in the Church: Jesus speaks in the voice of the suffering Christian. This principle is of particular significance where texts in the Psalter express spiritual desolation and struggle: the Psalms are the words of Jesus, the Word who speaks in all scripture. But how can we understand words that imply alienation from God when they occur on the lips of Jesus? Only by reading them as spoken by the whole Christ, that is Christ with all the members of his Body. He speaks for us, makes his own the protesting or troubled cry of the human being, so that his own proper and perfect prayer to the Father may become ours.[3]

---

[3]Examples abound, but see particularly *en.Ps.* 30.II.i.3, 4, 56.1, 62.2, 68.i and ii *passim*, 74.4, 87.14, 90, i and ii, *passim*, 140.5–7.

The outcome is a pedagogy of pastoral compassion, partially offered here. In the state of spiritual darkness, we are tempted to think that God is absent, yet when we hear Christ speaking 'our' words of anguish, we know that this cannot be so. His humanity is inseparably united with God so that, if he gives voice to our suffering, we know that such suffering does not silence God. This applies at the simplest level to the words of Christ in the gospels, yet it is also what grounds the possibility of interpreting the cries of the Psalms as Christ's.[4] Obviously, the opening of Psalm 22 (21 in the Lxx used by Augustine) is central, and Augustine reverts to it many times: 'My God, my God, why have you forsaken me?' is a kind of paradigm of how Christ as Head speaks for the Body.[5] There is also an interesting phrase in the *Enarrationes* on Psalm 66, where Augustine describes the cry as 'God appealing to God for mercy' (*Enarrat. Ps.* 66.5). It is as if we have an anticipation of the twentieth-century theology of Christ's dereliction developed by Hans Urs von Balthasar. The eternal difference in Trinitarian life between Father and Son is what makes possible the identification of the Son with even the most radical state of 'otherness' from God or separation from God.[6]

We are not here dealing only with a 'pedagogy of compassion'.. Singing the Psalms, in this perspective, becomes a means of learning what it is to inhabit the Body of Christ and to be caught up in Christ's prayer. Just as Christ makes his own our lament, our penitence and our fear by adopting the human condition in all its tragic fullness as the material of his Body, so we are inevitably identified with what he says to his Father as God (e.g. *en.Ps.* 30 (ii) 3–4; 74.4; 142.3). Our relation to Christ is manifested as multi-layered: '[H]e prays for us as our priest, he prays in us as our Head, he is prayed to by us as

---

[4]*en.Ps.* 93.19 refers specifically to Christ's agony in Gethsemane, but the pivotal question in relation to the Psalms is succinctly expressed in *en.Ps.*, 37.6 – how can Christ 'voice' the words of Psalm 21 (22):4 with its references to 'my offences'? Christ must have assumed the felt consequences of sin, even though he was sinless.

[5]On this point, in addition to the examples already mentioned, and the actual *enarratio* on Psalm 21, see *en.Ps.* 93.15. Bertrand de Margerie observes rightly that Augustine does not seek to minimize the actuality of Christ's concrete human suffering by connecting it with the human condition in general (*Introduction à l'histoire de l'exégèse, III.saint Augustin* [Paris: Cerf, 1983] 120 n. 31).

[6]See, above all, Balthasar's *Mysterium Paschale: The Mystery of Easter*, tr. A. Nichols (Edinburgh: T. & T. Clark, 1990) and the fifth volume of his *Theo-Drama* (San Francisco, CA: Ignatius, 1998).

our God' (*en.Ps.* 85.1). The meaning of our salvation is that we are included in his life, given the right to speak with his divine voice, reassured that what our human voices say out of darkness and suffering has been owned by him as his voice, so that it may in some way be opened to the life of God for healing or forgiveness.

Augustine does not offer an exact prescription for the imitation of Christ; it is more that he underlines the inevitability of passing through the cross if we are to speak fully with the voice of the divine Son. This is spelled out at some length in *en.Ps.* 119.1.[7] The Pauline or deutero-Pauline idea of 'making up what is lacking in the sufferings of Christ' (Col. 1:24) is given a fresh twist in *en.Ps.* 51.4, where Augustine speaks of paying our dues to the *res publica* of which we are citizens through our suffering: what we now endure is what the entire Body of Christ must suffer. The Body is – in historical terms – more than the Head regarded as a thing in itself. If we, therefore, as baptized Christians suffer, especially through persecution from non-believers, this must be part of what the *totus Christus* must endure – part of what the eternal Son has already accepted as the means by which Christ will heal the world. The Head-and-Body theology thus provides not only a pastoral understanding of what any believer suffers, but an interpretation of it as creatively building up the outworking of Christ's saving act in contingent history. It is not only that Christ accompanies the sufferer, sharing his or her pain; the sufferer is drawn into the action of Christ that ultimately overcomes all sin and grief.

A Christology of Humility

The interconnection between hermeneutics, Christology and the doctrines of grace, salvation and the Church is extraordinarily tight. As so often with Augustine, it is hard to disentangle anything that could be called a 'purely' doctrinal exposition, but it should be clear that the *Enarrationes* are a major source for understanding the heart of his Christology (and have been curiously underused in some accounts of that subject). Readers of the *Confessions* will

---

[7]Cf. *en.Ps.* 51.1, 52.2, 53.4, 93.5, 102.4.

be familiar with Augustine's insistence (especially in the concluding chapters of Book 7) that Christian faith cannot be understood without humility since Christ himself is only encountered when we come down to the level at which he has chosen to live, the level of ruined and scarred humanity (*conf.* 7.18.24). His own life is the way towards understanding the mystery of his person and work; sharing that life is the ground of true doctrine about him. Christ not only shows the way but *is* the way (*en.Ps.* 58.1.7). So the humility implicit in making the language of the Psalms our own – a language of doubt, near-despair, repentance, and lonely suffering, as well as praise and thanksgiving – is the acceptance of that human condition that Christ embraced in his incarnation.

As we truly assimilate the identity of the psalmist as paradigmatic human sufferer and struggler, we assimilate the identity of Christ who chooses those same words as his own; and thus we are given to speak the words that Christ speaks to the Father, because the humility and love that grounds his acceptance of our condition is the expression of the eternal love that unites him with the Father. What is distinctive about any hermeneutic of the Psalms is that singing them is quite simply and literally an appropriation of Christ's life, in history and eternity. And, from this act of appropriation, the church as a whole is revealed as the community where humanity is allowed full scope to say what it is, in terms of its failure and pain, so that it may fully become what it is created to be, the multiple echo of the Word's response to the Father. 'Do not hear anything spoken in the person of Christ as if it had nothing to do with you who are members of the Body of Christ' (*en.Ps.* 143.1).

The argument traced in both the *Confessions* and the *Enarrationes* has obvious and predictable affinities with that of the *De civitate Dei* (*The City of God*), whose definition of the divine commonwealth is set in opposition to any imaginable variety of individual or corporate self-assertion.[8] It also resonates with the themes that Augustine develops more fully in the anti-Pelagian works, which repudiated any idea that we could take as a theological starting point an individual will seeking to make peace with God. The dual foundation of the

---

[8] The *locus classicus*, of course, is *civ.* 14.28.

theology of our texts thus far is the eternal difference of Father and Son within the Trinity coupled with the decision of the Son to take human flesh so that the creature's difference might be subsumed in the loving and joyful difference that is the Son's response to the Father. The divine act, in other words, is necessarily the first thing we have to consider, an act that is primarily and simply the active being of God exercising the divine nature in the life of the Trinity and derivatively the Trinitarian action that is focused and expressed in the Son's incarnation. What effectively grounds substantial things in that reality is the highly distinctive activity of reciting the Psalms and so following the 'contour' of the act of incarnation.

The Church

The Church's worship, then, is not accidental or marginal to the Church's very being. Obviously Augustine has much to say about the Eucharist as the prime locus for discovering ourselves as the Body;[9] nevertheless, the singing of the Psalms becomes the most immediate routine means of identifying with the voice of Christ. And that identification carries implications for the kind of mutual relation that concretely defines the life of the Church.

We have noted the pastoral implications of Augustine's ascribing our expressions of weakness to Christ, who speaks for us. But the *Enarrationes* have more to say about the life that should be normative in the Body, since (following the classical exposition of the theme by Paul) Augustine clearly espouses the notion that such a community ought to be one in which each member supplies what is lacking for the other. The Body should also be a locus for attending to the other's specific needs, which may be material but are just as likely to be spiritual (*en.Ps.* 125.13). We should beware, as Paul warned us, of thinking we know what the most important gifts are (and so the most important people): why *worry* if you cannot work miracles? God has many services to perform, and the faithful action of a mundane task is no less an essential element of the

---

[9]See, e.g., *serm.* 229.1,272.

Body's life. Better a healthy finger than a diseased or blind eye, says Augustine with characteristic pungency, even though the eye is apparently a 'greater' *contributor* to the Body's life and welfare (*en.Ps. 130.8*).

So the notion of the Body as a place of mutual attention and service leads us back, yet again, to the central theme of accepting human limitation. The incarnational embrace of the prose of human existence means that the least spectacular act of authentic faith and obedience is validated by God, even though our preoccupation with dramatic success may hide it from our eyes. And the principle is applied also – with a clear aim at the Donatists – to living with the visible imperfections of the Church: we have absolutely no way of knowing whose faith will prove victoriously secure at any given moment, thus we have no way of deciding that a person needs no help from us or we from them. And if that is so, we take a considerable risk in trying to separate ourselves from the supposedly wicked (*en.Ps.* 99.9–11). The more there is love, the more suffering at the lovelessness of others in the Church (*en.Ps. 98.13*, referring to Paul in 2 Cor. 11). But such love is precisely what we have to offer the loveless within the Body; thus the cost must be borne.

Out of the Depths

Central to nearly all of Augustine's theology is the assumption that we think about God and speak to God only from our setting within time and the body. The *Enarrationes* address this in various ways. For example, *Enarrat: Ps.* 129.1 ('Out of the deep have I called . . .') identifies the 'deep' as this present life, just as *en.Ps.* 41.13 identifies the abyss with the human heart, which we never fully know during our earthly life (a recurrent theme in the *Enarrationes*).[10] The repeated emphasis on hope and unfulfilled desire as the heart of Christian discipleship (as in *en.Ps.* 89.15, 129.10, 138.20 and countless other instances) likewise places the psalm-singer firmly in the world of incompletion and yearning, with all the pain this entails. For Augustine, the 'spiritual' reading of

---

[10] Cf. *en.Ps.* 118, 15.7–8 on the 'night' of this world in which our hearts are hidden from each other.

at least these portions of scripture does not evade or relativize the 'historical' sense, which roots us in our own present history, not simply in a scriptural past. Perhaps more accurately, the voice of the incomplete and struggling past as recorded in scripture, most poignantly and directly in the Psalms, is allowed to become our voice when we renounce the temptation to grasp for a timeless peace without a time-bound discipleship of suffering and penitence. The connection with the themes of Book 7 of the *Confessions* is again very evident. Here Augustine's experience of what might be called frustrated mysticism (Platonic contemplation that delivers a vision but not a habit of life) is both countered and resolved by an apprehension of Christ in scripture that insists on a practice of reading that guides our growth and is rooted in humility (see particularly 7.21.27).

Thus, the most spiritual reading for Augustine will always lead us most directly to humility. Where literalism is to be rejected, it is because it proposes to us a static object of knowledge capable of possession and thereby fails to stir us to longing for the greater fullness of God.[11] So there is a paradoxical dimension to his hermeneutics: what most locates us in our earthly experience in all its reality is what most opens up the fuller sense because it most prompts desire. And, as noted earlier, the Psalms offer a particular way of structuring the time of the believer's life, so that the present is always oriented to Christ's future.

Holiness

We have seen how the holy life always begins with a Christlike acceptance of humanity's finitude, of an incomplete, sinful and frustrated present moment (including the sin of both myself and my fellow Christians). What makes this acceptance the gateway to a true *narrative* of the soul? The exchange between Christ and the human self, which the Psalms encode, moves the present moment toward the goal of created things because of Christ's action. What I am now is transformed into a moment in the history of Christ, who in accepting the conditions of this world employs what they offer so as to bring

---

[11]Spelled out in the first book of *De doctrina Christiana*; see below, Chapter 3.

about the fruition God intends. Christ is the supreme *signum*, the point of greatest transparency within the world to its divine origin. The human present, accepted by the believer, becomes therefore a kind of *signum* in Christ, a reinscription of scripture.

Augustine's definitions of holiness are thus bound up with scripture. However, it is not so much in the sense that the Bible *tells* us what holiness is (though that is undoubtedly part of what the Bible does) as in the fact that scriptural language models how the world manifests God – most explicitly in the language of penitence and growth. In *conf*. 7, Augustine turns to Paul when frustrated with Platonism (just as it is to Paul that he turns in Book 9 at the crucial moment when he recognizes once and for all how his unconverted will frustrates its own operation and liberty). The Psalms functioned for him as a dramatized version of Paul's analysis of the human state, of Paul rendered for performance. Scripture defines the character of a life in conversation and communion with God; and it is most fruitful for the believer when it provides a 'script' for such a conversation. First and foremost, however, we must recognize that the essence of Christ's own action in the incarnation is a matter of 'transfiguring' the human voice,[12] which, in turn, is essentially a matter of defining a *communal* voice that is nonetheless the only medium for the truly personal voice. Christian rhetoric is distinctive in that it gives unarguable place to stumbling or derivative performance. Such performance reminds us of the fact that *this* rhetoric seeks to persuade us not of this or that case or party in the world but of God's 'case'. Faithful discourse insists on its own inadequacy in unambiguous ways.[13]

Soul as 'Sign'

The Christian life that functions as a *signum* is fractured by the awareness of sin (and sorrow for sin). But it is also a life consciously identified with the *signum* of Christ's fractured and suffering life, culminating on the cross.

---

[12]See M. Cameron, 'Transfiguration: Christology and the Roots of Figurative Exegesis in St. Augustine', *Studia Patristica* 33 (1997), pp. 40–7.
[13]See *doctr. chr.* 4; cf. the study by Karla Pollmann, *Doctrina Christiana* (Freiburg: Universitätsverlag, 1996), and her article 'Hermeneutical Presuppositions', in *Augustine Through the Ages*, especially p. 428.

Such identification is enacted not only through sacramental practice but also through the recitation of the classic texts of frustration and hope, the Psalms, in which the divine adoption of the human voice is so keenly expressed. As these texts are recited, the *profundum* of the human heart, never known to us in fullness, is opened up by God. What we do not and cannot know about our past, present and future is given over to God, who will draw out of us cries and aspirations that more and more clearly give voice to what is hidden in us, knowing that all this elusive human agenda unrecognized within us is embraced in the incarnation and may be employed by Christ in his work.

Augustine describes in the *Confessions* the effect of the Psalms upon him as the process that, in *doctr. christ.*, he describes as being educated out of that mistaken love that tries to contemplate what it should be using – i.e. love that treats as ends what should be means. And although he does not put it quite like this, we could summarize his theology of the Psalms in terms of learning not to regard the soul as an object of contemplation but as a 'sign'. Augustine is so regularly treated as the great apologist of introspection that this may sound odd at first. But the point is that our examination of the self as Christian believers is meant to bring us to the recognition that the inner life, instead of being a sanctuary of stability, is both profoundly mysterious to us (the dark *profundum* of the *Enarrationes*, the 'caverns' of *conf.* 10.8.13) and the locus of our deepest awareness of frustration. The practice of psalmody as Augustine is already defining it in the 390s paves the way for the ultimate analysis of this theme in the later books of the *De Trinitate*.[14] Introspection can indeed reveal (as in *conf.* 7.17.23) the superior nature of the unchangeable. The mind looking on itself can glimpse the supremely desirable goal of beholding the reality that is not vulnerable to circumstance. But it is precisely the mind's capacity to recognize this and its incapacity to hold the vision that poses the problem that, for Augustine, can be resolved only through the incarnation with its summons to, and enabling of, humility.

---

[14] An excellent overview of recent shifts in the interpretation of this among Augustinian scholars may be found in L. Ayres, 'The Fundamental Grammar of Augustine's Trinitarian Theology', in *Augustine and His Critics: Essays in Honour of Gerald Bonner*, ed. R. Dodaro and G. Lawless (London and New York: Routledge, 2000), pp. 51–76.

So, to return to the beginning of the *Confessions*: the opening quotation from the Psalter sets the tone for the rest of the book. By electing to cast the story of his life in the form of a direct address to God, Augustine weaves his own apostrophes in with the language of the Psalms themselves. To tell a truthful story about myself, I must look to my memory not as a simple repository of impressions but as containing God (see *conf.* 10.24.35). My memory is thus a recording of the pervasive recognition of dissatisfaction with static and limited goals for desire, a record of the radical hopefulness that looks towards an end that cannot be fully determined or described from where I now stand. And so, to tell a truthful story about myself, I must be speaking to the only interlocutor who is not just another subject in time with another contingent perspective to offer. I must be exposed to Truth itself in person.

The Psalms demonstrate that such an address can be formed into a kind of unity. To call it an 'aesthetic' unity would miss the heart of Augustine's purpose and practice. It is certainly a unity not easily reducible to a simple record of the evolution of ideas or the accumulation of experiences, culminating in an optimal present situation. Augustine famously articulates in the tenth book of the *Confessions* that his present situation in no way resembles a plateau of achieved virtue or inner calm. Perhaps the unity more resembles a consistency of tone or register; I do not know at all what the substance will be of what lies ahead, but I know what key it can be sung in so that it accords with God's purpose. And if what lies ahead continues to engage with God directly and honestly, God will still be able to shape it as God pleases, whether or not its shape ever becomes visible to me on earth. It is in heaven that we shall read the text that is God without obscurity – a text that is simultaneously the ordered creation, scripture and the radical love of the Word, the Son (see *conf.* 13.15.18).

The psalmodic pattern explains why the *Confessions* is and is not an 'autobiography'. It seeks not to give an exhaustive account of this person's past, or to make a case in favour, but only to create a text that has the sort of unity that a Psalm has. This may explain why the concluding books turn with such apparent arbitrariness to the widest possible issues about time, creation and the Trinity. And in the creation of that narrative unity, we are not obliged to understand what cannot be understood, or to anticipate the judgement that can come only at the end of the temporal story. We must only continue to be faithful to the vocal 'register' of psalmody, with its personal address to God and its naked awareness of human need and failure. Put this alongside the repeated insistences of the *Enarrationes*, and it can be seen how this is also the prescription for identifying our individual narratives with that of Jesus. It is not that we are simply and instantly assimilated to his objective sinlessness, any more than he is assimilated to our objective guilt. What holds the two stories together is our reproduction of Christ's acceptance of the fallen and struggling condition to which we are without exception destined. And in that identification of narratives, the narrated human life of the believer becomes a sign of God.

Conclusion

I have attempted to systematize what Augustine, of course, did not. But the interconnections of what he was writing and preaching, especially in the last decade of the fourth century, are inescapable. These texts offer perhaps the clearest links that may be discerned between a doctrine of grace, a doctrine of Christ, a doctrine of signs and sacraments, and a practice of self-scrutinizing humility expressed in psalmodic prayer. Augustine's theological exposition is seldom systematic; we have to work with him and follow the connections he makes. And yet such labour at least clarifies the inseparability of these themes in what he writes and preaches, and warns against an abstraction of his doctrine from his pastoring. We may also, as I have hinted, learn better how to read some of the central arguments of both the *De civitate Dei* and the *De Trinitate* if we attempt an understanding of what (as he puts it) the Psalms 'made of him'.

In one of the passages already referred to near the end of the *Confessions* (13.15.18), Augustine imagines how the angels praise God: they 'read' without trouble the purposes of God that we must decode in a material text. From their reading, they know what to choose and how to love. *Legunt, eligunt, et diligent*, says Augustine in an untranslatable wordplay: 'they read, they choose, they love'. Although the angels are under discussion here, Augustine's analysis of what is involved in the simple act of singing a Psalm suggests that the same memorable triplet could be applied to us, once we have learned the skill of reading properly. Having once discovered how to make the voice of the Body of Christ in worship our own, we read in order to choose God (and not be bogged down in the world of signs), and to love the Father, to whom the Body of Christ by grace always speaks, and the Body itself, in whose historical imperfections and manifold human needs we discover the only perfection available to us, in the life of a community marked by hope.

Research on Augustine as reader of the Psalms has continued copiously and fruitfully. From William Babcock's 1971 Yale thesis[15] to a recent Cambridge dissertation relating Christ as mediator to the 'mediatorial' functions of memory in the human subject (i.e. as holding together apparently contradictory elements of our experience of ourselves) with particular reference to the *Enarrationes*,[16] scholars of Augustine's exegesis have agreed in seeing these sermons as a key both to Augustine's Christology (as we shall see in more detail later on, in Chapters 7 and 8) and to his exegetical practice. Michael Fedrowicz's magisterial study of 1997[17] offered a very full discussion of the core idea of Christ speaking in our *persona* in the Psalms: the Psalm text is always the whole Church speaking in the voice of its Head who takes to himself all the experiences and sufferings of the Body. In the English-speaking world, Michael Cameron's work has been of particular significance: in addition to the article mentioned in footnote 2 above, there have been several essays and a comprehensive book on Augustine's figurative exegesis.[18]

Apart from the theological importance of these connections, there is a methodological point that needs to be underlined. As noted earlier in the concluding note to the first chapter of this book, we shall misread Augustine if we forget that he is working as a teacher in a liturgical context. In contrast to some other early Christian exegetes like Origen, he does not have a 'school'

---

[15]'The Christ of the Exchange: A Study in the Christology of Augustine's *Enarrationes in Psalmos*.'
[16]Kevin Grove, 'Memory and the Whole Christ: Augustine and the Psalms' (Cambridge PhD thesis, 2015).
[17]*Psalmus Vox Totius Christi: Studien zu Auusutins Enarrationes in Psalmos* (Freiburg: Herder, 1997).
[18]Michael Cameron, *Christ Meets Me Everywhere: Augustine's Early Figurative Exegesis* (Notre Dame, IN: University of Notre Dame Press, 2012); also particularly 'The Christological Substructure of Augustine's Figurative Exegesis', in *Augustine and the Bible*, ed.Pamela Bright (Notre Dame, IN: University of Notre Dame Press, 1999), pp. 74–103, and '*Totus Christus* and the Psychagogy of Augustine's Sermons', *Augustinian Studies*, 36.1 (2010), pp. 59–70.

in which other professional interpreters are being trained; when he studies and expounds the Bible, he does so as pastor to a mixed flock. In his lecture, '"Heart in Pilgrimage": St Augustine as Interpreter of the Psalms',[19] the Orthodox scholar Andrew Louth provides a detailed reading of one particular sermon (on Ps.100) in order to show Augustine at work as a pastoral guide: his aim is not to elaborate a theology in a vacuum, but to enable believers to make the text of the Psalm their own, to speak it out of their own concerns and anxieties. And central to this is the recognition that Christ has first made these words *his* own. When this Psalm speaks of 'mercy and judgement' together, we are reminded that in Christ things otherwise separate are brought and held together, so that, because we are living in Christ it is possible for us to sing both of mercy and of judgement. In this present age, we sing of mercy, since this is the time when we must plead for God's forgiveness and grace while it is still possible, secure in the hope of mercy yet knowing we shall face judgement in the future. In Christ, present and future come together, so that we are able to 'inhabit' both, neither forgetting judgement in our praise of God's mercy nor fearing judgement as if God had not promised to be merciful. The point is that the *pastoral* goal of the sermon is inseparable from the clear theological principle of our incorporation into Christ and Christ's assuming of our human voice. If we are to understand Augustine, we need, as Louth says, to hear him negotiating this frontier between pastoral instruction and theological vision. Once again, we should be warned that a reading of Augustine that sees only the surface of his work as a speculative thinker will not reveal the fullest depths of his texts, even the most 'theoretical' of them.

Thinking about Augustine's preaching naturally prompts further reflection on his understanding of rhetoric, the art of persuasion, as it applies to Christian formation; so it is appropriate that we move next to examining some of what he has to say about this in his most extended treatment of the actual process of instruction, the *De doctrina Christiana*, whose first three books he was writing at the same period as many of the *Enarrationes*, and just before he embarked on the *Confessions*. This is a treatise on the formation of the Christian mind,

---

[19]*Orthodox Readings of Augustine*, ed. Aristotle Papanikolaou and George E. Demacopoulos (Crestwood, NY: St Vladimir's Seminary Press, 2008), pp. 291–304.

containing some of Augustine's most sustained thinking about the language of Scripture and its diverse senses. But it also sketches a number of significant ideas about the whole nature of language – moving on a good deal from his earlier theories about words and signs as found especially in the *de magistro* ('The Teacher'), where Augustine argues that nothing can really be learned from words: we learn the truth by looking at what we are internally taught by the living Truth, God. Words are not necessarily connected with the objects they denote: we learn to associate them with objects we already know by observation.

But, Augustine maintains (*De magistro* 33ff.: 'the sign is learned from our knowledge of the thing'), this means that a word is at best a kind of pointer to a mental content; if we are able to access that content for ourselves we do not need words to carry the information. And the ideal situation is, it seems, one in which language has been superseded by direct acquaintance with given mental content; when we are thinking about realities other than individual objects in the world (universals, for example), we rely on the intrinsic awareness of non-material realities implanted in us by God. This model has been much modified by the time we get to the *De doctrina*; and it is hard not to conclude that a significant part of what makes the difference is Augustine's experience of engaging with the words of Scripture as a preacher. What emerges from the *De doctrina* is, as the chapter following suggests, a more nuanced sense that the very tension between sign and thing becomes significant when seen in relation to Christology: Christ is both supreme truth and reality and also the sign on which all other signs converge, the context of all meaning in human speech and understanding; and so when we grasp that he indicates or articulates God in the world by his willing self-emptying in unconditional love, we learn, on the one hand, how to read all signs as pointing to divine love and, on the other, how we ourselves may become 'signs' of God by following Christ's self-emptying[20]. As the next chapter notes, it is not only Christology but specifically a theology of Christ crucified that now shapes Augustine's thinking about language; a conclusion entirely in accord with the theology in the *Enarrationes* of Christ's identification with human suffering.

---

[20]For a sophisticated recent discussion of these themes, see Susannah Ticciati, *A New Apophaticism: Augustine and the Redemption of Signs* (Leiden and Boston: Brill, 2013), especially chs 5 and 6.

3

Language, Reality and Desire: The Nature of Christian Formation

De doctrina Christiana, Augustine's treatise on Christian education (not 'doctrine' in the modern sense), has been called the first Christian essay in hermeneutics. It is not simply a discussion of biblical exegesis and the skills necessary for this, but a general consideration of how to understand strange texts, texts of an alien culture and language. Just *how* strange the Christian scriptures were to the literate late antique mind is almost impossible for those formed in an even residually Christian culture to imagine; Augustine is writing about the literature of what, from the 'civilized' point of view, is unmistakably a counter-culture. The Latin of the North African Bible would at times have been as bizarre to the educated reader as is the distinctive religious English of a Rastafarian for most of us. There is a good deal of room for exploration here – of the function and effects of specialized forms of language in the life of a religious community, of how this affects the way in which a community is perceived from outside, and, not least, of how it is possible for individuals to be bilingual and bicultural – like Augustine – in this respect; but my present task is less ambitious. Augustine's account of interpretation in the *De doctrina* (henceforward *DDC*) is a set of variations on a single theme, the relation of *res* and *signum*, thing and sign, reality and representation; I want simply to outline his account of this, and to look at one or two aspects of this scheme which may perhaps have some contemporary interest and pertinence. I have not entered into detailed consideration of the whole of the saint's thinking about language as it appears especially in *De magistro* and early in the *Confessions*.[1] Nor have I tried to examine in detail the background of the ideas in *DDC*, a job already done with distinction by others.[2] The following pages are a reading of *DDC* designed to bring into profile some features of Augustine's thinking on language that are both heavily theologically conditioned and in certain respects in tension with his professed theories of language. As so often with Augustine, he is most philosophically interesting when not being self-consciously philosophical.

'Things', says Augustine (*DDC* I.ii), 'are learned about through signs'; a *res* is, first and foremost, something whose being is not determined by the function of meaning something else. It is what it is, and does not belong in a system of representation. It may *become* part of such a system, and be both *res* and *signum*; and there are some things whose being is *in practice* wholly determined by the signifying function – words (clusters of sounds), whose reality has come to be bound up in pointing beyond themselves (though, as we shall see, this is convention: the clusters of sound remain *res* in that they do not signify by nature, being just vibrations of the air). This is not a wholly novel[3] nor, at first sight, a very sophisticated picture. There is an obvious problem with the notion of definable things standing independently of systems of representation, and Augustine does not help with this when he insists on the arbitrary nature of the relation of words to things (*DDC* II.i and ii), and the distinction between natural – involuntary – *signa* and conventional signs that refer to groundless consent.[4] But, unlike his classical predecessors, Augustine also insists that a doctrine of signs is a step towards a more general

---

[1] E.g. *conf.* I.viii.

[2] The seminal study is R. A. Markus, 'St Augustine on Signs', *Phronesis*, I.I, 60–83. See also R. Lorenz, 'Die Herkunft des augustinischen Frui Deo', *Zeitschrift für Kirchengeschichte*, 64, 34–60, and O. O'Donovan, '*Usus and fruito* in Augustine, *de doctrina christiana I*', *Journal of Theological Studies*, n.s.33, 361–97.

[3] It is outlined in *de magistro* IV and VIII. Markus, op. cit., pp. 60–3, summarizes the classical debates about signs, and notes Aristotle's definition of the sign as something that involves in its being the being of something else.

[4] He is eager to avoid the Stoic doctrine that signs are a natural effect of things, and his inclusion of words among signs is a highly important step towards freeing semiotics from a kind of naturalistic determinism and allowing room for a more culturally oriented account of language and meaning.

theory of language, and goes on to fuse this with a much more characteristic theme of his own. The world of *res* is not, after all, so simply defined. There are things which, on one analysis, do not 'speak' of anything further or 'make known' anything other than themselves; but human beings do not live only a cognitive life. We are engaged with the world, moving through it as subjects of will and of love, and each *res* operates in one of two ways upon our willing and loving. It may be something to be 'enjoyed', something which gives us a satisfaction entire in itself, not leading to or demanding interpretation in terms of anything further; or it may be something to be 'used', a means to a more final satisfaction, meaning or 'intending' more than itself. And, adds Augustine, there are things – subjects – that do the enjoying and the using – an important addition; Augustine assumes that 'signifying' is a threefold, not a twofold, affair, involving the subject *for* whom signs signify. We cannot miss the point that discussion of signification is also discussion of those beings who are involved in meaning or 'intending' or understanding.[5] The distinction between *frui* and *uti* (I.iii)[6] is thus superimposed on the *res–signum* distinction, and will pervade the whole of *DDC*; it is the means whereby Augustine links what he has to say about language with what he has to say about beings who 'mean' and about the fundamentally desirous nature of those beings – a link which is undoubtedly the most original and interesting feature of the treatise.

For the Christian, God is supremely *res* (I.v); he alone is what he is, determined by nothing else, confined by no function, requiring no context or interpretation. He is the 'context' of everything, paradoxically not a *res* at all in the strict sense, not one in a series (*non aliud*, as a later theological tradition would put it). He is beyond all naming (I.vi); though Augustine does not so express it, it could rightly be said that no *signum* is adequate to his being. Yet he has himself provided a

---

U. Eco, *Semiotics and the Philosophy of Language* (London: Macmillan, 1984), pp. 33ff. points this out, though considers that Augustine refuses to follow the path he himself opens up. This is largely true; but part of the purpose of the present paper will be to argue that he goes rather further than Eco believes – at least, if one reads his semiotic theory in close connection with his theological programme in *DDC*. I am enormously indebted to John Milbank's paper, 'Theology Without Substance: Christianity, Signs, Origins', in *Literature and Theology* Part I, 2.1 (March, 1988), pp. 1–17; 2.2 (September, 1988), pp. 133–52, for discussion of Eco's views.
[5]Markus, op. cit., p. 72, brings this out with exemplary clarity.
[6]On its possible sources, see Lorenz, and, much qualifying Lorenz's conclusions, O'Donovan, op. cit., pp. 365–7.

signum in the Word made flesh (xi–xiii). By God's own act and initiative, there is a speech available for talking of him: the mind of God is embodied in Christ as our thoughts are in our words, and by this means God can be truly enjoyed by us, perceived, contemplated and loved in his self-sufficient being.

God is *res*, and, in respect of him, all else is *signum*; God alone is to be enjoyed in and for himself, and in respect of him all else is to be used (xxii). As Augustine himself was well aware, such language is misleading if taken at its face value;[7] there is something odd in saying that the proper love of neighbour is a 'using' of the neighbour to draw closer to God, and there are very considerable problems (xxxi) in applying the scheme to God. The difficulties have been often noted. But we must be careful to avoid a superficial reading. Augustine is consciously playing here with a notion both ambiguous and challenging. Our last end is to enjoy self-sufficient truth and reality; since it is the glimpses and intuitions of this that make any understanding, any intellectual life, at all possible, it is not conceivable that anything should be preferable to this (xi).[8] Thus our last end is the contemplation of that which in no way depends on us or is defined in terms of us (we, rather, are defined in terms of it); and so we cannot for this end use other objects of love in a self-interested way. To 'use' the love of neighbour or the love we have for our own bodies (a favourite example of Augustine's) is simply to allow the capacity for gratuitous or self-forgetful *dilectio* opened up in these and other such loves to be opened still further. The language of *uti* is designed to warn against an attitude towards any finite person or object that terminates their meaning in their capacity to satisfy my desire, that treats them as the end of desire, conceiving my meaning in terms of them and theirs in terms of me.[9] 'If you settle down in that delight and remain in it, making it the end and sum of your joy, then you can be said to be enjoying it in a true and strict sense' (xxxiii); and no such cessation of desire is legitimate in relation to finite objects of love. It is painfully absurd, as well as destructive of

---

[7]Its contradictions are set out by O'Donovan, op. cit., pp. 383ff.: he argues that Augustine attempts to identify *fruitio* with love (so that what is not enjoyed is not strictly speaking loved), and that his understanding of *uti* wavers between an instrumental and an 'ontological' sense (the latter simply having to do with an object's place in the scale of being. I am not myself convinced that this latter point holds, as will become clear in what follows in the text.

[8]On the dependence of all intellectual perception on the tacit and occasionally realized awareness of eternal and unchanging truth, see, e.g., *conf.* VII. 10 and 17, *de libero arbitrio* II.xii, 33–4.

self and others, to conclude our exploration when we are in reality still *in via*, still being formed and transformed by what we receive (xxxiii).

The first book of *DDC* therefore offers a definition of moral and spiritual error in terms of confusing means with ends. God alone is the end of desire; and that entails that there is no finality, no 'closure', no settled or intrinsic meaning in the world we inhabit. And God is not an object among others, a *point in the world* to which other points relate and in terms of which they naturally and plainly organize themselves – except in the sense that there is indeed one 'point in the world' entirely transparent to God: the incarnate Word. There is one authorized 'sign' which for once we cannot mistake for anything *but* a sign. The life, death and resurrection of Jesus are *res* in the world's history, yet they are *signum* in a unique sense: they are God's speech, and so, like our speech, defined by what they teach, what they point to. Here is a worldly *res* that cannot mislead us into thinking that it is to be enjoyed in and as a purely worldly object. Because it is entirely and authoritatively marked out as an object of 'use', it can and does lead us to the ultimate *fruendum*, insofar as we can ever lay hold on this within our history. Thus the *way* God is present in our history preserves us from the proud illusion that we can step outside history or halt it (and we can compare Augustine's critique of the Platonists in *Confessions* VII, which echoes closely so much of *DDC* I on the incarnation). The Word's taking of flesh is not a dissolving of history as eternal truth takes over some portion of the world: it is not, says Augustine (I.xii), that God comes to a place where he was not before. Rather the incarnation manifests the essential quality of the world itself as 'sign' or trace of its maker. It instructs us once and for all that we have our identity within the shifting, mobile realm of representation, non-finality, growing and learning, because it reveals what the spiritual eye ought to perceive generally – that the whole creation is uttered and 'meant' by God, and therefore has no meaning in itself. If we do not understand this, we seek for or invent finalities within the created order, ways of blocking off the processes of learning and desiring. Only when, by the grace of Christ, we know that we live entirely in a world of signs are we set free for the restlessness that is our destiny as rational creatures.

---

[9]*conf.* IV.4–9 sets out the traps of loving other human beings as if their ultimate meaning and one's own were mutually definitory.

The coming of the Word in flesh establishes, we might say, the nature of fleshly being as word, as sign, the all-pervasiveness of 'use'. That is to say, we live in a world of restless fluidities in meaning: all terms and all the objects they name are capable of opening out beyond themselves, coming to speak of a wider context, and so refusing to stay still under our attempts to comprehend or systematize or (for these go together) idolize. As Augustine says at the very beginning of his discussion (I.ii), 'wood, stone and cattle' are all *res* at first sight; but there was a piece of wood with which Moses sweetened the waters, a stone on which Jacob laid his head and saw a vision of angels, a beast that Abraham slaughtered in place of his son. 'Not everything is *signum*' in the ordinary course of things (ibid.); but in the light of Christ, no *res* is left alone. It can be used, and so become a sign; it can mean what it is not.[10]

Book II of *DDC* turns to apply all this to Scripture. In Book I, Augustine has assumed that Scripture is a sort of primary derivative from the work of Christ, a unique object of 'use'. If we were perfected in charity, we should not need Scripture (I.xxxix) – just as, if we had known how to 'read' the created order, we should not have needed the incarnation (xii). As it is, Scripture arouses in us an appropriate love and delight when read properly, the delight fitting to a vehicle that is carrying us forward efficiently (xxxv). It is thus the supreme *signum* after Christ, and Book II reflects on the practical consequences of this in our study. Signs are various, and we need skills to read them; much of this discussion is, accordingly, a treatment of the linguistic, semantic and historical skills required. But in the light of what has gone before, one of the most significant passages is a rather awkward and inconclusive chapter early on in this second book (II.vi). Scripture is full of 'obscurities and ambiguities'; it does not lie open to the casual reader. If it is meant to be a pointer to the ultimate *res* beyond – the Trinity – why should such difficulty pervade it? The main point of Augustine's reply is that we do not properly value what we discover rapidly or easily, an argument

---

[10]It is the point that must lead us to qualify Eco's conclusions: Augustine still operates with a semiotic world of individuated substances referring to or pointing to each other, admittedly, but the way in which objects may be absorbed into the realm of sign does suggest something more than 'denotative unambiguity'. The word may, trivially, denote an object, and the object another object (as the ram 'means' Isaac); but the point of the ram denoting Isaac, and, through Isaac, Christ, is not either information or rhetorical decoration, but a warning against supposing we know exactly what 'ram' as a word means, and what the ram of Mount Moriah means, independently of the 'culture' of Christian *caritas*.

familiar from elsewhere in ancient rhetoric and patristic theology.[11] But this is combined with another fairly standard argument, that the unravelling of obscurity occasions delight. 'I don't quite know how', says Augustine, 'but I understand the saints in a more agreeable way when I see them as the teeth of the Church, cutting people off from their errors' (ibid.) – alluding to the allegorical interpretation of a passage in the Song of Songs, 'Thy teeth are like flocks of sheep' (4.2). The similitude contains no extra information, but, for reasons Augustine says he cannot understand, it makes reading proceed *suavius*.

Augustine lived in a culture that prized literary difficulty, and these words of his were to be a charter for later generations attempting to defend the legitimacy of difficulty, of polysemy and metaphorical fluidity in the understanding of Scripture. The Bible becomes a paradigm of what the late antique reader valued. But Augustine is doing more than simply commending it as a suitable field for the exercise of over-sophisticated literary critics. When he recapitulates the argument in the (later) Book IV (vi and viii), he stresses even more the function of difficulty in guaranteeing that learning from Scripture is a *process* – not a triumphant moment of penetration and mastery, but an extended play of invitation and exploration (the resonances of these metaphors are deliberate, and not wholly absent from Augustine's vocabulary). The Christian life itself, as we have seen, is in constant danger of premature closure, the supposition that the end of desire has been reached and the ambiguities of history and language put behind us; and thus the difficulty of Scripture is itself a kind of parable of our condition. We cannot properly enjoy what we swiftly and definitively possess: such possession results in inaction and ultimately contempt for the object (II.vi).

Obscurity in the words of revelation is one of the things that anchors us in our temporal condition; the search for instant clarity and transparency is like the Platonist's search for 'unattended moments' of ecstasy, as Augustine describes it elsewhere. A language which indefinitely postpones fulfilment or enjoyment is appropriate to the Christian discipline of spiritual homelessness, to the character of the believing life as pilgrimage. Yet Scripture is equally, as we have noted, an effective vehicle for the journey home, and its purpose is to perfect that unqualified and self-forgetting *caritas* which human beings

---

[11] E.g. Gregory Nazianzen, *Second Theological Oration* (*Or*.28), 12.

are made for. And so the tracing of the intricacies of scriptural symbol, the unending decoding of revealed obscurity must remain a morally controlled matter. It is not suggested that the difficulty of the sacred text offers a kind of elevated recreation for advanced souls, as an unsympathetic reading of Origen on allegory might imply.[12] The recognition that revelation is not obvious to the fallen mind is humbling, and humility is the indispensable soil for *caritas* to grow upon. Things are plainly stated elsewhere; Augustine admits (II.vi) there is nothing central to the Christian revelation that is restricted to those possessed of advanced hermeneutical skills; but the many transformations of what is plainly stated warn us of the folly of supposing we have rapidly and definitively grasped what is being said in a single successful event of communication.

Obscurity can also, for Augustine, include grotesqueness – the stylistic horrors of the Old Latin, the moral horrors of the Old Testament. The infidel reader may be simply put off (IV.viii), and this is probably just as well, since such a reader lacks the key to the text, which is conversion to Christ; though on the other hand, grotesquerie and strangeness may serve as at least a partly converting invitation. But, for the believer, these are a prophylactic against 'fastidiousness', the assumption that we have nothing to learn from what startles or offends our taste (we may recall Thomas Merton's remarks[13] about the 'difficulty' of the writings of Thérèse of Lisieux – a very considerable challenge to the young Merton's modernist sensibility). We are again being warned against closure; we can and shall learn from the unexpected and from what is not readily culturally assimilable. The bizarre as well as the ambiguous has its place in preserving our openness to the final non-representable end of desire.

The fact that we live in a world where, in a sense, everything is potentially *signum*, potentially speech, where the boundaries of meaning that seem to delineate the clear outlines of a *res* that is uncontroversially what it is are constantly being broken by the apparent metaphorical anarchy evident in Augustine's own exegesis – all this does not amount to a self-indulgent relativism, an exaltation of rhetoric and semantic ingenuity for their own sake. So much is clear from the later chapters of *DDC* II, especially xxiv to xl. We understand the

---

[12] Origen, *de principiis* I.praef. 3 and 8 sets out the principles on which his allegorical readings are based.
[13] *The Seven Storey Mountain* (New York: Harcourt, Brace and Company, 1948; London: Sheldon Press, 1975), pp. 353–4.

all-pervasiveness of use and sign only in the light of that reality which, as we have seen, points unequivocally to God and shows once and for all that creation is not our stopping place. Scriptural exegesis may have its surface anarchy – you never quite know what may stand for what – but *ultimately* its exchanges and substitutions converge on the cross, 'On which all Figures fix their Eyes'. II.xli spells this out a little further: the cross stands for the whole of discipleship; as we live it out, we learn the depth and riches of the *caritas* of Christ. The cross is the final 'passover', the point of disjunction between slavery and freedom; but only humility can grasp this – the humility, presumably, that has learned to live in the realm of time and symbol and not to 'enjoy' it as complete or final, the humility signified in the passover narrative by that insignificant plant, hyssop. 'Rooted and grounded' in this humble and accepting love, we see the scope of Christ's love in the cross. Relating this both to earlier passages, and, once again, to the almost contemporary *Confessions* VII, we can say that the scope of Christ's love lies precisely in his own supremely gratuitous acceptance of the limits of history: what is uniquely *res*, the eternal wisdom of God, becomes uniquely and entirely *signum*, a worldly thing meaning what it is not. To look to the cross, then, and to 'sign' ourselves with it, is to accept the same limits, and thus to live in hope – and, Augustine adds, oddly at first sight, to have proper reverence for the sacraments; not so odd if we see this as a further illustration of the need to see the symbolic life of the Church itself as pointing beyond itself, rather than providing a ground for spiritual complacency and stasis (as for the Donatists, perhaps, whom Augustine certainly has in mind here).

The cross in particular, and the incarnate life in general, display the distance between God and creation in displaying their union. How is God present in the world? In a death, in weakness, inactivity, negation, the *infirma divinitas* of *Confessions* VII.18, the weak God lying at our feet. It is the 'void' – in worldly terms – of Christ incarnate and crucified that establishes the *difference* of God; it is this emptiness of meaning and power that makes Christ supremely *signum*. He is God's speech *because* he is worldly 'silence'; he is what cannot be enjoyed or rested in. We can do nothing but 'use' this (if we relate to it at all) – that is, we can only allow it to detach us from self-sufficient satisfaction, from image and expectation. The unbridgeable distance between the eternal *res* and all earthly representation opens up through this 'anti-representation' that is the cross; yet in the recognition of distance is also buried the apprehension of gift or revelation. Here is an event that, in itself and in its long-term effect in the formation of the Church, speaks of absolution or re-creation, of grace; in challenging our 'possessing' of objects or events, challenging our urge to 'enjoy' the world, and so too the urge to close the question of meaning, it rescues us from the stasis of pride, the self-paralysis Augustine so vividly describes in the *Confessions* as the fruit of misdirected and misconceived desire. In the *Confessions*, Platonism serves first to liberate desire, to stop us enjoying limited objects, so that our longing can turn towards what is not in the realm of things; but desire must undergo a second purification. It is not to seek for timeless vision, for the true and the eternal, as a kind of *place* to escape into from the vicissitudes of the material world; it must enact its yearning through the corporate life of persons in this world (through the Church, ultimately, for Augustine). And it is directed or instructed and enabled in this by the fact that the crucial liberation from pride is effected by encountering the utter difference, the transcendence, of unchanging truth in the life, death and resurrection of a mortal man.

All this remains buried in what is very often a quite unreconstructed set of Platonic antitheses;[14] yet in the works of the later 390's, the breach with Platonism (Platonism as Augustine understood it and had experienced it) is perhaps more clearly marked than in any earlier or later writings. Having sketched with some care the Platonic vision of the superiority of the incorruptible and immaterial, Augustine is then obliged by his commitment to the incarnate Christ to *deny* that the incorruptible and immaterial can ever as such be an object for the cognition of material, historical and 'desirous' beings. Only in the non-finality of historical relationships and historical 'satisfaction', and in the consequent restlessness that keeps us active and attentive is unchanging truth to be touched. The language and the setting of *Confessions* IX.x, the famous Ostia 'vision', bring this out vividly: it is in the mutual stimulus, the urging further and further, of a *conversation* that there comes a momentary glimpse of sheer fruition. Cast as much of it is in the terminology

---

[14]For a brilliant interpretation of the tensions in Augustine between Platonic metaphysical resolution and questioning faith, see Joseph S. O'Leary, *Questioning Back. The Overcoming of Metaphysics in Christian Tradition* (Minneapolis, MN: Winston Press, 1985), ch. 4.

of a purgative ascent through creatures to the soul and thence to the highest being, this account is nonetheless a powerful challenge to the 'Platonic' model of individual escape from words and matter, because of its conversational character. Heaven would be a perpetuation of the moment of fruition, the *shared* reaching out *ictu trepidantis aspect* of Augustine and Monica; and now all that can be said or understood of that fruition is through the image of the moment of mutual transparency that can issue from the intense exchange of words: where the fluidity of utterance itself, a play of words that is also the modification and re-forming of a relationship between material persons, so indicates or rather embodies its own unfinishable nature that it expresses or introduces the irreducible 'difference' of God.

'There is no absolute knowledge but rather a textual infinite, an interminable web of texts or interpretation' (Geoffrey Hartman[15]). Allowing – as one always must with such statements – the widest possible sense to 'textual' (as relating to any structure of intelligible representation in words or acts), it is possible to see Augustine's treatment of reality and representation as moving in this direction. In the sense that no worldly *res* is securely settled as a fixed object 'meaning' itself, or tied in a fixed designation, that no worldly state of affairs can be allowed to terminate human desire, that all that is present to us in and as language is potentially *signum* in respect of the unrepresentable God, and despite the surface crudity of his distinction between things and names, Augustine's scheme in *DDC* certainly has affinities with the popular notion that everything is language, everything is interpretation. What we know is what we 'read'. But the point at which this ceases to be an adequate characterization of Augustine is precisely the point where this discussion began: the canonical text that witnesses to the canonical (normative) representation, Christ; the text that exists not simply for 'play', but for the formation of *caritas*. It is not textuality that is, ultimately, infinite, but the love of God, shaping our love.

Scripture is a text with a centre; it is to be interpreted in the light of Christ crucified and only so.[16] The central displacement of fixed concepts involved

---

[15]*Criticism in the Wilderness* (New Haven, CT: Yale University Press, 1980), p. 202.
[16]Well delineated in M. Pontet, *L'exégèse de s. Augustin prédicateur* (Paris: Aubier, 1945), esp. pp. 377ff. – 'La croix donne le sens même de l'Écriture' (p. 377).

here – God, flesh, time, eternity, mortality, creation, dissolution, power and impotence – reminds us that the sign-quality of the world is not to be trivialized into a mere system of ciphers, puzzles that yield solutions, fixed material symbols for a fixed immaterial object or set of objects (when you know the code, you read off the content). When Augustine in *DDC* III.v–x warns against the fundamental error of mistaking *signum* for *res*, he is not so much complaining that some people are ignorant of the code of scriptural symbolism as noting the importance of the central hermeneutical collision that occurs between Christians and Jews. In Augustine's eyes, the problem for the Jews is that they have long lived unconsciously under useful signs; without any theological overview to make full sense of it, the people of the Old Covenant knew how to 'use' the signs established in the Law, symbolic acts, ceremonies, modes of behaviour. By God's providence, these signs began to teach *caritas*, they did not invite enjoyment. But in fact the whole of this symbolic order looks forward to the point at which it is *shown* to be such, when it is finally revealed to be *signum*: with the coming of Christ and his passion and resurrection the full scope of divine and human *caritas* appears, so that the previous history in the light of which Christ is intelligible, and which he in turn makes newly intelligible, is seen to serve, to be 'useful', in relation to this decisively liberating event. Faith in Christ now renders the exact observance of the old symbolic forms redundant: from practices, they become words only, the written record of the Law, because the relevant 'useful' practice is now the resurrection of life in the Church, with its new and more restricted and austere symbolic life (III.ix).

A sign may be usefully observed in ignorance; but when it is shown to *be* a sign, a choice is introduced. To observe a symbolic form or deliberately go on inhabiting a symbolic structure of words and images in the old way, when the definitive sign appears that draws together all law, all rites, all images, is to turn the old order of signs into something different, to begin to 'enjoy' it, to choose it *for itself*, and so to refuse the summons to time and history and the possibility of *caritas* which the sign is meant to carry. The sign chosen for itself as against the liberation towards the one true *res* offered by the final sign of Christ is being turned into a pseudo-*res*: symbolic practice has lost its innocence.

Although this discussion is predictably cast in the rhetoric of anti-Jewish polemic (Augustine does not ask, for instance, what a *Jewish* exegete might want to propose as a focusing or definitive *signum*, or indeed what exactly the Law is a sign *of* for the Jew), he allows that the problem of confusing *res* and *signum* is a more general one. The Christian may so treat the sacraments of the Church as to cease properly 'using' them; there are useless interpretations of useful signs, and it is better to be ignorant of the explanation of a sign's use than to have a wrong understanding of it – presumably an understanding divorced from *caritas* (III.ix). But the importance of the application of all this to Scripture is that Augustine has in effect defined Scripture as the paradigm of self-conscious symbolic awareness: it is a pattern of signs organized around – and by – the incarnate Word in such a way that all the signs *remain* signs, all are kept open to the horizon of God, in virtue of their relation to the central acting out in cross and resurrection of God's otherness from the realm of representation. Only the God who is irreducibly different in this way (*non aliud*, not another in a series or class) can finally open up desire to the dimension of *caritas*, love which is both passionate (engaged, actively committed, exposed) and disinterested, self-forgetful. To know the difference between *res* and *signum* is, for the Christian believer, to know the difference of God, and so to be equipped for life in God's image, the unending expansion of love.

'It would be a great relief', writes Hartman,[17] 'to break with the idea of the sacred, and especially with institutions that claim to mediate it. Yet the institution of language makes every such break appear inauthentic. It keeps us in the "defile of the word", meeting, slaying, purifying what is held to be sacred or sublime again and again. The very persistence, moreover, of so many and various ideals of language purification betrays something religious in spirit, if not in name.' Hartman, like some other contemporary critics, comes close to a 'natural theology' grounded in the facts of language and interpretation, the unfinishable nature of discourse: the Other is inescapable, in that, once anything has been said, its incompletion, silences or embarrassments require a different utterance, 'friend or antagonist' to what has already been said.[18] When all has been said, we still face a question, even a claim, which expresses itself in language's pressure to self-purgation. This is a theme that needs careful handling (like all supposed

---

[17] *Criticism in the Wilderness*, p. 249.
[18] Ibid. p. 260.

natural theologies, it delivers only an abstract conclusion); but it could at least be agreed that no religious world-view could survive without an account of the unfinished and fluid character of the linguistic world, a conviction that atomistic 'systems of representation' purporting to label discrete objects are a snare and a delusion. The interest of Augustine's scheme is that he avoids giving a simplistic version of this conviction. He goes further than the argument, familiar from the Cappadocians,[19] that names leave a 'residue' undescribed and indescribable in things. Because he is ceaselessly attentive to the inseparability of knowledge from love, Augustine's own concern is not to secure such a residue, but to understand how language in its fluidity and displacements is inseparably interwoven with the restlessness or openness of desire that is what is fundamentally human. Language is not a set of discrete acts of unsuccessful naming any more than it is a set of discrete acts of successful naming. 'Success' in our discourse is the skill of *continuing with* the shifts of interconnecting perceptions that material history and relationship produce. To return to Augustine's example, we may start with the supposition that an animal is a *res*, a distinct object bearing a name; but the ram, once brought into the narrative orbit of covenant and sacrifice, slaughtered to redeem Isaac, is not to be so easily shepherded and penned in. Even the most trivial talk about rams is now liable to be haunted by this metaphorization. Only God means nothing but God.

And further, Augustine, by directing our attention to the particular set of signs we call Scripture, explains how the interweaving of fluid language and open desire is the locus of transforming grace. Cross and resurrection, to which all scriptural signs lead us, free us once and for all from the threat of an idolatry of signs. They are both inescapable and provisional. God has 'placed himself in the order of signs' (de la Taille's famous phrase), and so brought to light the nature of all signs in respect of his own nature as uniquely *res*. *Caritas* is the goal that lies in and beyond the skill of 'continuing with' the shifts of discourse; since, for the Christian, language is no more capable of being a 'neutral', closed, self-reflexive pattern of play than is human being itself. The 'realism' of such a view – to open up a rather unmanageably large issue – is implicit in the directedness of interpretation towards love, and the conviction

---

[19] Basil, *adversus Eunomium* I.i.6, ii.4, Gregory of Nyssa, *contra Eunomium* X, etc.

that adequate interpretation *begins* with the primordial 'non-worldly' love enacted in Christ. The world of human discourse is, for Augustine, extended between the love of God in creation and redemption, and the Beatific Vision.

The omnipresence of metaphor, then, is 'controlled', not by a breakthrough into clear metaphysical knowledge (though Augustine constantly struggles with the pull towards this resolution, not always successfully), but by a central metaphor to which the whole world of signs can be related, a sign of what all signs are. The Word incarnate and crucified represents the absence and deferral that is basic to *signum* as such, and represents also, crucially, the fact that absence and deferral are the means whereby God engages our desire so that it is freed from its own pull towards finishing, towards presence and possession. Christ can only be shown to be the enactment of God if, as bearer of ultimate promise, he at the same time defers and transforms that promise by a death that presages our baptismal death as believers (and our daily losing of and longing for the face of God in the practice we call faith), and a resurrection that does not destroy our creatureliness but at least strips it of creaturely 'attachment'. Wisdom elects to be mortal; and what prevents this from being a straightforward theophany that would lead us to *identify* Wisdom with the world of mortality is that it is precisely *mortality* itself, limit, incompletion, absence, that is the speech of Wisdom with us. A world of mortality can only be theophanic (in the sense of pure 'presence') if its mortal elements are erased: theophanies are seen in 'orient and *immortal* wheat'. But whatever the religious significance of such 'timeless' moments (and it is not something the mature Augustine dwells on; he is more inclined to see terror and mystery in the natural world than to sense God in it in any undialectical way), it is not here that Wisdom is active in the transformation of the world, but in the presence-in-absence of Christ hastening towards his death and calling us after (*DDC* I.xxxiv; the same image is found in *Confessions* IV.xii). Wisdom is mortal for and with us not to destroy but to affirm and then transfigure the world in which we actually live, the world of body, time and language, absence and desire. There is indeed a *requies* promised to the people of God, the 'presence' of heaven and the vision of God's face; but by definition this cannot now be talked about except in the mythological language of future hope (as if it were a future state like other future states, like what I shall feel tomorrow). It is the presence of God at our own end, our death, the end of time for us, and in some sense the end of desire in *fruitio*; not, therefore, for possession now in the language of belief, or any other language.

This discussion of Augustine's approach to language and meaning in connection with his preaching of Scripture underlines the importance of reading his theory of interpretation as bound in with a pedagogy of love: interpretation moves us to a more radical love for God, God's own love takes root in us, and we in turn become signs of that love; we are a 'text' in the world for others to read. Augustine, with his training as a public speaker, a rhetorician in the classical mould, is seeking (especially in Book IV of the *De doctrina*, written much later than the first three books, in 426/7) a way to articulate a set of Christian rhetorical principles consistent with classical method yet also appropriate for the very non-classical material he is handling (and the very non-classical spiritual goals of his interpretative activity).[20] Carol Harrison's essay 'The Rhetoric of Scripture and Preaching: Classical Decadence or Christian Aesthetic?'[21] gives a very lucid and fresh account of what is going on in this discussion, arguing that what is new in Augustine's rhetorical theory is the concern that good speech should produce 'delight', not in the skill of the orator but in the subject matter of the speech – that is, in this instance, the divine truth. 'It is', she writes, 'the notion of delight that transforms Augustine's very negative picture of language after the Fall, to make it one of the key ways in which God reveals himself to fallen man, in a manner which inspires his delight, and, therefore, pleases and moves him, so that he loves and performs the good.'[22] We noted in chapter two how Augustine reflects on the odd fact that metaphor increases the pleasure we take in what is said; and this acknowledgement of pleasure in the way language works is one of the ways in which the austerity of the model advanced in *De magistro*

---

[20]There is an excellent collection of essays on the *De doctrina*: De Doctrina Christiana: *A Classic of Western Culture*, ed. D. W. H. Arnold and P. Bright (Notre Dame, IN: Notre Dame University Press, 1995). See also R. A. Markus, *Signs and Meanings: Word and Text in Ancient Christianity* (Liverpool: Liverpool University Press, 1996).
[21]Pp. 214–30 in *Augustine and His Critics: Essays in Honour of Gerald Bonner*, ed. Robert Dodaro and George Lawless (London: Routledge, 2000).
[22]Ibid., p. 223.

is most clearly qualified. As Harrison argues, it is completely in accord with Augustine's general theology of beauty (the subject of Harrison's own doctoral thesis[23] that he should seek to show that Scripture is beautiful and must be so if it is to move us to love, which arises from delight; likewise, preaching must be beautiful, not as a matter of impressive ornament but through its appeal to what most deeply attracts, the self-giving love of Christ.[24]

Similar themes are taken up by Edward Morgan in his monograph, *The Incarnation of the Word: The Theology of Language of Augustine of Hippo.*[25] He notes that in his most mature work Augustine both sees language as the clearest marker of the difference between our situation and God's eternity and insists that only through language's materiality can we 'approach the being of God who is higher than both language and thought'.[26] Furthermore, he stresses Augustine's regular concentration on language used publicly – in preaching and liturgy – so that we can say that his theology of language always has a dimension to it that assumes the relation of speaker and hearer or author and reader.[27] There is, in other words, a dialogical element to his understanding and thus a social perspective always implied. Morgan's study traces how this is developed through the *Confessions* and the *De trinitate*: once again we are brought back to what has already appeared as the focal theme in recent Augustine scholarship, the recognition that Augustine is misunderstood if he is read as privileging a strictly individual interiority rather than a self formed in temporal interaction and speech.

But behind all these discussions about language and time and the self lies a cluster of wider issues. We have already seen how there is movement between that aspect of Augustine's thought, especially in his earlier work,

---

[23]*Beauty and Revelation in the Thought of Saint Augustine* (Oxford: Clarendon Press, 1992); ch. 2 is particularly relevant to the discussion of language in Augustine. Harrison very effectively (pp. 82–3) counters the claim by R. J. O'Connell *(Art and the Christian Intelligence in Saint Augustine* [Oxford: Blackwell, 1978]) that Augustine has no interest in the dialectical character of symbolism, both separate from and embodying what it signifies.

[24]Harrison, op. cit., pp. 224–7, 'The Rhetoric of Scripture and Preaching'. On the connection between preaching and spiritual development, see also the fine recent study by Paul R. Kolbet, *Augustine and the Cure of Souls* (Notre Dame, IN: Notre Dame University Press, 2010), especially ch. 6.

[25]London: Routledge, 2010.

[26]Op. cit., pp. 38–9.

[27]Ibid., pp. 95–100.

which encourages us to turn from the fractured world of external desirables towards the one truly desirable Other, God, and that aspect which increasingly embodies the recognition that the very diversity and fragmentation of finite reality (including finite language) is the necessary starting point for spiritual growth, and is to be valued for what it is – the indispensable base for our movement Godwards, the vehicle for God to communicate the promise of fuller joy and vision.[28] Without accepting our radical difference from God, we cannot be united with God.[29] But this requires some further examination of what we mean by creation itself. As the next chapter will explain, some readers of Augustine have understood him as claiming or implying that creation is an act of domination, in which the supreme God exerts power over a contingent and material world. This, I shall argue, is to misconceive completely what is actually being said about the relation of creator to creation – not only by Augustine but by all classical Christian theologians. It is as we reflect on how he understands what is involved in the creative relationship that we see the deepest roots of his conception of love itself.

---

[28] Ch. 3 of Hanby, *Augustine and Modernity* (op. cit., p. 22) is helpful here, especially pp. 82–90.

[29] Hence my puzzlement over some of Wayne Hankey's criticisms, especially in 'Stephen Menn's Cartesian Augustine' (for example, pp. 198–200) (op. cit., p. 22). He seems to be complaining that interpreters of Augustine who emphasize the importance of beginning with our incarnate state and its limitations are somehow creating an unbridgeable gulf between God and creation, and so (in the guise of distancing Augustine from Neoplatonism) reinstating a 'pagan Neoplatonism' (in which the transcendent One is beyond all relation, even to itself). But to say that, for example, our wisdom is never, even in grace and glory, *intrinsic* to us in the way God's wisdom is to God's being is simply to remark the grammar of createdness and uncreatedness, finite and infinite. And the curious statement that a concern with these matters condemns finite souls to an eternal hell (because they are never fully united with God) is, I believe, to misunderstand quite radically what Augustine – and pretty well any orthodox Christian theologian – would say about union with God. It never ceases to be the union of finite with infinite; it never becomes an identity of substance (such that our wisdom or virtue became identical with our being). But this is not to deny in the least the reality of union in Christ with the Father, a union that in heaven we believe will be eternal, inseparable and as intimate as is possible for created beings. Hanby, op. cit., pp. 145–6, has some pertinent remarks.

4

'Good For Nothing'? Augustine on Creation

'The received view [of the doctrine of creation] consisted of a nest of shared beliefs, but the two most important for our concern are that God created ex nihilo, *from "nothing", and that God created hierarchically, with the physical subordinated to the spiritual. . . . [T]he imaginative picture it paints is of a God fashioning the world, either intellectually by word (a creation of the mind) or aesthetically by craft (a creation of the hands), but in either case out of what is totally different from God, and in a manner that places humanity above nature, spirit above body.'*[1]

'A particular reading of this foundational text [Gen. 1–3] has given Western culture the fundamental idea that the universe is a hierarchy: a system of order imposed by spiritual power from above. . . . There is the idea that the physical world is an artifact, made or constructed by God out of inert matter. . . . Whenever we affirm belief in God as "Maker of the Universe" we are referring to this image, and reinforcing the claim to have and to exercise "spiritual power" over matter.'[2]

Two quotations from fairly recent critiques of certain aspects of traditional theology, both, as it happens, from women theologians with a strong ecological

---

[1] Sallie McFague, *Models of God: Theology for an Ecological Nuclear Age* (Philadelphia, PA: Fortress Press and London: SCM, 1987), p. 109.
[2] Anne Primavesi, *From Apocalypse to Genesis: Ecology, Feminism and Christianity* (London: Burns & Oates, 1991), p. 203.

concern. They represent something of a new 'received' view, impatient with what is understood to be involved in the classical doctrine of creation out of nothing; and both – in common, again, with a good many theologians of very diverse complexion – want to remove from our discourse about creation any element of *dualism*, any radical and unbridgeable gap between God and the world. It is just such a gap, we're told, that sanctions or grounds all sorts of other dualisms – not only spirit and body, but man and woman, and humanity and nature;[3] if we *start* with a basic disjunction between an active and a passive partner, and allot a massive metaphysical privilege to the former, we end up associating technocratic humanity, masculinity and distancing or dominating rationality with God. The result is the mess in which this planet now lives, as well as a model of God that signally fails to offer anyone good news (least of all those historically at the receiving end of manipulative dominance). Our crisis demands new models: both the writers I've quoted argue passionately for giving privilege now to the imagery of a God 'embodied' in the creation or a God who 'gives birth' to creation as something bound in with God's own being.

Augustine's is not a name of good omen in these theological circles.[4] He is regularly held responsible for making canonical all these assumptions about hierarchical dualism, as well as for bequeathing us the doctrine of original sin (or rather original *guilt*) in its most indigestible form, and for involving us in centuries-long muddles about sexuality. If we take, more or less at random, two quotations from his best-known and most accessible discussion of creation

---

[3]In addition to the works already cited, we might look at Elaine Pagels, *Adam, Eve and the Serpent* (London: Penguin Books, 1988), for a view of Augustine that tends in this direction; also Rosemary Radford Ruether, *Gaia and God: An Ecofeminist Theology of Earth Healing* (San Francisco, CA: Harper Collins and London: SCM, 1992/3). A more serious engagement with what is believed to be Augustine's legacy for ethics and metaphysics can be traced in the work of Colin Gunton, most recently in 'Augustine, the Trinity and the Theological Crisis of the West', *SJTh*, 43 (1992), pp. 33–58, and *The One, the Three and the Many: God, Creation and the Culture of Modernity* (Cambridge: Cambridge University Press, 1993).

[4]It is difficult to construct any profile of what unites the anti-Augustinians of contemporary theology, but it is probably true that they hold in common a radically anti-Cartesian perspective. Perhaps partly because of Descartes' own use of Augustine, Augustine is often read through spectacles strongly tinted by the way in which Descartes set up the problematic of knowledge and certainty. I have attempted to redress the balance a little in 'The Paradoxes of Self-Knowledge in De Trinitate X', *Collectanea Augustiniana*, 1993, pp. 121–34 (ch. 9 in the present volume).

(in the last three books of the *Confessions*), we seem to have clear evidence for the prosecution. Here he is, talking about creation and formless matter:

> In those days the whole world was little more than nothing, because it was still entirely formless. Yet by now it was something to which form could be added.
>
> For you, O Lord, made the world from formless matter, which you created out of nothing. This matter was itself almost nothing, but from it you made all the mighty things which are so wonderful to us. (XII.viii)

And on the radical distance and difference between God and creation:

> You had no need of me, nor am I a creature good in such a way as to be helpful to you.
>
> ... [F]or you do not withhold existence from good which neither benefits you nor is of your own substance and therefore equal to you, but exists simply because it can derive its being from you. (XIII.i, 2)

Surely these passages bear out the picture given by our contemporary writers? Augustine's creator is wholly alien from what is created, and, when creation is begun, it must be a story of the imposition of spiritual shape or meaning upon a recalcitrant and intrinsically worthless material life. In what follows, I shall argue that this is a complete misreading of Augustine's scheme; whether or not he is right about the relation of God to the world, he cannot simply be charged with inventing or reinforcing a simple matter–spirit dualism. And I want to suggest also that there are dimensions in *any* intelligible Christian theology of creation that oblige us to reckon with some of Augustine's characteristic insights, and so to tread cautiously in exploring some proposed modern correctives, such as those I cited at the beginning of this chapter.

To understand what Augustine is saying about creation, we must grasp the way in which he sees both the continuity and the discontinuity between God and the universe. That created things are 'in' God he does not for a moment dispute; indeed (as Books VII and X of the *Confessions* make clear), coming to a Christian mind on the subject of creation involves recognizing that all things are 'in your truth' (VII.xv), in contrast to the Manichaean doctrine that matter is essentially something impenetrable to the divine, though containing 'granules' of divine life, undigested and unintegrated – and also in contrast to the transitional view described in *Confessions* VII.i and v, where the universal presence of God is thought of as a sort of universal permeation of the world by a very refined material stuff.[5] Existing 'in God's truth' is, in the *Confessions*, primarily to do with existing in reality rather than fantasy, and (consequently) existing in coherence: that is to say, the transparency of the world to the prior reality of God lies in the perception of things *actively* existing and maintaining a pattern of interaction that we can follow or chart in certain ways, a pattern of interaction that leaves no room for a final self-fragmentation, a chaos of arbitrary events. This orderliness is the essence of what we call beauty; and our ability to make judgements about beauty, our instinctive appeal to a standard of ideal harmony, is one of Augustine's most familiar grounds for asserting an innate God-directedness in the mind (*Confessions* VII.xvii; cf. for example, *De vera rel.* 21, 56, 67, etc.).

We can say, then, that creation shares or participates in God *by being a coherent system*. It can't participate in any other way, in Augustine's scheme of things: it can't be a literal 'bit' of God, since God is not a material substance, and it can't be an overflow of the divine essence, since Augustine is quite clear that being God is being outside the realm of change and interaction (we shall look at this again later). How this participation is structured Augustine discusses in a number of places by referring to a text from Wisdom (11.21), where we read that God has ordered all things *in mensura, et numero, et pondere*.[6] In perhaps his earliest use of this text, Augustine quotes it as he considers the question of why there are unattractive or repellent animals in the world, and (as in *Confessions* VII.xvi) he concludes that their unattractiveness and even their hostility to human beings has to do with our sin and spiritual blindness: 'I can't think of any animal's body or members where I don't find the measure and proportion and order that goes towards harmonious unity. And where all this comes from I can't understand unless it is from the supreme measure, proportion and order that exist in the changeless and everlasting sublimity

---

[5] This is, in effect, a Stoic view, though not identified here as such; see, for example, *Stoicorum Veterum Fragmenta*, ed. J. von Arnim, II.774.

[6] *Gn. adv. Man.* 1.16.26 and 21.32; for a seminal study of these terms, see W. Roche, 'Measure, Number and Weight in St. Augustine', *New Scholasticism*, 15 (1941), pp. 350–76. See also *de nat. boni* for *forma* as a variant of *numerus*.

of God' (*Gn. adv. Man.* 16.26). By the time Augustine came to write Book IV of *Gn.litt.*, fifteen or more years later, the 'measure, proportion and order' of the earlier text have turned into the more familiar alternative of 'measure, proportion and *weight*' – which allows him to make some powerful connections with his use of the metaphor of weight in the *Confessions*, where it may well owe something, directly or indirectly, to Plotinus.[7]

I want now to look at what he has to say in *Gn.litt.* IV.3.7ff. about this text from Wisdom. Obviously, to say that God 'follows' measure, proportion and weight in creating cannot mean that God's creative work is dependent on anything other than God; what God 'follows' is the divine life itself. But this in turn cannot mean that God is identical with measure, proportion and weight as elements in created reality. Rather, God is what fixes a *modus* for everything, a specific way of being; what gives a thing *species*, a formal structure that appeals to both aesthetic and intellectual judgement; and what draws a thing towards a state of equilibrium. God is *qui terminat omnia et format omnia et ordinat omnia* (IV.3.7) – the one who limits all things, gives intelligible shape to all things and directs all things to a goal. We can see that these principles do not apply only to material quantities, but to the active mental subject: the moral or spiritual agent acts (ideally) by measure (action limits itself, it is not a stream of undifferentiated energy), by proportion (wisdom involves an appropriate exercise of feelings and virtues, or, as we might put it, a fitting response to circumstances), and by weight (in choosing or rejecting courses of action according to whether they fit the goals of our love). And here we see more clearly how *our* reality is shaped by a formative agency beyond our minds. For Augustine, to be a thinking being is always to be *responding* to something prior to us, and the ordered shape of mental life (which, remember, includes *emotional* life in this context; Augustine never denies that emotion belongs to the mind), the purposive character of action and our attempts to make sense or balance of our experienced history, shows that the principles of *mensura, numerus* and *pondus* are active in our regard; and since they cannot act on God (nothing acts *on* God), they must be the act *of* God (Ibid.4.8). They represent the direct impact of God on the world, not a sort of afterthought: as

---

[7] *Enneads* II.1.3.

a matter of fact, everything in the world has colour, but this is not a sign that colour is a divine activity; the intelligible structure of things does not depend on colour, and so we say that God has organized things in such a way that they are coloured, but not that God made them 'in' or 'according to' a principle of coloration (Ibid.5.11). So the conclusion is that the beauty and intelligibility of the world communicate to us the truth that God's action is the kind of action that produces harmonious effects, and therefore tells us, obliquely but unmistakably, that God's nature is to be, not one harmonious or lovely thing above others, but the cause of all harmony and loveliness.

This is a version of familiar Platonic themes, and picks up the commonplace[8] that when God is called good it is because God is the *source* of good, not one among a class of good things (just as, in Aristotle's famous discussion,[9] you can call food 'healthy' when it is the sort of thing that *produces* health). It is the cornerstone of all classical theories of analogy in speaking of God. So if we say, as we must, that the measure and proportion that govern all things belong in God's life, it is because they represent the way God acts, not the 'rules' dictating how God must act. The natural shape of divine action is what produces beauty; no cause controls this action except the being of God as such. Thus, if the world is orderly and purposive, we can conclude that the activity that moulds it makes for order; and this is brought home to us most vividly in thinking about our own mental life, in recognizing that it is shaped by response to unchanging standards. And if we understand that divine activity is not controlled by anything but God, we shall see that God's *nature* is such as to produce beauty; it is in this way that the world's beauty tells us something of what it is to be God – not because God stands at the summit of an ascending scale of beautiful things, but because we grasp that, whatever God's life is (and we can never catch it in a concept), it is what makes for harmony.[10]

---

[8] Articulated, for example, by Albinus, *epitomé* X.5; on the whole question, see R. Williams, *Arius. Heresy and Tradition* (London: Darton, Longman and Todd, 1987), III. B and C.

[9] *Cat*. I. la; for an important expansion and refinement of the point, see Porphyry's commentary on the Categories, esp. 66. 15–21.

[10] This is to recognize the (often ignored or minimized) apophatic element in Augustine; see the classic discussion by Vladimir Lossky, 'Les éléments de "théologie negative" dans la pensée de saint Augustin', *Augustinus Magister* (Paris: Edition des Etudes Augustiniennes, 1954), pp. 575–81.

This helps us to negotiate what may seem a difficult corner in the argument. Augustine is not claiming that the world is, crudely, 'like' God, reasonable and harmonious in all ways: of course it isn't. It is a place of risk, frustration and terror from where we stand,[11] as he was to insist with increasing stridency in his later years: a place which is not amenable to our understanding or control, and in which the frustration of purpose by contingent happenings leads to what we call evil.[12] How does this sit with the vision of a world pointing to God by its orderliness? The answer is that, for Augustine, all good except God's is the product of a process; hence the importance of *pondus* as well as *mensura* and *numerus* in his thought. Measure and proportion govern the reality of things that are made to change, and 'weight' is what pulls them to their proper place. Some of this interest in process is of course carried by Augustine's well-known doctrine, Stoic in origin, of *rationes seminales*, the inbuilt principles that regulate the development of organisms according to predictable patterns (acorns grow into oaks, not daffodils or cows). But, more generally (and it is a theme that plays an important part in the discussion of peace and order in *de civ.* XIX), the world is so ordered that at any point in time the balance of things or agencies is being adjusted towards equilibrium: as individual things develop and their relation to other things consequently alters, *pondus* continually guarantees an overall balance, so that there is not, in the natural order, a chaos of conflictual agencies. Energy is conserved, as we might say in the twentieth century. Things are made to change and grow, to realize their optimal form over time; but this change is woven into a universal mobile pattern, consistently reclaiming its stability. In rational beings, as Augustine famously says, *pondus* is *amor* (*Confessions* XII.ix.10): it is love that draws us back to our proper place, that pulls us back to stability and harmony. And we know ourselves most fully and truthfully, as he so often says, when we know

---

[11] See, for example, *op. imp.con.Jul.* VI, for some of Augustine's most eloquent evocations of the world's miseries.

[12] In the sense that we identify as 'evil' the ways in which our wills become incapable of effecting their own good intentions because of the history of fallenness we inherit. Not all sin, Augustine insists, is naked rebellion against God; it may be the simple fact of defeat by reason of intolerable circumstances, by ignorance or by plain weakness; see, e.g., *De nat. et gratia* xxix.33 and Peter Brown's admirable summary in *Augustine of Hippo* (London: Faber and Faber, 1967), p. 350.

both that we are desiring beings and that our desire is ultimately and freely itself when it consciously becomes longing for God.[13]

Two points here, then. First, Augustine's is a universe in motion: he takes up a philosophical cliché about regular principles of development, and links it with a more comprehensive picture. Everything 'seeks' its own level or its own place; but that place is a place within a network of sensitive interaction, and to grasp the ordered and purposive beauty of the world is to see this ordered mobility and interdependence as a whole,[14] to see – we could say – what a *world* is, a coherent system. We do not have to be able to chart each process in it to understand that it operates as a whole. Augustine is expressing in a very different idiom the often misunderstood conclusions of the *Tractatus*: 'it is not the *way* the world is, but *that* it is that is mystical. The vision of the world *sub specie aeterni* is a vision of it as a (limited) whole. The sense of the world as a limited whole is what is mystical.' Wittgenstein's analysis of logic requires us to recognize that to talk coherently is to deny that there is such a thing as *pure* contingency, anything that could not in principle be described in some sort of intelligible way: it is not that any given system of description (such as scientific 'laws') delivers a final or exhaustive account, but that we have an irreducible insight or intuition, based in the logical form of our discourse, that coherent description is possible.[15] So what is significant is that we intuit a whole, and that we recognize that we cannot *think* of a particular in isolation (Hegel as well as Wittgenstein is on the horizon here). Augustine's vision has all sorts of points of contact with what has gone before in the Platonic tradition, and his originality cannot be overstated. But the use of *pondus* as a central metaphor, with its connotations of 'finding a level', *seeking* something in shifting circumstances, certainly brings into sharp focus the idea of a purposive totality, rather than just an ensemble of specific orderly processes.

Second, this universal motion of seeking or (analogically) 'desiring' equilibrium is part of the way in which creation manifests God, part of the world's 'continuity' with the life of God. As we have seen, God cannot fall under

---

[13]See *civ.* XIX.12–14 in particular.
[14]*Gn adv. Man.* I.xxii.33.
[15]Ludwig Wittgenstein, *Tractatus Logico-Philosophicus*, (London: Routledge & Kegan Paul 1961), p. 149.

the same rules as the world; God could not (logically) be simultaneously the cause of a whole interlocking system *and* a member of it, and so we can never talk of features in common between God and the world. If we use the language of continuity, it is as we trace the character of creative action in its manifest effects, in the fact that we can make sense of the flux of things around us. Once again, it is a Platonic commonplace that time is 'the moving image of eternity': Augustine gives a little more edge and definition to this in the idea that God is imaged or reflected in the 'desire' of things for the divine stability.[16] Turn to the *trin.*, and you will see how this perspective introduces something quite fresh into theological discussion of the image of God in the human subject, which is no longer to be identified with a single feature or cluster of features, but with the orientation of the subject to God, with the radically *unfinished* character of thinking and wanting.[17] Creation, in other words, tells us most about God when it is most clearly *different* from what we conceive to be the divine nature; it speaks of God by being temporal and changeable, a process of endless adjustment that still remains capable of being thought and talked about coherently.

Continuity and discontinuity between God and creation are thus very hard to pull apart in Augustine's thought. The continuities, the ways in which creation shares in the sort of life that is God's, steer us inexorably back to the fundamental difference. But what this secures is a model of creation that should never, in fact, produce the ideas attacked by the writers I quoted at the beginning of this paper. For there to be a world, a limited whole, there must be coherence, a convergence on stability, though it is a stability that continues to alter and reinvent itself at every moment, as time advances: there is no question of 'imposing' anything from 'outside' or 'above', since there is no above or outside the universe in the sense of a rival system acting causally on it from a competing position in logical space. There *is* simply the system, and without intelligibility it cannot be spoken of at all: order is not an extra. But what then does Augustine's language about 'form' and 'matter' mean? This has to be

---

[16] *Gn.litt.*6.32ff., 6,36ff., 6.362, 6.372.

[17] Again, this can be compared with Plotinus' suggestion that the One is somehow mirrored in the *erōs* of intellect towards it; see, e.g. *Enneads* VI.7 and 8.

answered by a longer look at the quite complicated arguments of *Confessions* XII, especially vi–xiii. Having established earlier that creation is not a point at which God changes (since time can only be correlated with the changes of our world, and, once again, God does not share an environment with us and so does not change in response to an environment as we do),[18] Augustine and his readers can only conclude that creation is caused by God's will alone; and what that will establishes as the logical precondition of everything else is that the world will be capable of change (XII.vi). We can understand nothing about the world without granting that this is primary. For the world *not* to be God, to be itself as a limited whole, it must be a complex of processes. What does change entail? A *medium* of change or a vehicle of change; or, to put it another way, an interaction between stability and variety. If change were total, global transformation, we couldn't talk about it at all, since there would be no conceptual structures to hold together a before and after. So Augustine proceeds to interpret Genesis 1.1, 'God created the heavens and the earth', in the light of these requirements. We are told that the earth was originally 'without form'; 'heaven', presumably, is at the opposite end of the spectrum from 'earth'. Thus Augustine postulates two extreme cases of created reality – a level at which formal stability is at its highest because the creature is directly open to God, and a level at which there is minimal form, virtually indeterminate reality. The former (the 'heaven of heavens') must be the condition of intelligent agents wholly devoted to the love of God, so that, while still changeable in principle, they are *in fact* unchanging – angels and redeemed souls in the state to which we can now only aspire: they don't need to get better and, if their love is truly purified, they can't get worse; and so they experience a kind of pure duration, beyond 'history' (XII.xi). At the other end is matter without form, or rather with hardly any form, minimal stability (we could not give content to the idea of an actually existing state of *total* formlessness, as this would be nothing but potential: what could that mean?): all we can say of it is that it is capable of being further formed (XII.viii). The creation we know exists between these two poles, with form constantly and steadily moulding matter into a coherent world. And time, as we experience it, belongs in this in-between. Without

---

[18] See the article referred to in n. 4 above for a fuller discussion.

form there is no change (XII.11), since there could be no measurement of difference: matter alone could have no history. And a state in which form had attained stability would have no history either, since it would no longer be in search of its optimal condition. In between, form and matter are in ceaseless interrelation: we could, indeed, say that the creation we concretely know *is* the process of form acting on matter, the story of increasingly sophisticated organization and interdependence in the universe.

At this point, we had better pause to clarify what 'form' and 'matter' really mean. The post-seventeenth century mind tends to draw a neat distinction between solid things and ideas, with the result that Augustine's statements about form and matter are read in the way our opening quotations seem to assume – some 'spiritual' force struggling with the world of concrete stuff. But this is a travesty. For Augustine,[19] as for Plotinus,[20] 'matter' is pure potentiality. If we say that matter is not of itself good, or even (as Plotinus very nearly says) that it is the source of evil, we are not saying that there is something wicked about flesh, trees, stones or even amino acids. This would be nonsense – the kind of nonsense Augustine spent a lot of time exploding in his writings against the Manichees: only minds can be wicked, because moral evaluation is only relevant to beings who have desires and make decisions. The point is that we cannot make any evaluation at all of pure, empty possibility: we can comment on potential only as potential *for* something or other. And once we start talking about potential for something or other, something with recognizable features and structure, we have started talking about *form*. Potential that isn't realized or that is frustrated is, in this perspective, at best a deficit, an incompleteness, and at worst something that erodes the proper purposive action of a thing. The action of form on matter is not the imposition of one thing on another, let alone one system on another: it is simply the process of actualization itself, the process by which organization appears. In reading these pages of Augustine, we must lay aside the imagery of a primitive stuff shaped into alien structures by God through an act of triumphant power. The point could be

---

[19] *conf.* XI, passim.
[20] See, e.g., *Enneads* II. 4 and I.8; J. M. Rist's article, 'Plotinus on Matter and Evil', *Phronesis*, VI.2 (1961), pp. 154–66, may be recommended as a thoroughly reliable guide to some of the complexities here.

better put by saying that God wills that there be reality quite other than God, and that this entails the positing of a reality that can change: if so, it entails also the dialectic of the possible and the actual, it entails a world of purposive fluidity, things becoming themselves, organizing themselves more successfully or economically over time. Possibilities are continually being realized, but realized in orderly and intelligible fashion: changes in form mean measurable changes, the only sort of change we can talk about (which is why, incidentally, Aquinas could say[21] that the act of creation was not itself a change or a process).

Creation, then, is the realm in which good or beauty or stability, the condition in which everything is most freely and harmoniously itself in balance with everything else, is *being* sought and *being* formed. This is, of course, why there can be no short route to heaven: we must *grow* into new life, as the *Confessions* constantly reminds us.[22] And we must learn to start where we are, as moving, material beings: God's definitive clue to the divine life, and to how we may open ourselves to it, is the event in which the everlasting Word and Wisdom shapes and speaks in and acts out a human and material history, telling us that there is no way to God but through time. To know God, we must follow the course of the incarnate Word,[23] not look for a timeless penetration of God's mind. Two of Augustine's most important themes converge here: the universal implicit recognition of order in the story of things, and the impossibility of fully living in that order without humility, the recognition that we encounter God truly *only* when we accept our mortal fragility for what it is, do not seek to escape it, but put our trust in a God who speaks and relates to us through flesh. A full exposition of Augustine on creation would have to go hand in hand with an exposition of the role of the incarnate Word; understanding Augustine, especially the Augustine of 395 onwards, has often suffered from a failure to keep these themes in view together. And it is essential, in reading Augustine, to recognize that he becomes more and more preoccupied with growth rather than accomplished vision, so that, at any given moment, we are faced with our inability to master the whole process of things: 'As for me, though, I am broken

---

[21]*Summa Theologiae* I.xlv.2 ad 2.
[22]E.g. VII.x,20, X, passim; cf. en.Ps 37.
[23]For the image of the believer running after the incarnate Christ, see *conf.* IV.xii and *doctr. christ.* I.xxxiv.

apart in time, whose shape and meaning I do not know; and my thoughts, the most intimate organs of my soul, are split up by time's stormy changes, until, purified and melted by the fire of your love, all of me will flow together into you' (*Confessions* XI.xxix). Just before this passage, he has been discussing the experience of singing a well-known psalm: bit by bit, expectation shrinks and memory expands. So it is, he says, with the whole of my life and the whole of our common history (XI.xxviii); but in such a perspective, no individual knows the song to its end.

Creation is the constant process of realizing potential goods; and that is why the difference between God and creation cannot be elided. There is nothing that is *potentially* good for God. If there were, God's self-realization would be imperfect; and since the processes of self-realization are bound up with interaction, an agent bringing some other (passive) entity to its fuller life by supplying what it lacks in itself, this would entail treating God as part of a system, in which independent factors could provide for God what the divine being required and did not possess. This is what Augustine is battling against in *Confessions* XIII.i–iv in particular, and it remains a fundamental objection to any theory that regards creation as augmenting God's life or consciousness or whatever.[24] Either God has the resource within the divine life for fullness of bliss, in which case no divine act changes or enlarges this in its essence; or God does not have such resource, and this divine lack can only be supplied by another agent – and to postulate such another agent would be to abandon any commitment to the notion of a coherent universe. Hence Augustine's insistence in XIII.i and ii on the notion that Creation does not 'benefit' God. This has become a profoundly unpopular doctrine in

---

[24] I should say, in passing, that, while this sets Augustine firmly against all varieties of process theology and any other scheme that proposes to reduce the radical (non-competitive) difference between God and the world, Augustine's relation to Hegel represents a far more complex question, worthy of longer discussion. I do not myself believe that a doctrine of creation faithful to what Augustine and the great majority of traditional theologians take for granted is necessarily hostile to the Hegelian account overall, since this could be read as another way of dealing with what I have called non-competitive difference, in a drastically different idiom. The one thing Hegel does not teach, despite the assumptions of some, is that there is an augmentation of Spirit through the processes of creation, or that God is in any sense a subject of history. But this takes us further afield than is convenient for present purposes. I hope to develop the point more fully in an essay on Hegel's religion for a planned volume on philosophers and faith to be edited by Phillip Blond.

some circles of late, on the grounds that it builds into the relation between God and world a wholly non-negotiable asymmetry, absolute dependence opposed to absolute self-sufficiency: the problems of dualism and hierarchy or patriarchy are seen as focused here. But what needs to be said is that dualism and hierarchy become problematic as relations *within* a system that ought to be unified and interdependent.[25] Enough should have been said by now to make it clear that God, in Augustine's terms, is in no sense within the same frame of reference. God's action cannot *compete* with created agency, God does not have to overcome a rival presence, the creative power of God is not power exercised unilaterally over some other force, but is itself the ground of all power and all agency within creation. God does not (*pace* McFague, Primavesi and others) make the world by imposing the divine will on some recalcitrant stuff, and no serious theologian has claimed this. Rather, God causes an entire process in which intelligible structure comes to view. In response to the act of God, created life shapes itself as a balanced whole, seeking all the time what the physicists call dynamic equilibrium; but all this, and the possibilities thus realized, is simply the result of the divine freedom.

Thus creation really is 'good for nothing': its *point* is not to serve a divine need. Our difficulty with the idea is (depressingly) the difficulty of imagining a need-free love, and it is a difficulty felt as much by ancients as by moderns. The early Christian claim that God creates out of nothing presupposed the possibility and reality of a love *not* based on kinship or similarity, since it presupposed a God willing to make real something wholly other than the divine life and to endow it with beauty, rationality and liberty. As Clement of Alexandria put it,[26] this is a love that goes beyond the natural claims of *koinonia*. Now *koinonia*, community of kind – perhaps 'solidarity', if you want a fashionable word – is, in the Christian vocabulary, not the ground but the effect of love, of a free reaching out to what is and remains ineradicably strange and other. So St Paul implies; so Augustine too implies in his lengthy

---

[25]For some shrewd observations on this, see M. J. Scanlon, 'The Augustinian Tradition. A Retrieval', *Augustinian Studies*, 20 (1989), pp. 61–92, esp. pp. 80–4.
[26]*Stromateis* II.xvi (GCS edition, pp. 151.27–152.26).

discussions of love and communion in the anti-Donatist literature.[27] There is a thread of connection between a repudiation of tribal or sectarian accounts of love and what has to be said about the gratuity of creation. It is a point that receives a subtle, almost ironic, twist in the *doctr. chr.* (I.xxxi–ii). If all loving is to be divided into instrumental and contemplative, using and enjoying, loving something for the sake of or in relation to something else and loving something for its own sake, what can be said of God's love for us? If God 'enjoys' us, contemplates us as we do God, that would suggest that God requires us so as to be happy, and so that we augment or enrich the divine life; and this will not do, because light is not kindled by the objects it illuminates. So God's love for us is 'instrumental'? Yes, but God does not 'use' us for the sake of something more ultimate, since God *is* the ultimate good, for whose sake all things in the world are to be loved, and so has no ultimate goal but the self-contemplation of the divine life, which, once again, needs nothing else to complete it. So we must say that God 'uses' us for the sake of our greatest good, which is, of course, loving God: God loves us so that we may come to *our* highest good, not so that *God's* good may be served. Our good is God, and, consequently, the love of one another for and in God. God's love is instrumental for our good, and so is wholly selfless, since my enjoyment of God is the greatest possible bliss for me, but adds nothing to the endless bliss of God.

The pure desire for the joy of another: that is what the Augustinian doctrine of creation presupposes, and that is where it challenges our supposed improvements on his synthesis. There are all sorts of proper objections to a theology that drives a wedge between God and what God makes – and, as we have seen, Augustine would understand and share them. But what is problematic is when these objections lead us towards a theology in which God and creation have virtually indistinguishable interests, and where God's love for creation becomes a function of God's love for God, understood as a furthering of those 'interests'. Ultimately this impoverishes our spiritual and moral imagination in intimating that there is no love beyond kinship and shared interest. I suspect that the difficulty has something to do – in the widest sense – with politics. In the Western world, we have rightly become

---

[27] See esp. Book III of *bapt.*

suspicious of certain models of love that take for granted an unexamined system of power relations – love as the benevolence of the one who possesses towards the one who is dispossessed, a love that does nothing to transform the structures of possession and dispossession. For all kinds of groups, love has been rediscovered in the experience of solidarity, the mutual nurture of those who share the same pain or privation. Such nurture is the source of strength, a beginning of empowerment, and so of transformation. This has been the experience underlying so much of liberation theology, whether in the Third World or among women and black people and others in the global north, and it plays a central role too in various kinds of peace movements. But – as Ellen Charry points out in a powerful and controversial recent essay[28] – there is a risk that different victim groups or marginal groups remain locked in their specific frames of reference, lacking a way of realizing a substantive unity with each other, or of imagining a situation beyond the mutual empowerment of those sharing privation. The underlying question of how we love the radical stranger (let alone the oppressor, in some new and rectified order) is evaded if love's paradigms are rooted solely in common experience and common need.

This is not to brush aside – God forbid – the moral weight of solidarity, and the immense force of the discovery of power in powerlessness that emerges from a politics of solidarity. Nor should it lead us to gloss over the fact that Augustine undoubtedly *does* endorse a hierarchical and patriarchal picture of the universe. But his fundamental structures for thinking about creation place firmly on the agenda a set of issues we cannot safely ignore. The desire for the good or the joy of another who *remains* other, perhaps disturbingly, certainly uncontrollably, other, should remind us that solidarity doesn't say everything; and the more that has to be said has a great deal to do with how we understand the love of God in creation and redemption.[29] Without a belief in a love without self-directed interest, we may find that the gospel of a human community beyond faction and rivalry is harder to preach than we might

---

[28]'Literature as Scripture: Privileged Reading in Current Religious Reflection', *Soundings*, lxxiv (1991), pp. 65–99.

[29]On the significance of such 'otherness' as fundamental for ethics, see Edith Wyschogrod, *Saints and Postmodernism: Revisioning Moral Philosophy* (Chicago, IL: University of Chicago Press, 1990) (allowing for the reservations expressed in my review of this work, *Modern Theology*, 8 (1992), pp. 305–7).

have imagined. Augustine's theology of creation treats the world eminently seriously as the self-communication of God; but, like all God's 'rhetoric', the world does not simply offer a bland reproduction of recognizable and timeless truths.[30] To be serious about creation's meaning and value is to weigh properly its integrity as a moving and changing image, as a limited and fluid whole that is not God, yet is saturated with God. Above all, Augustine invites us to bring our thinking about love under the judgement of a causeless act of origination, whose purpose is nothing but the joy of the other; for him, we can say of creation itself what the poet said of redemption – that it is:

Love to the loveless shown,
That they might lovely be.

If creation is to be understood as a supremely non-self-interested act of God, it cannot be thought about without reference to the eternal nature of God and to the trinitarian relations. Michael Hanby's *Augustine and Modernity*, already referred to, traces these connections so as to make it clear that creation, for Augustine, *is* grace, in the sense that God's making of the world is inseparably linked with the specific purpose of the world's well-being – and thus, in the particular case of human existence, with sanctification and union with Christ.[31] The creative act of the Trinity is grounded in the Father's delight in the Son and his infinite goodwill towards the Son; what comes into being in creation and is re-created in the incarnate Word is the *beauty* of the eternal Son, that in which the father delights; our growth in wisdom and holiness is thus a growth both in longing for the ultimate beauty which creation intimates to us, and our growth in spiritual beauty.[32] As Hanby argues, this casts helpful light on the hinterland of the Pelagian controversy: the Pelagian self, freely able to choose between moral alternatives, is, for Augustine, cut off from the fundamental motivating energy of *delight*, and thus from an authentically Christ-centred account of the willing self. The Pelagian subject cannot really be what Hanby

---

[30] On God's 'rhetoric', see particularly the 1992 Oxford D.Phil. thesis of Robert Dodaro, OSA, *Language and Justice: Political Anthropology in Augustine's De Civitate Dei*.
[31] See, for example, Hanby, op. cit., p. 22, pp. 82–3, 87–8.
[32] Ibid. p. 84, on 'our differential participation in the beauty of the Son'.

calls a 'doxological self'. 'Once human agency is no longer constituted by its participation in the doxological agency of God; once, subsequently, one's status *in Christ* is reduced from participation in the hypostatic union to *mere* mimesis or imitation [. . .]; once we are no longer understood to be moved to action by the Father's delight in the Son; then *voluntas* ceases to name a relation of love between lover and beloved but rather a "Cartesian" relation of cause to effect.'[33]

Put slightly differently, Hanby's argument could be summarized by saying that we need to keep firmly in focus the way in which Augustine's doctrine of God conditions everything he writes, whether about creation or about human freedom in relation to God. We cannot sensibly discuss Augustine's theology in any specific area without acknowledging the central significance for him of belief in a God whose eternal life is joy and mutuality. Of course this theme becomes more marked and more thematically focused as time goes on, reaching its fullest expression in his work on the Trinity; but it is crucial to see how it is at work in the whole of his thinking. Once again, the *Confessions* displays this interweaving of concerns with particular clarity – as, for example, in Book XI.viii./10– ix/11, where creation, knowledge of the truth, salvation from sin and Trinitarian theology come together in a 'confession', and acknowledgement, of Augustine's present dependence on God's grace. The Word spoken in the flesh of Christ is the Word which is the beginning of all things; to hear this Word in the flesh is to be summoned to the unchanging centre within our existence – to be summoned to learn the truth by 'standing still and listening'. The effect of this is that we 'rejoice with joy on account of hearing the voice of the bridegroom' (a reference to John 3.29), and yield ourselves to this bridegroom. Our source, our 'beginning', speaks to us and engages us totally through the delight offered in the words uttered by the incarnate Christ; but what it draws us to is the eternal reality in and by which God makes the universe and fills it with his light – which is also his saving will and action. It is a dense passage, but its very density confirms the point: there is no way of separating the interlocking themes of free creative love, incarnation, delight, nuptial union with the Son, reconciliation with the

---

[33]Ibid., p. 104.

source of our life. Hanby is right to speak of the human self which emerges through this rich interweaving of relation as a doxological self, becoming itself in glad acknowledgement of where and what it is within the pattern of divine gift and bliss.

Basic to all this is the conceptual discovery which Augustine charts in the middle books of the *Confessions* (especially Book VII), the point which allowed him to break the intellectual deadlock that held him back from baptism: if God is the sole creator and God is as Christians say he is, there can be no substance to evil. God does not make anything that is incapable of being drawn into further communion with his wisdom and love. This wording is important: it is not simply that God, being good, makes a world of good things, but that God makes that which can share progressively more deeply in his joy in his own being. The inanimate creation shares through its order and proportion; conscious souls share through receiving the adoptive grace communicated in Christ and Christ's Body on earth, the baptized community. As we shall see in Chapter 6, our capacity to 'live well' or 'blessedly' depends significantly on the community we live in, on what that community lives by, what it loves and desires; so that Augustine's view of the Church is again inseparable from what he believes about God and our growth towards God. But the point about God not making anything incapable of being in communion with him is, of course, Augustine's response to the 'problem of evil' – as he puts it, *unde malum*? Where does evil come from? The superficial reading of Augustine's approach which sees it as somehow weakening the seriousness of evil is, as the next chapter argues, confusing the nature of our proper moral response to evil with the appropriate conceptual framework to understand it; something may be both metaphysically 'insubstantial' and morally hideous, actively destructive. If our growth into human maturity and spiritual alignment with the eternal Word is a matter of desire and delight, as we have seen it to be in the context of looking at Augustine's doctrine of creation, we have to reckon with the possibility of misdirected desire and inappropriate delight; there is no *automatic* growth towards wisdom and the supreme joy associated with it.

But it is crucial to his argument that there can be no embodiment of evil as such; God is such that he cannot, consistent with his own character and purpose, make a substance or subject that is not capable of being in some sense 'at one' with him. Equally God is such that he cannot consistently with his character and purpose make a conscious being who is compelled to love him as he should be loved. In other words, what Augustine has to say about this subject is fundamentally about the God he believes in; and that is why in his discussions in the *Confessions*, his thinking about the nature of evil and the nature of God advance in step. Once you have broken the hold of a certain kind of picture in which God and evil are, as it were, competing entities, like two physical masses in a limited space, it becomes possible to see that God, the soul and evil are none of them solid substances taking up space but spiritual realities, i.e. forms of agency. God is unqualified and unconditioned act; the created self is finite and responsive act; evil is finite and responsive actuality turning inwards on itself as its object or goal and away from that infinite act to which it is meant to be united. And this is the picture which ultimately shapes not only a perspective on the problem of evil but an entire social ethic.

5

Insubstantial Evil

Mali enim nulla natura est; sed amissio boni mali nomen accepit.[1] Thus Augustine most epigrammatically sums up his view on what might best be called the 'grammar' of evil. Talking about evil is not like talking about things, about what makes the constituents of the world the sorts of things they are; it is talking about a *process*, about something that happens to the things that there are in the universe. Evil is not some kind of object – so we might render the phrase from the *City of God* – but we give the name of 'evil' to that process in which good is lost.

As all students of Augustine know, the formation of this principle is described in the *Confessions* as a crucial moment in Augustine's liberation from both Manichaeism and the kind of problems that had brought him into Manichaeism in the first place. It is not too much to say that the sorting out of the grammar of evil is an indispensable part of that sorting out of the grammar of 'God', which cleared the way for his return to Catholic Christianity. This also suggests two preliminary considerations for any discussion of the strengths and weaknesses of his theodicy (to use a word that is, in fact, misleading where Augustine, and most pre-modern theologians, are concerned).[2] First, we shall not understand Augustine on evil without some attention to Augustine on God, and, by obvious extension, Augustine on humanity and salvation. Second, if Augustine's account of evil is to be challenged or rejected, we have to ask what the implications might be for his doctrine of God; can the two

---

[1] Augustine, *civ.* 11.9.
[2] See particularly the Introduction to K. Surin, *Theology and the Problem of Evil* (Oxford: Basil Blackwell, 1986).

grammatical concerns with which he wrestles, especially in *Confessions* 7, be sufficiently disentangled for his doctrine of God to emerge unscathed? Since Augustine is, by common consent, one of the formative influences on what has passed as the orthodox doctrine of God in western Catholicism, this is a serious consideration.

In what follows, I do not intend to offer a full summary of what he has to say about evil; there are several satisfactory accounts available.[3] I shall be taking up four specific points of criticism from modern discussion of the question, and attempting to assess their gravity. Three of these are given eloquent and clear statement in John Hick's near-classic survey of the history of theodicy, *Evil and the God of Love*.[4] The fourth, less easy to state, is sketched in a recent and very searching essay, *Escape from Paradise: Evil and Tragedy in Feminist Theology* by Kathleen Sands.[5] As the argument advances, it will, I think, become clear that all these criticisms in fact focus on a single issue which might be represented as the question of what it is to speak of 'a' world at all, with all that this implies about the universe's relation to a maker.

Existence and Goodness

John Hick, in the work mentioned above, is careful to acquit Augustine of the charge of teaching that existence is a sort of variable property of things, a quality of which a particular existent may have more or less.[6] It may occasionally sound as though Augustine is confusing the 'axiological' sense of 'existence' – the degree of intensity or energy of being that might allow us

---

[3]G. R. Evans, *Augustine on Evil* (Cambridge: Cambridge University Press, 1982), remains a magisterial summary; the chapter on 'Evil, Justice and Divine Omnipotence' in J. Rist's *Augustine: Ancient Thought Baptized* (Cambridge: Cambridge University Press, 1995), is useful, though (surprisingly) does not extensively discuss the logic of evil as privation; D. A. Kress, 'Augustine's Privation Account of Evil: A Defence', *Augustinian Studies*, 20 (1989), pp. 109–28, concentrates on this aspect, and offers some rebuttals of recent philosophical critiques; and B. Horne, in ch. 4 of *Imagining Evil* (London: Darton, Longman and Todd, 1996), gives a very brief but splendidly eloquent and imaginative summary of the Augustinian position.
[4]London: Collins, 1966; chs 3 and 4 are a lengthy discussion of Augustine.
[5]Minneapolis, MN: Fortress Press, 1994.
[6]Op. cit., pp. 56–8.

to say that an artist, for example, lives more fully than another person – with the sense of existence as sheer thereness: a 'lower' form of existence is not less *existent*. However, Hick grants, this is not fair to Augustine, who does not have a concept of sheer thereness: to be at all is to have a particular place in the interlocking order of things, to be possessed of 'measure, form and order'.[7] That is to say, to exist is necessarily to exemplify certain 'goods', to be, in a certain way, actively exercising the ordered and interdependent life that belongs to the creatures of a good God. In this sense, to say that existence can be 'graded' is not to make any crass mistake about the possibility of different degrees of 'thereness', but simply to observe that the exercise of the goods that go with existing may be more or less constrained in its environment, more or less capable of modification of that environment; within the overall notion of interdependence, some realities are more dependent than others.

Nevertheless, this does not quite meet Hick's doubts. *Why*, he asks, should we assume that 'measure, form and order' are good? In any case, for whom are they good? For the particular realities in the world, or for God?[8] This is not a wholly clear challenge, but it seems to mean something like this: to say that ordered existence is good from the point of view of an individual being is to say that such a being would rightly and intelligibly desire the persistence of their life. However, not all beings in the universe are destined to live for ever: for the merely animate, as opposed to the spiritual, creature, continued existence is not properly desirable beyond their allotted span. In God's eyes, it is good that they perish when they do (whatever they might think about it or desire). Likewise, it is good that a spiritual creature, however depraved, should continue in being, so as to go on exhibiting the specific kind of good associated with spiritual existence. Hick characterizes the whole of this scheme as 'aesthetic rather than ethical': God is perceived more as 'the Artist enjoying the products of his creative activity . . . than the Person seeking to bring about personal relations with created persons'.[9] The perspective offered by Augustinian theodicy is ultimately determined by metaphysical considerations,

---

[7]Op. cit., p. 57: 'For Augustine there was no such thing as bare existence.'
[8]Ibid., pp. 58–9.
[9]Ibid., p. 59.

considerations – to use the language I employed earlier – about the grammar of 'essences and substances' in a created universe. This objection is, as we shall see, close to the others Hick advances: in so far as this is a theodicy governed by aesthetic criteria, it fails to do justice to the personal. The justification lies in the eye of the divine beholder, the one 'subject' to whom the whole system is present or visible.

I have argued elsewhere that a theodicy that privileges the observer's standpoint is theologically and spiritually vacuous; that an 'aesthetics' of evil is not, in any helpful sense, a properly theological response at all to the question.[10] Is this, however, what Augustine is doing? Hick's stress on the problematic nature of whose 'point of view' is being invoked in the argument very definitely treats his scheme as one in which the resolution is achieved by an appeal to an intrinsically inaccessible standpoint, a non-human (and, therefore, strictly non-thematizable) perspective. I suspect, however, that this is to iron out some of the complexities of Augustine, even to impose an anachronistic interpretative grid upon him. The discussion of evil in *Confessions* VII has quite a lot to say about points of view; but there is no appeal to a divine point of view, to an idea that existence is 'good' in the eyes of God, never mind the concrete perspective of actual existents.[11] Time and again, Augustine writes of learning to 'see' afresh; when, in VII.xiii, he acknowledges to God that *tibi omnino non est malum* – 'for you, evil is just not there at all' – he goes on at once to say that the same must be true of creation as a whole. There simply is not any such *thing* as evil; not just because it doesn't exist from 'God's point of view', but because it cannot exist, for all the reasons that Augustine is in process of elaborating. If there is no evil in the eyes of God, that is not because God is in a position to make a *judgement* for which we have insufficient grounds; it is because that which is evil is not a subject to which qualities can be ascribed, not a *substantia*. There is no thing for God to see. Of course, God is *aware* of the states of affairs we call evil; but,

---

[10] R. Williams, 'Redeeming Sorrows', in *Religion and Morality*, ed. D. Z. Phillips (London: Macmillan, 1996), pp. 132–48, especially 135–6.

[11] The prevalence of the language of seeing and failing to see is notable; see especially VII.i.1–2 (the mind's eye clouded by materialistic images, the failure to be *conspicuous* to oneself), VII.iv.6 (seeing that the incorruptible is better that the corruptible), VII.v. 7 (materialistic images again), VII.vii.11 (the inner light of the mind, blocked by false images), 7.8.12 (God's healing touch reducing the swelling that obscures sight), VII.xi.17–xv.21 (what the renewed mind sees when it 'looks' at the world) and so on.

unlike us, God is not tempted to short-circuit the argument and ascribe to evil a substantive life it does not and cannot have.

The point is not therefore an aesthetic one, in Hick's sense: God looks at the whole of creation and approves of the value or goods it exemplifies as a whole, irrespective of the standpoint of particular existents. I can learn to 'see' exactly what God sees, in a rather simple way, by grasping the conceptual nonsense of thinking of evil as a sort of stuff. However, this is not really the most adequate response: the whole language of views and standpoints presupposes an observing subject, when what Augustine is talking about is the capacity simultaneously to grasp the nature of evil as the perversion of my own capacity to see or know, and to become open in love and knowledge to the reality of God. To see evil as privation is to see it as something that affects my own perception of what is good for me: if evil is the absence of good, it is precisely that misreading of the world which skews my desires; so that to read the world accurately (in its relation to God the creator) is also to repent. Furthermore, that accurate reading of the world arises from the renewal of my own creaturely relation to God, my own shift into a relation to God that worthily represents what God truly is, and that thus overcomes the evil which is constituted by imperfect, corrupt or nonsensical pictures of the divine.

There is, in other words, a tight connection between the adoption of a particular 'doctrine' of evil and the reordering of desire towards its proper end. Within the Augustinian frame of reference, it will not make sense to think of God and God's creatures as having comparable and potentially competing points of view: the point of view of a creature, considering itself *in* itself, is not a neutral *locus standi*, but is itself an illustration of what evil is; an account of the good of a creature abstracted from its place in the universe overall as ordered and loved by God.[12] And the 'point of view' of God, if one can even begin to use such language, is not a perspective alongside others, the divine 'interest' considered alongside other 'interests' to be satisfied. Augustine is clear in the *De doctrina Christiana* that God's relation to creatures (unlike the mutual relations of creatures) cannot be strictly categorized either as 'use' or

---

[12] It is one of the virtues of Evans' study (above, n. 3) that it emphasizes this dimension of the problem: evil as *alienatio* of the mind.

as 'enjoyment'.[13] 'Use' is any relation to another being that furthers the user's ends, that makes the item used an instrument for some further good, while 'enjoyment' is finding one's fulfilment in concentrating one's action, vision and energy on some reality outside oneself. God has no need of anything to further the divine purposes, since God does not act, as we do, by strategy and skill in deploying finite resources; nor can God find fulfilment in anything other than God, being wholly self-sufficient, necessarily and eternally possessed of bliss. The only sense, according to Augustine, in which God 'uses' creatures is so as to make them instrumental to their *own* fulfilment; as if we were to work on some portion of the world, treating it as deserving of an attention wholly independent of the possible benefit it could be to us.[14]

In the light of all this, it could never be said that God has a 'point of view' competing with ours or that of any creature, that God has a definition of the good relating to the divine perspective or concern (in terms of aesthetic satisfaction for God?) that takes no account of the creature's perspective. The creature's perspective simply *is* defined by God's creative purpose; but that divine purpose is to maximize all possible fulfilment for the creature, since the good, the joy, the flourishing of the creature could never be in any way a threat to the divine bliss.

To understand evil is not to look at detached phenomena and (by some curious mental gymnastics) arrive at the conclusion that the beauty of the whole outweighs the deficiencies of the parts, let alone rationalizing such a conclusion by asserting that this is how God sees things. It is part of a many-layered spiritual reconstruction, the process traced in *Confessions* VII. At the beginning of the book, Augustine is still in thrall to a kind of sophisticated materialism.[15] What exists is a complex of extended realities, one of which (God) is invulnerable to the erosion or invasion that diminishes and damages others. In such a universe, the question of where the erosion comes from

---

[13]*doctr. chr.* I.iv for the basic distinction of use from enjoyment; I.xxxi.2 on God's 'use' of us *ad nostram utilitatem . . . ad eius autem tantummodo bonitatem* (for our benefit . . . but only for God's goodness).
[14]Ibid., I.xxxii: God 'makes use' of us for the sake of the exercise of God's own *bonitas*, which is the ground of our existence; so the divine use of us is always to that divine end which is *our* blessedness.
[15]*conf.* VII.i on God as infinite extension; VII.v on creation as an immense mass both permeated and spatially exceeded by God.

might make sense: we could properly ask, if the 'territory' of one reality is being invaded, what force is it that takes up the space lost by the original entity. *Unde malum?* 'Whence is evil?' is an intelligible query. The breakthrough to a new frame of reference comes when Augustine reflects on the activity he is, in fact, engaged in: thinking itself. The mind does not take up space; there is a mode of presence in the world that is not an occupying of concrete territory, the possession of an exclusive and impenetrable block of the finite room there is in the world of material objects. If this way of being in the world that we call mind or thought is conceived as if it were a kind of material thing, the more free and flexible mode of presence is being subjected or reduced to the less, the 'higher' to the 'lower', the more active to the more passive. If we go on to ask how the mind evaluates and orders or unifies its environment, the question arises of whence the mind derives its standards, its sense of real and mutually relative (ordered) structures. The answer given to Augustine by the Platonist literature he is studying is that the mind is itself activated by a yet more free and active presence, the radiance of a truth that is not static or passive. It is at this point that he returns to the problem of the 'derivation' of evil, and finds the difficulty dissolved, or, at least, so redefined that the original question has to be discarded.[16]

The source of all things is the light and truth of the divine, that agency that is wholly unconstrained and, thus, immaterial and invulnerable (incapable of being modified by any other agent). As such, the divine is not ever on the same level as, or in competition with, finite agency, which is always in some measure constrained and vulnerable (were it otherwise, it would be indistinguishable from the divine). In what is not divine, there must be a plurality of agencies, and this means a variety in the level of freedom or self-determination realized by an agency. The world is, therefore, an interlocking system of action and passion. *Purely at the level of the natural order at large*, what may look to the unreflective observer like 'evil' – the aesthetically disagreeable, the contingently annoying – is no more than a particular arrangement of action and constraint,

---

[16]Ibid., VII.xii, where Augustine returns to the issue of evil in the wake of learning to 'see' afresh the nature of created being, and understands that corruptibility is not *ipso facto* incompatible with good in some measure.

perhaps, specifically, a case of action more unstable or vulnerable or liable to variation as a result of circumstances than human action, and, above all, that distinctive action that is mental functioning.[17]

Likewise, at the level of my actual experience of the world, evil is a failure of the appropriate balance between action and constraint that ought to be operative in a specific interaction in the world: paradigmatically, it is the submission of the mentally active human subject to the dominance of selfish and materially defined goals, with all the consequences of such an imbalance in the wider human and non-human environment. The characteristic problem of the human agent is twofold: it is the subordination of spirit to trivial and finite desires but at the same time it is the confidence of created spirit that it is able by its own immanent action – self-knowledge and self-improvement – to free itself from this subordination. The solution lies only in the reconnecting of the finite mind with infinite agency, with the loving wisdom of God; and the opening of that connection depends on the initiative of God in Jesus Christ.[18]

I have laboured the argument of *Confessions* VII in this way in the hope of demonstrating more clearly how inadequate it is to describe Augustine's concern as 'aesthetic', and how misleading it would be to think of Augustine as privileging a divine 'point of view'. The process being depicted in the book is highly complex: it makes no sense at all without the prior conviction that all finite agency considered simply *as* agency or free self-adaptability is animated by God, and directed by God (through its location in a certain place in the scheme of things) towards its fullest possible orderliness or balance, which for sentient creatures means its fullest possible joy. The positive point of the argument, as laid out in the text of the *Confessions*, is to rule out any statement of the cause or source of evil that treats it in a spatialized way; and it is essential to this goal that God and the created mind are simultaneously 'despatialized'. If God – the most fundamental form of activity that there is – cannot be properly thought of as occupying a territory,

---

[17]Ibid., VII.xiii and xvi on the unavoidable rub of conflict in the 'lower' reaches of creation, which is none the less *conveniens* (fitting) within the whole. The argument is not without obscurity, but the general point seems to be that we do not need 'local' and obvious harmonies at every level of existence in order to believe that the creation is coherent overall.
[18]Ibid., VII.xviii.

and if the human mind or spirit reflects this primary activity in its own non-territorial character, if, in short, the relation between God and the mind is rightly spoken of in terms of time, rather than space, evil, as that which interrupts the relation of creator and creature, belongs in the same frame of reference. Its origins are to be sought in the interactions of the world's history, not in a classification of substances within a single territory, a single medium of extension. Furthermore, if this is what Augustine is pursuing, the charge of teaching a resolution of the problem of evil in terms of 'essences' rather than 'personal relationships' is a caricature; and the aesthetics of Augustine's model cannot be reduced to the idea of a resolution by appeal to a divine perspective, a divine satisfaction with the cosmic picture, unconnected with the subjectivity of created beings.

Moral Personality

The above attempt at clarification has a good deal of bearing upon the next major area of criticism articulated by Hick. He observes that there is, or should be, an important difference between 'metaphysical' and 'empirical' accounts of the reality of evil: whatever the accuracy of the metaphysical definition of evil as privation, it cannot be accurate to speak of evil *as experienced* in such terms. 'Empirically, it is not merely the absence of something else but a reality with its own distinctive and often terrifying quality and power.' An evil will is not automatically one that tends towards disintegration and final extinction: 'it may retain its degree of mental integration, stability, coherence, intelligence, lucidity, and effectiveness . . . one thinks, for example, of Milton's Satan or of Iago in fiction, and of such men as Goebbels in recent history'.[19] Evil activity has a power and 'integrity' of its own. Furthermore, if evil is to be described as the absence of good, does this not mean that, for example, pain has to be described as the absence of pleasure, which is a grossly inadequate account of something that manifestly *impresses* itself upon the subject?[20]

---

[19] Hick, op. cit., pp. 61–2.
[20] Ibid., p. 62, on pain as 'intrusive'.

This is intuitively quite a powerful point; but it reveals a profound confusion. What the Augustinian argument claims is that the 'terrifying quality and power' of evil derives from those elements, in whatever reality we are talking about, that are most alive and active. Evil is dreadful and potent because of the kind of world this is, a world in which the active, joyful goodness of God is mirrored or shared by creatures. Because the 'underlay' of worldly reality, so to speak, is this intensity of action, the diversion or distortion of worldly reality is appalling. For evil to 'impress' in the way already touched upon, it has to employ the vehicle of action and, in the human sphere, intelligence. The corrupted will is certainly not, *ipso facto*, a weak or powerless will, so long as it shows the typical excellences of will: liberty, energy, persistence or whatever. What makes its evil terrible *are* those excellences; nothing else. What is distinctively *evil* in the evil will is simply not capable of being spoken of or understood in terms of liberty, energy and so on. It is true that the passionate desire for what is false ultimately leads the subject to destruction; but this does not mean that the quest for falsehood is automatically half-hearted or vague.

To say that a Goebbels – or a Radovan Karadžić or a Saddam Hussein – exemplifies lucidity, coherence, effectiveness and so on in his actions is certainly not to claim that his pursuit of his desires is a simple instance of homogeneous 'evil', exercising power and effectiveness. It is to recognize that, if evil itself is never a subject or substance, the only way in which it can be desired or sought is by the exercise of the goods of mental and affective life swung around by error to a vast misapprehension, a mistaking of the unreal and groundless for the real. The more such a pursuit continues, the more the desiring subject becomes imprisoned, enslaved, hemmed in; the more the typical excellences of will and intelligence are eroded. However, that does not mean that the effects of this nightmare error are lessened.

To put it more pictorially: the more power, dignity and liberty adhere naturally to a created being, the more energy there will be for the pursuit of false or destructive goals, illusory goods. The corruption of a human will is a more far-reaching disaster than the corruption of an animal will, because the latter has a severely limited range of possibilities for innovation on the basis of reflection. A wicked human is an immeasurably greater problem than a wicked hamster (if, indeed, we could give much content to such an idea); and

Augustine and the majority of Christian theologians up to the Enlightenment would have added that a corrupted *angelic* will is an immeasurably greater problem than a corrupted human will, and that a fair number of our difficulties in this world derive from just this problem. The dispositions and habits of intelligent beings have a wide range of effects, because intelligences exist in conscious and creative interaction and interdependence: that is why they can do more damage; and it is one reason for the disproportion between the experience of evil and the level of moral culpability in any individual's life.

An Augustinian would have to say that this and this alone does proper justice to moral personality, however paradoxical that may sound. Consider the alternative. Evil possesses – as such – a power of initiative, a capacity to set intelligible goals and to advance those goals in a lastingly coherent manner. This implies that evil impinges on a finite agent in the way that another finite agent would, and that there is nothing absurd in proposing, or having proposed to one, a set of objectives specified as evil in themselves and claiming to be proper objects for rational pursuit. The first point pulls back towards Manichaeism: evil as an invasive 'other', struggling with the moral responsibility of the finite person, so that the victory of evil is the victory of a subject, or substance, distinct from the finite person. The second allows that what is good for one subject is not necessarily good for any other: that there is a plurality of intelligible goods, goals that may be pursued without absurdity by reasoning subjects.

This undercuts a fundamental aspect of Augustine's theology: that the good of all persons is both unified and interdependent (I can not specify what is good for me without including what is good for you in the same calculation), and that any alternative simply makes the entire process of human moral and spiritual reflection impossible.[21] As we might now put it, *discourse* itself fails if one party is allowed to talk about wanting the dissolution of its own mental or spiritual identity as a discussable option, or to claim to be pursuing goals that are incapable of being described to other agents as consonant, or convergent with, their own purposive desires. Augustine's assumptions and arguments about the unreality of evil as an independent substance, cause or agency are bound up with a conviction about the location of evil in the malfunctioning

---

[21] Of signal importance here is the discussion of loving the Good in others in *trin*. VIII.

of relations between subjects, not in the relation of this or that subject to some other *thing* called 'evil'. Any notion that the latter could be a possible grammar for talking of evil has to be recognized as subverting the very idea of intelligibility as something relating the individual's mental/verbal life to a system or order transcending the individual frame.

In other words, if the Good is in some sense one, evil cannot be allowed a place of its own, outside the system of balancing and interweaving relations that actualize the Good for particular beings, and which, in a contingent world, are vulnerable to malfunction and distortion. A discord on a musical instrument is not the result of the instrument being interfered with by an external agency *called* discord, it is a function of the workings of what is there, of what constitutes the instrument itself. Some years ago, Ed Koren, the *New Yorker* cartoonist, depicted a garage mechanic explaining the situation to his customer: the car bonnet is open, revealing a fanged and hairy creature smiling a little sheepishly at the owner. 'Well', says the mechanic, 'there's your problem'. It is an admirable illustration of exactly what Augustine wants at all costs to avoid. So, far from undermining the idea of moral personality, this scheme in fact seeks to defend the integrity of personal agency from a mythological conception of something outside that agency displacing the person's own responsibility.

If it is argued that a person's agency can be powerfully motivated by evil desires, or that a person's intelligence can work strongly and consistently for evil ends, Augustine's reply would have to be along the lines sketched in Book XIX of the *City of God*. It is an *analytic* truth (as a modern person would say) that desire desires satisfaction, that the disequilibrium represented by the acknowledged lack that fuels desire seeks the restoration of equilibrium. All things seek 'peace'; even twisted and nightmarish desires are movements towards order, an order hideously misunderstood, it may be, but order or harmony, none the less. What is sought is sought *as* good; what is sought is a peaceful universe. The degree to which an agent's perception of peace is blinkered by their own self-concerned definition of the good is the degree to which their desire is destructive of their own ultimate reality, or integrity, and of whatever order or harmony there is immediately around.[22]

---

[22]*civ.* XIX.12–13.

To return to Hick's original statement of his difficulty, what we experience and call evil is, indeed, not simply a void, a lack; but it is the effect of a lack, the displacement of true by untrue perception. A vacuum is a 'lack', an absence; but its effects within a system of forces may be powerful. The complaint that evil-as-privation does not do justice to the experienced reality of evil presupposes that the Augustinian account is a blend of 'metaphysical' and 'experiential', and that an adequate account should balance both. However, this is a misunderstanding. As any reader of Augustine will be aware, what he can say of specific *mala* in no way weakens their substantial and historical reality. An 'evil' is, by definition, a concrete state of affairs, and a great evil is a massively effective disruption of the world's order; evil perpetrated by an intelligent being is grave and terrible because of the power of intelligence in the order of things. How one describes *mala* is, in an important sense, irrelevant to the programmatic question of what evils should be ascribed to. Furthermore, to ascribe them to anything other than skewed, or damaged relations between agencies in the world, is finally to threaten the entire possibility of intelligible talk.

The Principle of Plenitude

The last of Hick's objections I wish to examine has to do with the alleged involvement of Augustine's scheme with a Neoplatonic assumption that must be questionable for a modern reader.

> God acts deliberately to form a universe, and He acts in terms of the principle of plenitude, considering it better to produce all possible forms of being, lower as well as higher, poorer as well as richer, all contributing to a wonderful harmony and beauty in his sight, than to produce only a society of blessed archangels.[23]

As becomes clear in the lines following, this is really another version of the objection to an allegedly 'aesthetic' emphasis, obscuring the priority of personal relationship in God's purposes. All that Augustine does to Christianize the

---

[23]Hick, op. cit., p. 83.

Neoplatonic emanacionism underlying the 'principle of plenitude' is to substitute God's creative will for the automatic 'radiating' of being from the One; but this, in fact, intensifies the difficulty. Why should God act according to any 'principle'? Once we have imagined that creation's form is in some sense dictated by a principle, we have lost sight of the all-importance of God's will to engage with finite persons whose freedom mirrors God's own. The love of God is being conceived in 'metaphysical rather than personal terms'.[24]

This is not all that easy to assess as an argument. Augustine certainly speaks in *Confessions* VII.xiii of the totality of beings as better than the higher elements alone (*meliura omnia quam sola superiora*), and in *City of God* XI.22 of the principle that things must be unequal for there to be any particular things at all (*ad hoc inaequalia, ut essent omnia*). However, what he does *not* do is to advance a simple claim that God creates the maximum possible variety of creatures. His argument, where it occurs (and it is found less clearly elaborated in *De natura boni* and *De Genesi ad litteram*), turns on the appropriateness of there being diverse levels of being; not necessarily 'every conceivable kind of being'.[25]

Furthermore, the justification of variety or inequality that is offered takes us back to the point already variously articulated in these pages: the universe is a system of interdependent agencies; by the creator's providence, each thing is what it is in virtue of where it stands in the universal order. Thus, things further down the scale that contribute to the good of things higher up, find their *own* good in so doing. Without that use of the lower levels of creation, the higher elements would not be what they are, or flourish as they should. Thus, the principle Augustine is elaborating is not one of 'plenitude' in the sense of a realization of absolutely all possibilities of being, or even of all 'compossible' outcomes, to use a modern logical term, but one of universal interdependence. Of course, it is expressed in a strongly hierarchical idiom that undoubtedly owes an uncomfortably heavy debt to Neoplatonism and falls harshly on the modern ear; but the fundamental point, that inequality in the sense of variegated levels of capacity or resource in the natural order is

---

[24]Ibid.

[25]In *De natura boni*. see especially 1 and 8; in *De Genesi ad litteram*, see for example, III.16, on beasts of prey.

necessary in a world in which things become, in which things acquire their concrete identity through *processes*, is less obviously mortgaged to problematic patterns of thought.

Certainly, the aesthetic is a significant consideration: Augustine's remarks about the importance of the eyebrow to the well-proportioned face, or his confidence that a world containing sin can still as a whole be beautiful, as is a picture with dark patches, come close to the aestheticism Hick and others criticize so sharply.[26] The apparently unimportant detail (the eyebrow) is the object of God's care and craft for the sake of a larger picture. The darkness of sin in itself is terrible, but yet the entire universe does not, because of it, cease to reflect the order of God's wisdom; the implication is that the ultimate punishment of sin, in manifesting God's just laws, balances once again the order of the whole. However, this is not simply either a celebration of unstructured diversity, or a claim that sin would be less offensive if we somehow knew how to look at it. The 'unimportant' detail *serves* the proportion and beauty of a more complex reality; it is part of a system, but also part of a convention of seeing and valuing, the social practice of recognizing and appreciating beauty. Furthermore, the manifestation of God's justice in the punishment of sin is something worked out in the passage of time: it is, once again, in the *process* of the world that order is shown, not in the perspective of a timeless observer. Sin is not in some way 'good', or even bearable, when seen against a sufficiently broad backdrop: what is good is the process of the universe which, in God's providence, includes in its final reckoning the manifestation of the gravity of sin and the triumph of God's healing and rectifying action.

The principle of plenitude, as articulated by Hick, sounds as though it is claiming that the world is simply an accumulation of as many different kinds of thing as possible, and that God has virtually no 'choice' but to create such a maximal diversity. What Augustine actually says is that, once God 'chooses' to make a world that is both temporal and interdependent, the logic of that free determination requires variety and the oscillation of circumstances as agents act upon each other, never at any one point attaining perfect balance within the world's history.

---

[26]*civ.* XI.22.

This is, I think, compatible with what Augustine says in *City of God* 11.23, that, without human sin, the world would have been full 'only with good natures'; there is a difference between the protracted mutual adjustment of natures that are imperfect (that is, temporal and contingent), but not corrupt, and the mutual erosion of natures that are corrupted, destructive of their own integrity and that of others. However, this is admittedly not something Augustine clarifies with any precision, here or elsewhere. What he is reasonably clear about is that the ascription of evil to 'lower' elements in creation is a mistake, a failure to see how they fit into the good of 'higher' levels of organization, and so into the good of the whole. Their relative passivity, or even ugliness and imperfect or unpleasing forms, are not marks of an *eroded*, corrupted life, a life that is less than it *should* be, but are simply the signs of a particular place in the interweaving of finite agents, a place in which little transforming initiative can be taken. Without sin, the hierarchy of the universe would have been a steady flow of interaction in which what is conventionally called the 'corruption', the disintegration, of elements is only a moment in their proper temporal unfolding and mutation, which is, in itself, good. It is only with the corruption of will and intelligence that change and passivity become problematic, infecting the whole of the world's order. Hence, Augustine's conviction that the Fall has *physical* consequences (human death).[27]

Thus, it would be a mistake to read Augustine as subscribing to a simple belief that God 'had' to make the maximum possible variety of creatures. For the creation to be the kind of creation it is, there must be an *interlocking* variety of some kind, so that the 'goodness' of any one agent or agency in the world cannot be assessed in and for itself. The implication is also present, in this, as in other parts of Augustine's general argument, that for there to be *any* kind of creation, variety and interaction are inevitable. For the world is, by definition, not God; therefore, it is subject to change. The contents of the world are mutable and passible, and thus are bound to be acted upon by each other, and if the world as a whole is good, then its good must be realized through interactive processes; all things are good in virtue of where they stand in a system of acting upon and being acted upon. Thus, a creation of *any* kind entails variety,

---

[27] Among many possible instances, see *civ*. XIII.19 and 23; *op.imp. com. Jul.* VI.39.

variety of freedoms and variety of dependencies. To see this only in terms of a 'principle of plenitude', or a primarily aesthetic understanding of the world's variety, is to miss Augustine's always crucial interest in time and change as, paradoxically, intrinsic to the good of finite things.

The Possibility of the Tragic

Kathleen Sands' essay on feminist theological perspectives in theodicy offers a clear, and rather novel, typology of theodicies, together with a nuanced appreciation of how her ideal types mingle, and even spill over into each other, in the work of particular theologians. Classically, she argues, Christian (or, at least, Western Christian) thought deals with evil on either a 'rationalist' or a 'dualist' basis.[28] Rationalism designates a metaphysic that assumes that the universe is basically harmonious and intelligible; evil is the refusal of intelligibility, the refusal to occupy a rational place in the order of things. One implication of such a model is that there is no evil 'beyond comprehension or rehabilitation'; and this survives even in a secular culture, as the dominance of a rational order of discourse, an order without bias or interest, which must always work to assimilate and correct the rebellious discourses of those who refuse 'objectivity and universality'. Dualism understands evil as a real moral other, the object of an unconditional hostility and an unremitting struggle. In some sense, evil has its own ontological presence: there is no fore-ordained identity between the true and the good, or the real and the rational, so that this approach 'provides ideological frameworks for strategies of withdrawal, resistance, and destruction'.[29]

However, these are not simply two neatly defined alternatives: they tend to collapse into each other. Religious dualism struggles and hopes for a *victory*, a creation or restoration of identity. Rationalism's struggle against the otherness of rebel discourses, non-standard modes of understanding and engagement in the world, can have the excluding energy and hostile passion of dualism.

---

[28]Sands, op. cit., pp. 2–6.
[29]Ibid., p. 3.

While both have real strength, both have the same weakness: they ignore the realm of the truly contingent and, thus, the experience of the genuinely tragic. They suppress plurality and chance.

Martha Nussbaum's brilliant study in classical ethics and tragedy is invoked to powerful effect here to argue for a conception of the good that is various, mobile, vulnerable, rather than unified and stable.[30] There is a gulf that cannot be crossed between 'first principles', ideals and goods on the one hand, and the 'rough and bloody theatre of history', the realm of actual human choices.[31] Unless this is recognized, theological discourse will simply enshrine the interest of the particular elites who are fluent in it, who set the canonical standards of intelligibility, and will always create and sustain a 'counterworld', a sphere whose darkness and disobedience provide a sort of negative reinforcement of the dominant discourse, and into which can be bundled the non-resolution and provisionality of that dominant discourse. In short, we have a recipe for denial and for oppression, the demonizing of the other. In a world of postmodern sensibility, the struggles that matter are not between the clearly good and the rebellious or resistant, but between competing goods and competing powers. We are at once obliged to take stands *against* certain things and to allow that they may have an integrity, a good, proper to them, yet unacceptable *here*.[32] This conviction that not all interests can be harmonized is central to the tragic vision, which accepts 'the inevitability of our involvement in evil'.[33] Tragedy obliges us to 'find every form of conflict and suffering *question-worthy* and *wonder-worthy*'.[34]

Augustine, recognized as the most influential figure in the construction of the Western Christian perspective, illustrates precisely the mutual implication of rationalism and dualism.[35] Rationalism allows Augustine to argue against Manichaean dualism and to construct an orderly hierarchy for desire to

---

[30] *The Fragility of Goodness: Luck and Ethics in Greek Tragedy and Philosophy* (Cambridge: Cambridge University Press, 1986) (see especially chs 11 and 12).
[31] Sands, op. cit., p. 6.
[32] Ibid., pp. 8, 11–12.
[33] Ibid., p. 9.
[34] Ibid., p. 11
[35] Ibid., pp. 17–20.

move upwards to God. But there is a directly moral dissatisfaction with the force of evil that this structure cannot contain; and this finds expression in Augustine's analysis of sin, with its own perverse power, its status as an apparently autonomous force that binds the will. Because sin is manifest in the perversion of the will to the lower elements in creation, these elements take on a sort of moral colouring, and all pleasures connected with the purely bodily order are the objects of suspicion and interrogation. In the post-Fall environment, things that are still good in themselves have become the carriers of moral corruption. Thus, there is, after the Fall, an effectively dualist drama being enacted, even though the beginning and end of the story are dictated by rationalism. In neither context is there room for the tragic. Sands notes Augustine's 'disdain for tragic and comic dramas', and his anxiety about the reaction of readers to his own story: he dreads equally being pitied and being mocked.[36] Behind all this anxiety to secure moral fixity – by the adversarial definition of evil in the present, and the negative account of it in the distant metaphysical horizon – is an anxiety about the maintenance of the threatened dominant position of the male, reasonable will; so that woman, in particular, focuses concerns about evil or rebellion, even though Augustine grants that such rebellion may, in fact, be the effect of the 'higher' agent's failure in the ordering of desire.[37]

Although Sands' discussion of Augustine is brief, and her references often seem to depend on secondary sources, or to relate to a narrow band of Augustine's work, the case is an interesting and challenging one, which does not simply repeat standard feminist charges against Augustine, but allows his schema a degree of moral seriousness and weight. In effect, she is claiming that the tradition of which Augustine is the classical exponent – if not the creator – is preoccupied with what a contemporary critic would call 'closure', a damaging impatience because, whatever the metaphysical good intentions,

---

[36]Ibid., p. 19. The passages cited from *civ.* on Augustine's hostility to drama should be read in context as part of a specifically anti-pagan polemic, concerned with the representation of 'divine' agents as involved in rape or violence. The general conclusion proposed here is poorly supported by these particular texts, and it is not easy to see how they are to be connected to an alleged fear of pity or mockery in Augustine.
[37]Ibid., pp. 19–20.

it is constantly slipping into polarizations of the Good' and 'the not-Good' in the present moment; polarizations that encourage the identification of actual agents here and now with the Good and the not-Good, and the projection of failure and lack on to certain classes and categories of existence (matter, woman).

What is interesting here is that what Sands wants to reinforce is, in important respects, exactly what Augustine wants to reinforce: there is no timeless and stable goodness in this world; there is no incarnation of evil. All creaturely good is realized in *time*, and the perfection of goodness exists not as something that issues from a process, but as the eternal standard and direction of creaturely good. However, it is in relation to this last point that the division opens up. Sands seems to want to deny that there is a transcendent measure of good: the good is rather what emerges as a possible, a 'viable', wholeness and balance in the life of moral communities. 'Moral judgements . . . are strategic, contextual judgements about how the diverse goods of life might best be integrated and unnecessary suffering minimised in a particular place and moment.'[38]

We need to look harder at some of Sands' case. The assumption is made that, if there is an uncrossable gulf between ideals and the harsh choices of history, those who articulate ideals and who defend the notion of a transcendent good, are almost bound to become a self-perpetuating elite, surviving by demonizing the 'other' who represents disobedience and disorder. That this has often been true hardly needs saying; that it is the consequence of an Augustinian schema requires more argument to be established. It could as well be said that the practical dualisms of Christian history arise not from too faithful but too careless a reading of Augustine. Part of Augustine's gravamen against both Pelagians and Donatists is to do with their identification of possible states within history as bearers of a goodness that is somehow complete or adequate. The Donatist absolutizes the purity of the empirical church; the Pelagian affirms the possibility of keeping the commandments of God. Both take the Church out of time, in their different ways. The Church which continues to pray 'forgive us our trespasses', is a church whose purity and integrity are

---

[38]Ibid., p. 15; see also p. 136.

inseparable from continuing self-questioning and penitence.[39] And this is because the Good *is* God: the divine self-identity means that the 'ideal' is precisely, in one central sense, not available for realization. God is not another agent pursuing (successfully, as we pursue unsuccessfully) a proper moral balance. God is not, in any sense, a rival in our universe, so that the divine Good cannot be appropriated by any finite agent as simply identical with its own. If so interpreted, the idea of a transcendent good becomes a decisive *prohibition* against the use of an ideal as the reinforcement of a particular interest. What prevents this itself becoming a claim to a universal and rational perspective is its essentially negative and provisional character: as Augustine insists against the Donatists, the Christian community continues to be immersed in possible and actual sin.[40]

The resolution of historical struggle is, for Augustine, the work of grace and, thus, ultimately a victory never produced by history itself, never the triumph of a moral programme. Augustine certainly fails, in a variety of ways, to spell out what might be needed to make this explicit in such a way as to challenge, discipline or overturn particular bids for the power to exclude or discount; yet the scheme proposed retains a logic that Sands' critique does not wholly answer. If we examine the positive content of what is suggested as an alternative, I suspect that we may find the option collapsing into just the same polar oppositions Sands identifies in the classical account. Say that the Good is, indeed, properly conceived as 'various, mobile and vulnerable': this might mean that the Good is different for different created subjects, to the extent that what is good for one subject is necessarily and permanently at odds with what is good for another; that the Good genuinely differs from circumstance to circumstance, without any 'grammar' of continuity; that the Good of or for certain subjects might simply and finally fail or prove impossible of realization.

The first reading implies that there are genuine (truthfully conceived) creaturely goods that can be realized only at the expense of the genuine goods of others; a view hard to reconcile with any properly emancipatory ethic, since

---

[39] See, for example Augustine's *ep*. 185.9.39.
[40] See, for example, the argument at *bapt*. 2.6 on the 'contamination' of the African Church, even in the time of Cyprian, by the communion of the righteous with apostates.

it is the argument, implicit or explicit, of the slave-master. The second suggests that particular developments might render good what once was not, that torture or racial discrimination might be *made* good by historical changes. The third suggests that there are worldly subjects 'predestined' to final and irredeemable frustration. To appeal to the notion of a viable balance in a community's life as a way of avoiding the Hobbesian consequences of these possible readings (the war of all against all, the *inevitable* non-convergence of creaturely good) will not really meet the case. It assumes that the reconciliation of partial and competing goods is itself a good to be pursued, without qualification, it seems. There is no argument to establish why this good should be exempt from the general prohibition against general goods. An absolutist assumption is being smuggled in under the guise of pragmatism.

Part of the problem comes in the definition of what Sands (or, indeed, Nussbaum) really understands by the tragic. An Augustinian might say that the world *is* tragic, in the sense that our fallen perceptions of the world are so flawed that we are constantly, and inevitably (since the Fall), involved in mistaken and conflictual accounts of our true interests. In so far as the Good, in the fallen order, requires a measure of coercion if total incoherence and fragmentation are to be avoided, *loss* is always bound up with creaturely virtue, even sanctity. And since there is no coercion that can ultimately overcome the perverse will, there are creaturely subjects whose good *is* eternally frustrated, lost souls. However, this frustration is contingent on a history, not intrinsic to the nature of their good. What such an interlocutor could not accept would be a definition of tragic conflict as a *necessary* feature of created order. That would be to return to naked dualism: there is not one Good, therefore there can be no convergence of goods, therefore there is (even if not dramatized in Manichaean terms) irreconcilable cosmic struggle, with no ontological priority accorded to either side. Against this, the Augustinian would have to marshal the saint's own arguments, already considered here, on the grammar of evil in a world created by a good God. In another kind of universe . . . but, for the Christian, there can only be a universe made by a good God; and for such a universe to be at all, the grammar of good and evil must be as Augustine argues. It is not clear whether Sands, for example, accepts any doctrine of a creative origin that can be articulated in anything like traditional Christian terms; and in fairness to her, her book does not pretend to be an essay in Christian dogmatics, and gains much of its moral strength from this standing back from conventionally doctrinal concerns. Nevertheless, I do not believe that an option for the tragic, conceived in terms of necessarily conflictual goods, absolves from attention to the potentially very stark metaphysical implications that begin to arise.

Conclusion

Augustine's account of the character and logic of our discourse about evil is not, by any means, tidy or exhaustive; it is still marked by elements of argument that his theology as a whole is moving beyond or away from. I have tried particularly to put in appropriate perspective the 'aesthetic' aspects of his case. My main concern has been to propose that he was himself right to see this issue as involved with the logic of talk about God. As *Confessions* VII makes plain, he is engaged in 'de-spatializing' talk about both God and evil: neither has a *place* in the universe, neither is a subject competing with others.

In relation to evil, this means that talking about evil is always talking about temporal processes, the processes we learn to identify as loss or corruption, and that we identify more clearly and truthfully the more we grow in understanding of the whole interlocking pattern of the world's activity. In relation to God, it means that talking about God is always talking about the temporal processes of clarification, reconciliation, self-discovery in love, the processes that lead us beyond rivalry and self-protection; talking about God is the articulation of a self-knowledge that grasps the central dependence of the self, a knowledge of the self as lacking and searching and, thus, as presupposing a goal of desire that exceeds any specific state of affairs in this material world.

Augustine's argument is a pincer movement, driving us to concentrate precisely upon the bloodiness of the world's processes and the obscurity of our decisions, mingling as they do reason and longing, with all the risks attendant on a reasoning that is always interest-bound and a desire that is always haunted by self-obsession. The alternative is, in fact, hard to frame coherently without dissolving the central vision of a God who is able to transfigure our desire and heal our blindness *because* this is a God who has no interest to defend, no limited and self-referring good to promote in negotiation with others. It has become fashionable to promote the idea of a God who is 'really' affected by the world's history, or whose life is, in some rather hard to specify way, bound up with the world's destiny. Augustine's discussions of evil leave us with the question of whether any such God can, in fact, be understood, except as one who has concerns that are other to ours as another inhabitant of a common moral world.

There may be ways of defending the compatibility of this model with the traditional Christian (and Jewish and Muslim) commitment to the divine freedom, and with the doctrine that God creates the world from nothing (and is, therefore, in no way constrained by what is made); but they would have been strange to Augustine. His concern with finding an adequate grammar for evil (not a justification of evil, a rational account of the proportion of evil to guilt, let us say, or a calculus of how much evil is necessary to produce a good cosmic outcome) is, I have been arguing, at every point inseparable from his discovery, as he believes, of the nature of our discourse about God as self-subsistent and therefore without limit, miraculously generous in creation and salvation. If we do not share his understanding of evil as privation, no-thing, no-space, can we in any way share his understanding of God as subsistent and overflowing fullness, no-thing, no-space, the noncompetitive other whose freedom makes us free?

One of the difficulties in doing justice to Augustine's account of evil is that many of its aspects have been taken up and promoted by writers who have no great interest in those wider Augustinian concerns that have been so often mentioned in these pages. Some of those who have declared themselves 'Augustinian' have in fact done as little service to the saint as those who have criticized him on the basis of an equally selective reading. This problem is set out and analysed with great sophistication and skill by Charles T. Mathewes in his monograph on *Evil and the Augustinian Tradition*.[41] He discusses in particular the influence of Augustine in the work of Reinhold Niebuhr and Hannah Arendt in grounding a political vision in which due allowance is made both for human perversity and for the necessity of coercion – a realist or pessimist vision concerned to ward off sentimental utopianism or excessively high expectations of human social

---

[41] Cambridge University Press, 2001.

and political existence.[42] Mathewes treats these two writers with sympathy and insight, but concludes that they both misread in significant ways the Augustinian tradition's scepticism about the possibility of moral innocence, and that both work from an anthropology much narrower than Augustine's own. The recognition of ignorance and corruptibility within our own mental life which is intrinsic to Augustine's analysis of how evil works is connected by Niebuhr with the need for 'acknowledging responsibility' in public life, acknowledging both complicity in public evil and the need to leave behind any dreams of moral purity won at the expense of public involvement. For Arendt, the priority is to overcome the passivity (and 'banality', to use the term most associated with her understanding of evil) that allows atrocity to flourish by positive political association and action. As Mathewes notes,[43] both are at one with Augustine in demystifying or 'demythologizing' evil: it has become a *practical* challenge. We are summoned to participate more fully in the goodness of *agency*, even when this commits us to acts that are not unequivocally good in the abstract.

The problem is, though, that this leaves the impression that it is still *human* agency that will resolve political impasse or disaster; there is not in either Niebuhr or Arendt any sense of what it might mean to be called to become signs of divine meaning, divine self-bestowal.

This means that the supposed moral realism of a Niebuhr is actually deficient in what it takes reality to be;[44] and Arendt's appeal to basic and prosaic political activism comes dangerously close to suggesting that all we have to do is activate in ourselves a primordial free will which can deliver a renewal of agency and motivation of itself: which can 'begin again'.[45] Niebuhr, Mathewes

---

[42]Compare the influential book by Jean Bethke Elshtain, *Augustine and the Limits of Politics* (Notre Dame, IN: University of Notre Dame Press, 1995), which gives one of the most intelligent accounts of this general approach without adopting the more questionable aspects of Niebuhr's or Arendt's rhetoric.

[43]Op. cit., p. 227.

[44]This is argued at length by John Milbank in 'The Poverty of Niebuhrianism', pp. 233–4 in *The Word Made Strange: Theology, Language, Culture* (Oxford: Blackwell, 1997).

[45]Mathewes op. cit., pp. 189–92. Arendt lays great stress on the importance of Augustine's belief that humanity has a beginning and that humanity exists in order to make beginnings (p. 196). This is the heart of a belief in human freedom. But, as we have already seen, Augustine's understanding of 'beginning' is a good deal more than this, since we are created in the eternal beginning which is the divine Word.

suggests, ends up internalizing evil in a problematic way: all our best ideals are corruptible, we must be ready to forswear innocence. Arendt *externalizes*: the politically virtuous agent distinguishes himself or herself from the victim of banality by what can only be an exercise of internally reinforced will against the pull of corrupt moral conformity; not innocence, exactly, but certainly access to a wellspring of inner renewal bound in with the *amor mundi*, love of the world, which Arendt sees as the cornerstone of proper public engagement. Both leave us with disturbingly unfinished business. If corruptibility is real, we need both absolution and discernment of the point at which we can become collusive with our fallibility, using it as an excuse for not growing towards transformation or not acting to change what can and must be changed. And we are also bound to recognize our inability to 'begin': we have always already 'begun', in Augustine's world, beginning the doomed project of organizing our own moral world and refusing to return to our true beginning, which is not in us. The action we are called on to initiate is 'an imitation of God's creative action',[46] and the pedagogy or therapy that leads us deeper into this; it is a 'project of participation' in which 'we are transforming ourselves, or are being transformed, in ways that enable us to inhabit (and love) the world more fully'.[47]

But this implies that an Augustinian analysis of evil as privation or as the misdirection of desire will make no sense if removed from its context within the whole of that pattern discerned by Augustine in the course of the narrative of the *Confessions*. Evil as privation makes sense because of the recognition of what it is a privation *of* – the harmonious outworking of finite agency united with infinite creativity. Evil is possible because the harmony of finite agencies must be worked out in the passage of time, in processes of change, and so through contingencies in which agencies may collide. But the point is that it is not a generalized malfunction that constitutes evil but the specific departure from harmony with the pattern of mutuality and 'self-displacement'; which is God's own life and thus the heart of life well-lived within creation. Consequently, for us to be delivered from evil is to be fully attuned to the order

---

[46]Ibid., p. 219.
[47]Ibid., p. 223.

we did not and could not make, an attunement that happens in the life of grace as experienced in the baptized community; and this grace is made available to us because of God's act to restore broken harmony in the earthly presence of Jesus Christ and all that flows from this. God enacts his being in the history of Jesus so as to heal our diseased desires and renew our delight.

Thus at every point the treatment of evil is drawn back to consideration of the grammar of God's being and the specific events of the incarnate life.[48] An 'Augustinianism' divorced from these themes is a pale shadow at best of the integral argument that Augustine is developing; and at worst a painful distortion, implying either a 'tragic' understanding in which we are always doomed to do what is not in accord with our deepest nature or destiny, or else a naive faith in the self-renewing capacity of human agents, despite their historical location and heritage. Augustine does indeed have a tragic element in his understanding, in that he envisages actors in the public sphere being hemmed in by unwelcome choices, greater and lesser evils; but we are not encouraged to see these choices as intrinsic to our condition in such a way that we are anything other than responsible for them and for the damage they do. We do what we can in order to preserve the conditions for further transformations, neither shrugging our shoulders about the moral risks involved nor holding back from action because of those risks. And we are able to do this because of a basic confidence in the persistence of divine purpose, the fidelity of grace as it is offered to us in the common life. What we say about politics and the public sphere does not and cannot belong in a different discourse from what we say about the soul's therapy.

---

[48] Although he does not directly refer to Augustine, the late D. Z. Phillips, in his book *The Problem of Evil and the Problem of God* (London: SCM Press, 2004), seems to come close to a similar argument about the grammar of divine life and action; see especially chs 4 and 8.

6

Politics and the Soul: Reading the City of God

'Augustine seems to have been the last to know at least what it once meant to be a citizen.'[1] Hannah Arendt's judgement is all the more interesting because she clearly considered Augustine to be the single thinker most responsible for the Christian repudiation of the 'public realm' – a repudiation which she regarded as, in its modern guise, one of the major threats to the security, peace and sanity of the human world. The 'public realm' is seen by Arendt as the world we consciously have in common; to paraphrase her rather condensed exposition,[2] we could say that the common world is what provides us with an identity in terms of language; it is the possibility of securing what I have been and done and said as an individual by locating it in a *tradition* of speech and recollection. It is what makes it possible for me to be remembered, for me to be part of the conversation of a future generation. Thus it is the sign of a *common humanity*, existing independently of my will or imagination: to engage in 'public' life is to accept that I am finite and timebound, born *into* a continuum of language and interaction I did not choose or invent, and yet also to transcend my finitude in the only way I can, by striving to contribute to the language and interaction of the group some new qualification or nuance that can reasonably and properly become part of a tradition, a heritage. Our goal should be to make our lives 'a symbol perfected in death'.[3] Without this, we are doomed to the

---

[1] H. Arendt, *The Human Condition* (Chicago, IL: University of Chicago Press, 1958), p. 14.
[2] Ibid., pp. 50–8.
[3] T.S. Eliot, *Little Gidding*, III.

futile insignificance of purely private and individual life, futile insofar as its value is perceptible only to my subjectivity and the subjectivities of those I am immediately in contact with, and because its conduct is likely to be constrained and dominated by my need to survive and meet my necessities and those of my dependants. In this sense, says Arendt,[4] classical thought considered the public realm to be the sphere of true freedom: rule, coercive power, even violence, belong in the household, since they are the means of mastering necessity, organizing the threatening incipient chaos of daily life. Without the patterns of dominance securely fixed in the domestic order, no one would be able to go out into the *polis* among equals, freed from private need so as to engage in the creative, intelligible work of constructing shared meanings and shared futures, in action worthy of remembrance, action establishing a human continuity that transcends the immediate and the local. The private has no history, because the struggle for survival and the meeting of needs has no history. And without this public realm of active, creative persons taking responsibility for the integrity and continuation of a form of talking and understanding, we are condemned either to the animal pointlessness of the mere effort to subsist, or to the more typically modern unfreedom of 'mass society', in which financial achievement and reward or security replaces glory and repute, the notion of worthiness to be remembered, and the quality of public action as creative, as formative of a 'conversation' extending beyond individual death, is undermined. Society becomes increasingly incapable of intelligent speech, common imagination, increasingly enslaved to idolatrous objectifications, fetishes and slogans.[5]

How then does Christianity – or Augustinian Christianity in particular – carry forward this subversion of the public? The early Church, Arendt suggests,[6] is a community of people more or less marginalized by their refusal of Roman imperial authority and their anticipation of the end of the world: humanly speaking, the 'conversation' is simply not going to continue. What then can 'replace the world' as a bond between such persons? The sense of belonging to a

---

[4]Ibid., pp. 28–30. See also the excellent article by Paul A. Rahe, 'The primacy of politics in classical Greece', *The American Historical Review*, 89 (1984), pp. 265–93.
[5]Arendt's analysis here should be compared with that of Adorno on objectification and the menace of the 'totally administered society'.
[6]Arendt, *Human Condition*, pp. 53–4.

community which is in important respects more like a kindred, a family, than a *polis*, a community in which achievement, excellence or creativity are irrelevant to membership, even damaging. It is a body held together by love, *caritas*: 'the bond of charity between people, while it is incapable of founding a public realm of its own, . . . is admirably fit to carry a group of essentially wordless people through the world'.[7] *Caritas* is, in the Augustinian system, a love which is indifferent to merit and achievement: it sees the bonds between persons as resting simply on their common createdness and equal sinfulness, and thus operates impartially and, in a sense, impersonally. In her doctoral thesis of 1929, *Der Liebesbegriff bei Augustin*,[8] Arendt had argued that *caritas* means 'loving the eternal' in ourselves and others, and that this is the essence of Christian 'neighbourly love': we see in one another tokens of both the creative and the redemptive work of God. As creatures, we love still at a distance, we 'coexist'; but as sinful objects of the saving work of Christ, we are brought together in communion. A non-worldly society is thus created, the 'City of God'.[9] By the time she came to write *The Human Condition* in the 1950s, Arendt was far more openly hostile to the idea of non-worldly community than she had been in 1929 (that, as she would no doubt have said, is what the twentieth century does to you); but the analysis of Augustine and the principle of 'worldless' love remains much the same. The *civitas Dei* is a substitute for the public realm, and thus its enemy.

Yet Augustine knew 'at least what it once meant to be a citizen'. This is a remark made in passing, puzzling in the light of the conclusion that it is Augustine who makes it more or less impossible for a Christian to *be* a citizen. In this paper, I want to explore precisely why Augustine might be said to understand what is involved in citizenship, and how far he may at the same time be rightly seen as a subverter of the values of the classical public and political realm. Hannah Arendt is, I believe, right, though not perhaps for the right reasons. And on

---

[7] Ibid., p. 53. Note that Arendt, in alluding to the Augustinian ascription of some kind of 'political' virtue to even the robber band (*civ.* XIX, 12), misses Augustine's point. There is no assimilation of the 'worldlessness' of the saint and the criminal to each other: Augustine is making a general observation on the universality of the desire for peace, without which no corporate life or action can exist.

[8] Berlin, 1929; see esp. pp. 62–8 (there is a good summary of this rather rare and inaccessible work on pp. 490–500 of Elizabeth Young-Bruehl's fine biography, *Hannah Arendt: For Love of the World* (New Haven, CT and London: Yale University Press, 1982).

[9] Ibid., pp. 75–90 (Young-Bruehl, pp. 496–7).

the other hand, a recent defence of Augustine as a fundamentally political educator – Peter Bathory's *Political Theory as Public Confession*[10] – seeks to correct the imbalance that prompts the notion that Augustine commended passivity or disengagement, yet does so at the expense of any analysis of the saint's radical assault on the conventionally political as such. Both Arendt and Bathory, in fact, seem to resolve what many readers of Augustine have found to be an irresoluble set of tensions. As will appear, I do not believe Augustine is guilty simply of flat contradictions; but I see little value in trying to extract a wholly consistent programme from the *City of God*. We should look less for a systematic account of 'Church' and 'world' (let alone Church and state), more for a scheme for reflecting on the nature of social virtue.

Robert Markus, in what remains probably the finest survey of Augustine's political thinking in English, argues for a tendency in the *De civitate* to 'atomistic personalism' where Augustine is reflecting on what we should call state power. Augustine may write of a *civitas terrena*; yet his discussion deals not with anything that could be called an institution, but rather with persons and processes.[11] Thus we cannot really say that he has a theory of *the* state at all (even in the attenuated sense discussed by Figgis, who is careful to warn against the translation of *civitas* by any strictly political term).[12] Augustine does not think – or at least does not consistently think – of two distinct kinds of human association, the sacred and the secular, or even the private and the public. His concern is with the goal of human life as such. Thus, at the end of Book XVIII of the *De civitate*, we read that both cities, of God and of this world, experience the same vicissitudes of earthly life and make use of the same temporal goods, but *diversa fide, diversa spe, diverso amore*: their goals are distinct, and so will be their eternal rewards.[13] Book XIX then opens the

---

[10]New Brunswick, NJ and London: Transaction Books, 1981.

[11]*Saeculum, History and Society in the Theology of St Augustine* (Cambridge: Cambridge University Press, 1970), pp. 149–52.

[12]J. N. Figgis, *The Political Aspects of Saint Augustine's 'City of God'* (London: Longmans, Green and Company, 1921), pp. 51ff.

[13]*civ.* XVIII, 54; cf. XIX, 17 for the distinction between *communis usus* and the diversity in *finis utendi* as between the city of God and the city of the world. It is important to recognize that the common use/diverse ends model has nothing to do with pluralism *within* a society; this clarification is forcefully made in an unpublished paper on 'Augustine's *City of God* XIX and Western political thought' by my colleague, Oliver O'Donovan, and I am much indebted to him for allowing me to read and discuss this essay with him.

discussion of the end of human existence; and the 'political' debate of this book must be read in this light. Augustine is not here seeking to pronounce on what might be an appropriate relationship between the two cities; he has just completed[14] a fairly full account of the history of persecution, and concluded firmly that there can be no guarantee of persecution ever being a thing of the past. The last thing he is likely to wish to do is to draft a concordat between the city of God and its avowed enemies. His question in Book XIX is, rather, about the optimal form of corporate human life in the light of what is understood to be its last end. At this level, the *De civitate* is not at all a work of political theory in the usual sense, but sketches for a theological anthropology and a corporate spirituality. The political and the spiritual are not separate concerns: Book XIX seeks to show that the spiritual is the *authentically* political. Although it is in one sense quite true to say, with Markus,[15] that Augustine abandons the classical idea of 'creative politics', of life in the empirical city as the sphere of the free development of moral persons towards the human goal, this does *not* mean that the saint repudiates the public realm for something else, or even that his perspective is 'atomistic' in quite Markus' sense. Rather he is engaged in a *redefinition* of the public itself, designed to show that it is life outside the Christian community which fails to be truly public, authentically political. The opposition is not between public and private, Church and world, but between political virtue and political vice. At the end of the day, it is the secular order that will be shown to be 'atomistic' in its foundations.

In both Books II and XIX, Augustine refers us to Cicero's *De re publica* for a definition of 'the public realm' or the 'commonwealth', as Healey accurately renders it. A *populus* is not just any contingent gathering of persons, but a group bound together *juris consensu et utilitatis communione*.[16] This, then, is where discussion of the properly political, consciously and articulately shared life, must begin: in agreement over what are and are not legitimate moves within the social grouping, and in some sort of guaranteed common access to the things that sustain life (not too far from access to the 'means of

---

[14]*civ.* XVIII, 49–53.
[15]Markus, op. cit. ch. 4, esp. pp. 94–5.
[16]*civ.* II, 21; XIX, 21.

production', perhaps; there are worse translations of *utilitas*!). In a celebrated polemical section,[17] Augustine demolishes the claim of pagan Rome to be a 'commonwealth' on the grounds of what seems to be a piece of lexical sleight of hand: *jus* gives to each his or her due; but pagan society cannot give God his due. It offers sacrifice to demons; only the Christian community offers sacrifice to the true God, and, what is more, the only acceptable sacrifice, itself as a totality redeemed in Christ.[18]

This is not, however, quite as disingenuous as it sounds. A social practice which impedes human beings from offering themselves to God in fact denies that central impulse in human nature which Augustine defined as the unquenchable desire for God and his truth.[19] It provides *ersatz* gratifications, finite substitutes for the infinite. And as such it diminishes humanity itself, in that it takes away the one principle that can rightly order our wills and affections. *Quando quidem Deo non serviens nullo modo potest juste animus corpori aut humana ratio vitiis imperare.*[20] There are, indeed, other factors which may regulate the passions; but the supposed virtue resulting from this kind of control is really vice – pride and vainglory – insofar as it is not referred to God.[21] So *beate vivere* is made impossible for us when society directs us to goals other than the glory of our maker. Thus if the pagan *res publica* is deficient as a commonwealth, it is not because Augustine polemically sets a standard of unattainably high righteousness or religious probity, but because a society incapable of giving God his due fails to give its citizens their due – as human beings made for the quest and the enjoyment of God. Where there is no *jus* towards God, there is no common sense of what is due to human beings, no *juris consensus*. And this theme proves to be the main burden of the *De civitate*'s vision of political virtue.

---

[17]*civ.* XIX, 21–3.
[18]*civ.* XIX, 23; cf. XVIII, 54; X, 4, 5, 19 and 20. Markus (op. cit., pp. 64–5) rather misleads the reader by eliding most of the detail of Augustine's argument, when he says that the saint identifies Ciceronian *jus* with Christian righteousness; this would make the argument about sacrifice redundant.
[19]*conf.* I, 1.1, etc. On the vast subject of desire as a theological theme in Augustine, see recently Isabelle Bochet, *Saint Augustin et le désir de Dieu* (Paris: Edition des Etudes Augustiniennes, 1982).
[20]*civ. Dei* XIX, 21.
[21]*civ.* XIX, 25.

If this reading of XIX, 21-3 is correct, then the argument about true and false commonwealths cannot be resolved by appealing to Augustine's allegedly more pragmatic definition of the *res publica* in XIX, 24. Normally[22] this has been seen as indicating that Augustine has exhausted his polemic, and is now attempting to work a more constructive vein. The definition of a *populus* as united by *jus* has been shown to be inapplicable to any but the people of God; is the Roman republic then no more than an arbitrary *coetus*? No, for there are other possible definitions; let us try one. We might define the commonwealth as unified *rerum quas diligit concordi communione* – by harmony as regards the things it loves or values.[23] On this showing, of course, there is a sense in which Rome counts as a commonwealth; so would *any* empirical political unit (we may as well say 'state' from now on, misleading as the term is in many respects). But what is often missed in this chapter is the note of *irony*: in the catalogue of nations thus admitted under the definition of a *res publica*, Athens begins the list, and Babylon ends it. There is a continuum between the ideal of classical politics and its antithesis, the tyrannies of the Orient; for without God's justice, the one is merely on the way to becoming the other. *Justitiae veritas* is by no means secured by this putative harmony about values. In this chapter, Augustine recalls the arguments of earlier books to the effect that, while Rome may once have been in principle committed to a genuinely common harmony, it has long since become an empty word. A state may claim to possess the necessary concord as regards the objects of its *dilectio*; but what degree of stability can such a society possess? It is doomed to vice (XIX, 25) and its security is transitory (XIX, 26). In short, while it may be empirically an intelligibly unified body, it is constantly undermining its own communal character, since its common goals are not and cannot be those abiding values which answer to the truest human needs.

---

[22] As, e.g., by Figgis (op. cit. pp. 61-4), Ernest Barker, in his introduction to the Everyman printing of Healey's translation of *civ.*, (London: Dent, 1945), pp. xxxi-xxxii, Markus (op. cit., pp. 65-6, 69 ff., where he speaks of the 'neutral, positivistic terms' of Augustine's definition), and others. Markus' identification of the concept of a neutral secular realm in *civ.* was challenged by Gerald Bonner, 'Quid imperatori cum ecclesia?' St Augustine on History and Society', *Augustinian Studies*, 2 (1971), pp. 231-51, esp. pp. 244-7; see also more recently, J. van Oort, *Jerusalem and Babylon* (Leiden: Brill, 1991), pp. 127-9.

[23] Cf. *civ.*, II, 21.

So, far from XIX, 24 representing a shift in Augustine's analysis towards a more pragmatic and positive view of the state, it is in its context a final stage in the argument begun in XIX, 21. Take even the most minimal and trivial definition of a political body – the unity of common aims – so that you include tyrannies as well as the classical *polis*,[24] and you will still have a picture of societies that cannot *cohere*, that are their own worst enemies, condemning themselves to abiding insecurity. We may call them commonwealths if we will, since there is no doubt that they exist as identifiable social units, but their character and structure are inimical to the very nature of an ordered unity in plurality, a genuine *res publica*.

To understand this more fully, we must refer back to earlier books of the *City of God*, those more directly formed by controversial interest. Book II, 21, in its summary of the argument attributed in Cicero's *De re publica* to Scipio, lays great stress on justice and harmony as the conditions of unity in the state: the various orders of society collaborate rationally, each contributing its own particular note to the harmony. This, of course, assumes that the function of each person or rank in the *civitas* is uncontroversial. And if any class or functionary acquires disproportionate power, 'injustice' is created, and the *res publica* therewith ceases to exist.[25] Thus all members of a society must know their place in a universal *ordo*, they must know how to live in accord with natural law. But, Book II argues, how are they to know this? Chapters 4 to 7, 14 to 16 and 22 to 26 in particular demonstrate that neither the pagan gods, nor the antique philosophers (for all their achievements) enable citizens to live well, in accord with a *lex aeterna*. A poet like Persius may exhort men and women to learn *ordo*, the bounds of aspiration, the will of God;[26] but he writes as a private individual. Such are not the values celebrated in the public worship and festival of antiquity: how then are such values to be established as the common human heritage?

---

[24] Augustine has already noted in *civ.* XVIII, 2, 22 and 27 that Rome is to be seen, both chronologically and spiritually, as the heir of Assyria or Babylon.

[25] *sic ex summis et infimis et mediis interjectis ordinibus, ut sonis, moderata ratione civitatem consensu dissimillimorum concinere, et qua harmonia a musicis dicitur in cantu, eam esse in civitate concordiam, artissimum atque optimum omni in re publica vinculum incolumitalis, eamque sine justitia nullo pacto esse posse.*

[26] II., 6.

The classical world is thus shown to be without any authentic conception of public virtue. Book V takes this still further in its treatment of the motivation of virtue in Roman society. We have noted that in XIX, 25 it is admitted that virtue of a sort is possible where vice is restrained from motives other than the fear of God; that brief aside is meant to recall the bleak reductionism of V, 12-20. The longing for public praise, for glory and good name, controls that *libido dominandi* which so ruins the unity of any state.[27] In this way (under the providence of God) a specious unity is given to the existing order, even a measure of stability. A small number of persons taking a leading role in the state, obsessed with their desire for glory, are enabled – one would almost think, supernaturally – to resist the greater power of other nations. The remarkable successes of the early Roman republic are not due to the favour of the Roman gods (we have already seen in Books II and III that they show little sign of being concerned for the welfare of their worshippers),[28] nor simply to immanent causes like the extraordinary power of disinterested virtue. Augustine's explanation is at once cynical and theological: the lust for glory restrains the more obvious factors making for disintegration in the state; and God elects to raise up a new empire over against the ancient tyrannies of the East, one which at least represents some kind of judgement upon the unbridled *libido dominandi* of those older systems.

Yet the Roman polity is still vacuous at its core. Cicero recommends that the ruler of a city should be educated in the longing for glory;[29] thus the rebellious impulses to tyranny, prodigality or whatever are governed and ordered by one supreme sin, pride. This means that the classical republic is shut out from *ordo* and *lex aeterna*: it is built on disorder, in that what should restrain passion is itself replaced by a passion. That sovereignty of spiritual over material interest which is the essence of *ordo*[30] is parodied by the elevation to supreme status of a material or worldly interest capable of masquerading as spiritual. But this is not the only problem about a glory-dominated public ethic. 'Glory' is of its very nature an individual matter, won

---

[27] E.g. *civ.*, I, 21; II, 20; V, 12-13 etc. as well as V, 19.
[28] *civ.* II, 16, 22ff.; cf. V.l.
[29] *civ.* V, 13.
[30] E.g. *civ.*, XIX, 13.

by competition, not open to all. Augustine mentions without stressing it in V, 12 that the classical Roman story is of the achievements and virtues of the *few*;[31] and while this is, in the context, part of a testimony to the striking nature of the republic's triumphs, it is also made clear that the majority of the population, politically inactive, are kept united only by fear of external enemies.[32] The desire for glory is not a universal moral instructor or preserver of social order: it can assist the unity of a society only negatively, as we have seen, by restraining tyranny. And in Book XV, Augustine has still harsher things to say. Romulus and Remus are alike prompted by the desire for glory in their work in founding the Roman state: but glory is not easily shared. *Qui enim volebat dominando gloriari, minus utique dominaretur, si ejus potestas vivo consorte minueretur.*[33] Preoccupation with achievement brings in its wake a preoccupation with power and pre-eminence: the whole point of the quest for glory lies in the urge to gain advantage over another. In contrast, the love and longing for goodness which marks the city of God is of its essence a desire which seeks to share its object: *tanto eam reperiet ampliorem, quanto amplius ibi potuerit amare consortem* – more is gained by the love of those others who share the quest and the goal. But the search for glory means that the *civitas terrena* is torn by constant strife. The very thing which can in certain circumstances save a society from total dissolution is also potentially a murderous and divisive force.

The conclusion is clear enough: classical society and classical political thought provide ideals for the corporate life of humanity which they cannot provide the means to realize. Already, in the *Confessions*,[34] Augustine had had much to say about those (in that case the Platonists) who offered the possibility of vision without transformation: here, in the *De civitate*, the same complaint can be heard. It is all very well to talk about the public realm, about justice and commonalty; but, empirically speaking, the means employed to make a *coetus* of persons more than a chance aggregate consistently subvert true

---

[31] *civ.* V, 12 repeats several times *pauci . . . paucorum*.
[32] Cf. *civ.* V, 12; I, 29, on the effects of the destruction of Carthage upon the internal affairs of Rome.
[33] *civ.* XV, 5.
[34] E.g. *conf.* VII, 17–21.

common life. It does not greatly matter whether or not we decide to accord the *name* of *res publica* to this or that political order: the reality of common or public life is not there. Unity will always be something imposed from outside rather than growing from within; and so it comes about that states need enemies. As Augustine observes in Book I, Carthage played a highly significant role in securing order and justice in Rome. The destruction of the Republic's great rival meant that the *libido dominandi* hitherto checked by the need for discipline and unity and to some extent exercised in defence against an external aggressor came to be exercised within the state, producing gross inequality and injustice.[35] Aggression not dealt with in the inner ecology of social beings seeks outlets – if not against a stranger, then by making strangers of fellow citizens. Fear, hatred and the struggle to survive become characteristic of relations between those orders of society which, for Augustine as for Cicero, ought to live in interdependent harmony. But such a vision of interdependence is empty without the undergirding of a vision of humanity in the purposes of its maker.

This interdependence, and the critique of internal social aggression must not be misconstrued: it is nothing to do (as a modern liberal might hope) with collaboration and exchange between equals. Augustine believed that we enjoyed a measure of equality as God's creatures;[36] but his universe, including his social world, is unmistakably hierarchical. The subordination of the less rational to the more is certainly part of the *ordo* spelled out in Book XIX, and the authority of the Roman *paterfamilias* over family and slaves is accepted and defended as a model.[37] Slavery as such is a punishment for sin,[38] the way in which God conserves the *ordo* menaced by Adam's transgression. Yet the implication

---

[35] *Delata quippe Carthagine magno scilicet terrore Romanae rei publicae depulso et extincto tanta de rebus prosperis orta mala continuo subsecuta sunt, ut corrupta disruptaque concordia prius saevis cruentisque seditionibus, deinde mox malarum conexione causarum bellis etiam civilibus tantae strages ederentur . . . ut Romani illi, qui vita integriore mala metuebant ab hostibus, perdita integritate vitae crudeliora paterentur a civibus* (civ. 29).

[36] The image of God is equally in all, irrespective of the differentiation of more and less rational; cf. the discussion of the *imago* in women, *trin.* XII, 7, 9.

[37] *civ.* XIX, 16 on the *paterfamilias*; the theme is not unfamiliar from Augustine's correspondence.

[38] *civ.* XIX, 15.

of much of what Augustine says, here and elsewhere,[39] is that, although it may be a decline from primitive liberties that some human beings are so drastically at the disposal of others, it is servitude, not subordination, that is the new thing. That subordination needs reinforcement by mechanisms of compulsion is the consequence of our fallenness; and that compulsion so readily converts itself into a tool for selfish interest, a means of exercising the *libido dominandi*, is the sign of how far fallen we are. Markus argues persuasively that the origin of strictly political rule, like the origin of slavery, lies in the necessities of our fallenness; and that therefore (on Augustinian principles) the empirical state will be distinguished from the city of God insofar as it is always characterized by the exercise of coercive power.[40] Eschatologically this holds true: there will be no compulsion in heaven.[41] But meanwhile the citizens of the heavenly city certainly *do* exercise coercion,[42] nor are they necessarily compromising with the *civitas terrena* when they do so. They are merely working within the inescapable constraints of fallen finitude. No, the city of God is not set over against 'the state' as a body which invariably exercises its power in a different manner from the secular arm (Augustine is emphatically not a Tolstoyan); the difference is, as we should expect, in the ends for which power is exercised, and the spirit in which it is exercised. While it is true that the hierarchy of command in the *res publica* does not have to correspond to any natural hierarchy,[43] the purpose under God of the former is, so far as possible, to restore the rebellious wills of human beings to some approximation to the divine *ordo* – which, as

---

[39]*civ.* XIX, 13 on the natural hierarchy in citation; the discussion of woman's post-lapsarian subjection to man in *Gn.litt.* XI, 37,1 brings out the distinction he wishes to make between natural subordination experienced as joy and fulfilment and the (necessarily) enforced domination of the status quo. It is kindest to say that Augustine is seldom at his best in passages like this. Figgis (op. cit., pp. 52–4) draws a helpful distinction between natural power over the inferior being and 'dominion' in the strict classical sense of absolute right, almost possession, exercised by master over slave, and suggests that this is the distinction Augustine has in mind in the relevant portions of *civ.* XIX.

[40]Markus, op. cit., p. 95 and ch. 6; naturally he observes that Augustine himself cannot be made to say that coercion is alien to the Church's life, but the point is that his principles *ought* to move him in this direction.

[41]*civ.* XIX, 6: . . . *caelestem domum, ubi necessarium non sit officium imperandi mortalibus.*

[42]The anti-Donatist literature is clear enough on the rights of the Church to coerce recalcitrant members back into the fold, though there is no suggestion that it can use force against non-members; see the texts quoted by Markus, op. cit., pp. 148–9, esp. from *epp.* 173 and 185.

[43]This is implicit in *civ.* XIX, 15, 17 and 26; cf. IV, 33.

Augustine repeatedly reminds us, is also the right ordering of our *internal* lives, the dominance of soul over body, reason over passion. In household and society, coercion is properly aimed at restoring the offender *paci unde desilueral*;[44] and as we have been told by Augustine in XIX, 13 that 'peace is indivisible', so to speak, that the *pax* of the individual soul and the *pax* of the universe are parts of a single continuum, so that attempts at peace on the lower levels without regard to the higher are doomed to disaster, it is clear enough that just rule (including, where necessary, the use of force) must aim at a peace which is not restricted only to temporary adjustments or passing convenience.

Hence the significance of the link which Augustine makes between *imperare* and *consulere*: *imperant enim, qui consulunt*.[45] *Consulere* is spiritual nurturing. Because it is itself an activity based on a lively apprehension of the true meaning of *ordo* and of the indivisibility of peace (as XIX, 14 explains at length), it does not run the risk of slipping over into *libido dominandi*. The exercise in authority as *consulere* takes it for granted that the body's peace must serve the soul's, and that the soul's peace is in the love of God and neighbour. The natural order of family life – with the not-quite-so-natural appendage of the household slaves – is the primary locus for the exercise of such an office: a dramatic reversal of what Hannah Arendt saw as the classical set of priorities. So far from being the sphere of bondage and necessity, the household has become a 'laboratory of the spirit', a place for the maturation of souls (the soul of the ruler as well as the ruled). This may sound like a privatizing strategy – creativity being shifted into the domestic sphere. Yet Augustine makes it plain in what follows in the same discussion (two chapters later) that the *pax* of the household is to be 'referred' *ad pacem civicam*,[46] even that the *paterfamilias* should derive his standards from the law of the city. The implication seems to be that the *civitas* is itself, like the household, ideally a creative and pastoral community, educating the *paterfamilias* as to his priorities as he educates his own subjects. The family has become, in some sense, the paradigm political community; but instead of this meaning either that family is opposed to

---

[44]*civ.* XIX, 16.
[45]*civ.* XIX, 14.
[46]*civ.* XIX, 16.

large-scale *civitas* (as in certain sorts of bourgeois politics) or that the *polis* is conceived in organic and 'totalizing' ways, the implication here is that both the small and the large-scale community are essentially *purposive*, existing so as to nurture a particular kind of human life: in both, authority is determined in relation to a specific goal.

This is not spelled out in any detail; but it helps us to see why Augustine, despite his distaste for blandly triumphalist ideologies of the Christian empire, can wax so lyrical in Book V[47] about the virtues of the Christian emperor, who is not afraid of sharing or delegating authority, who uses his power to point to the majesty of God, whose primary longing is to possess and rule his own soul in *ordo*, and whose motive in all he does is love and not the lust for glory. Theodosius I is regarded (V, 26) as a ruler well on his way towards this ideal. We should not read this as any kind of uncritical eulogy for a despot, however: Augustine is not doing for Theodosius what Eusebius did for Constantine, but depicting those features of Theodosius' reign least congenial to an ideology of the emperor's sole authority and unlimited right. He does not cling to undivided supremacy, he is not swayed by private grudges, when (as a result of sharing his responsibilities and being influenced by counsel?) he makes mistakes such as the Thessalonian massacre, he accepts the role of penitent. We may be more suspicious of Theodosius than was Augustine, but we should note what exactly it is that Augustine picks out as the marks of good government – law and coercion employed for the sake of the subject by one who is manifestly not in thrall to *libido dominandi* or vainglory, because he is capable of sharing power and accepting humiliation.

This is *good* government, but it is not, Augustine is careful to tell us, necessarily *successful* government in the world's sense. The well-governed state is not automatically the victorious state; God gives or withholds extensiveness and duration of dominion as he pleases. The government of the commonwealth by the redeemed rationality of a Christian prince is precisely a government whose policy is not determined by considerations of worldly

---

[47] Pp. 24–6. On the portrait of Theodosius, see Y. M. Duval, 'L'éloge de Théodose dans la "Cité de Dieu" v. 26', *Recherches Augustiniennes*, 4 (1966), pp. 135–79. Markus' comment (op. cit. p. 149, n. 2) that Augustine's picture emphasizes the 'private' virtues of Theodosius is odd; he is commended, after all, for *ruling* in a specific way.

triumph. And this leads us to consider a final and very searching paradox in Augustine's reflections on power and rule. The commonwealth is, ideally, a pastoral reality, its ruler a director of souls. Thus it is understandable that Augustine is happiest with the idea of a world composed of small states, comparable to the households of a city:[48] only so is the *pax* and *ordo* of the individual city truly related to the *pax* of the whole world as it should be. 'He favoured', wrote Figgis, poignantly, at the end of the Great War, 'a League of Nations'[49] – though for theological reasons rather than pragmatic ones. Augustine's devastating critique of imperialism in Books III and IV of the *De civitate* displays the impossibility of an expansionist state doing the proper job of a *civitas*: imperial adventures, arising out of the *libido dominandi*, are always a distraction from the real problems of a community, an attempt, conscious or not, to create an *ersatz* unity in a fundamentally fragmented and disordered group. Occasionally, Augustine grants, there is a case for a war waged to subdue an enemy whose aggression directly menaces your own survival; but he has severe words for those who seek, in effect, to provoke another's aggression, to harden attitudes, to provide themselves with an object of hatred and fear, with the goal of reinforcing or extending a nation's power (words not without some contemporary pertinence). And he adds, wryly, that the Romans have been fortunate in being confronted with enemies sufficiently unjust and unpleasant to give their own cause some semblance of righteousness.[50]

However, to go to war is to enter the arena of historical risk and uncertainty in a most dramatic way; the just community is *not* guaranteed protection in such a conflict. In a not very much discussed passage in Book XXII,[51] Augustine takes the issue a little further. Cicero considers that state to be just which goes to war only in self-defence or for the sake of its *fides* – its honour, in particular its treaty obligations; and the obligation of self-defence rests, for him, on the fact that the perishing of a *civitas* is the perishing of a whole 'world'. Death for the individual may be a happy release; 'death' for the state is the dissolution of those bonds of speech and meaning which make the world rational and

---

[48]*civ.* IV, 15.
[49]Figgis, op. cit., p. 58.
[50]*civ.* IV, 15.
[51]*civ.* XXII, 6; cf. III, 20 on the incident in question.

properly human (hence the connection of its fate with the preservation of *fides*, covenanted loyal mutuality). But, Augustine responds, the city of God as such *never* goes to war even in self-defence; for to go to war is for it to lose its integrity, its *fides*. In this case, *fides* and security are one and the same, for the *fides* of the Church (there is an obvious but nuanced play on the word) is its trust in the abiding city of God, which is not found on earth. Ultimately, the true bonds of human speech and meaning, the *sense* of the human world, are preserved in God's eternal will and in the *ordo* of the universe as a whole. It is not contingent upon the survival of any human system of meaning. To defend the city of God would thus be a sign of unfaith, an abandonment of the Church's integrity.

Cicero's picture is, in fact, Augustine implies, a naive one. What of those tragic circumstances in which a *civitas* seems to be faced with the choice between integrity or loyalty and security (as in the well-known case of the Saguntines in the Second Punic War)? The secular politician has no means of deciding here; the city of God has no need to decide. This poses a considerable problem for the interpreter. There are, it seems, legitimate – if risky – defensive wars which may be waged in self-defence; yet such wars cannot be waged in defence of the city of God. The wise ruler will refrain from conquest and aggression, and will only reluctantly and even penitently take up arms to pacify an aggressive neighbour: it is not recommended that he abstain entirely from defence. But what it seems he must beware of is supposing that what he is defending is the city of God. Insofar as the commonwealth is just and orderly, it is worth preserving, and its ruler will take steps to preserve it; that is, insofar as it is *imperfectly* just and orderly, it justifies defensive action. True justice and orderliness cannot be defended by such means, because they participate in the city of God, which depends upon defenceless trust in the continuance of God's *ordo*.

The Christian ruler is thus left with a stark and more or less theoretically insoluble dilemma: if he makes the state's earthly triumph or survival his over-riding goal, he betrays any real 'justice' in the *civitas* he seeks to defend. There can be no crusades, no victory at any price: he has the alarming task of discerning the point at which what he is defending has ceased to be defensible because the means of defence beyond this point undermine the real justice in the state by implicitly treating it as an absolute, to be preserved at all costs.

No particular *ordo* is identical with the order of God's city, and so no state can rightly be defended as an absolute 'value' in itself; the potential tragedy of the ruler is in his responsibility to determine the moment at which he must condemn his *civitas* to defeat.

At first sight, this seems to confirm Markus' conclusion that Augustine points towards a 'secular' neutral space for the state; no political system can be regarded as sacred, as having final legitimacy in itself. But the conclusion is not in fact quite so clear. All this is true; but, for Augustine, there is only one person who can be trusted to perform the task of the ruler in such circumstances – the detached and mature believer, who in his own soul knows the true nature and the true *ordo* of sovereignty. In such a situation, what will the unbeliever do but yield to the *libido dominandi*, with all its ruinous consequences for the genuinely common or public character of the commonwealth. So we arrive at the paradox that the only reliable political leader, the only ruler who can be guaranteed to safeguard authentically *political* values (order, equity, and the nurture of souls in these things) is the man[52] who is, at the end of the day, indifferent to their survival in the relative shapes of the existing order, because he knows them to be safeguarded at the level of God's eternal and immutable providence, vindicated in the eternal *civitas dei*. Politics and the art of government take on the Socratic colouring of a discipline of dying; and only so do they avoid the corruption of the *civitas terrena*, the anti-city, the realm of what Bathory aptly calls 'anti-politics,'[53] in which value and unity rest on essentially divisive and contingent factors and yet are bitterly and unscrupulously fought for.

This is not precisely to say that only the saint should be 'allowed' to govern. Augustine does not envisage a situation in which anyone is able to *decide* about the structures of governmental authority, nor does he ever provide any basis for an abstract discussion of what might be the best form of government, or who the best persons to administer it. In this, he is conspicuously a man of the *bas-empire*, assuming, unclassically, the givenness of the existing order. Indeed, the most disturbing and uncongenial feature of this analysis for most

---

[52] I use the masculine advisedly.
[53] E.g. op. cit., p. 165.

modern students is probably the absence of any idea that the actual *structures* of government and society are answerable to some critical principle. Christians are to be indifferent to the mores of the nations among whom they live[54] – and the word is wide enough to include many of the institutions of public or civil life. It is demonstrably *good* that the state should be ruled by persons aware of the right order of sovereignty because of their own spiritual maturity; and insofar as anyone has the choice of assuming or rejecting the exercise of official power, it is good for them to accept, however reluctantly;[55] but he is not interested in reinventing the inherited forms of power or guaranteeing a succession of saints in office (a form, surely, of defending the city of God by worldly means). Here lies Augustine's great difference from all sides in the medieval debates about sovereignty – from the ardent defenders of papal hegemony to Thomist rationalists. However, we should also remember that he is not a Luther, for whom the Law of God in the earthly kingdom can be dispensed equally well by Duke Frederick or Sultan Suleiman. The Christian has – at least – the authority and the duty to point out what will happen in the land whose king is a moral and spiritual child, incapable of unifying his people through the evangelical exercise of command as nurture.

Where, then, are we left as regards Hannah Arendt's strictures on Augustine as the great enemy of the public realm? In one obvious sense, her criticism is well directed: Augustine is profoundly at odds with anything resembling Arendt's notion of public involvement (and its motivation, which is so precisely what he castigates in Book II). Yet it is not right to see him as replacing it with a more 'private' love ethic. Two points need to be remembered: first, that Augustine's condemnation of 'public' life in the classical world is, consistently, that it is not public enough, that it is incapable of grounding a stable sense of commonalty because of its pervasive implicit élitism, its divisiveness, its lack of a common human *project*; and second, that the member of the city of God is committed *ex professo* to exercising power when called upon to do so, and, in responding to such a call, does not move from a 'church' to a 'state' sphere of activity, but

---

[54]*civ.* XIX, 17 (cf. 19).
[55]See Augustine's correspondence with Marcellinus (e.g. *ep.*138) and Boniface (*ep.*220) on the duties of public involvement; cf. Markus, p. 94.

continues in a practice of nurturing souls already learned in more limited settings. Bathory considerably overstates his case in arguing that Augustine provides a universal political *paideia* for all believers, fostering in them the spirit of authentic public responsibility: such a picture, of an Augustine devoted to the cause of 'community politics' over against late Roman bureaucratic centralism, is seductive but anachronistic. It is true, however, that Augustine assumes that a person nurtured in the Church and in the ordered *caritas*[56] it inculcates is uniquely qualified to take responsibility for wielding political power.

Arendt's further gravamen, that Augustine's model of community relationships represents a flight from *time*[57] is a weighty one. For Arendt, we are summoned to join a conversation that was begun before our birth and will continue after we die, accepting, as we do so, precisely the fact that our participation is temporary, bounded by mortality and 'natality': this is the conversation that constitutes rationality, and, frail as it is, can and must be celebrated as we join in it. But Augustine would have replied[58] that the decision to 'inscribe' ourselves within the human conversation in the terms described by Hannah Arendt is bound to that quest for reputation and secular immortality that actually itself represents a deep denial of the temporal. The guarantee of a place in the human story, gained by active participation in the public realm, seeks to assuage the fundamental restlessness that is *constitutive* of our human creaturehood by offering us the glamour of an assured historical future. For our souls' sake, we need to know that there is no guaranteeable future such as Arendt's neo-classical vision might suggest: real temporality is more vulnerable, and so also more open to radical hope (hope in God). It is the awkwardness and provisionality, the endlessly *revisable* character (morally

---

[56] A notion excessively personalized and psychologized in Arendt's earlier discussion, and to some extent in *The Human Condition* also. We must bear in mind that it is more than a sensation for Augustine, more even than the fact of mutual acceptance for God's sake, but is ultimately the activation of what is ontologically basic in us, our humanness itself, and expresses itself in firm institutional ways, as the Holy Spirit binds us to Christ in the Church.

[57] This is implied in the opposition sketched out between the Christian view and Arendt's own analysis of our involvement in *the human conversation*; see pp. 54ff. in *The Human Condition*.

[58] In the terms especially of *civ.* Books IV and V.

[59] As indicated, Augustine does not think in terms of structural revisability; this is not within his political horizon.

speaking) of our social and political relationships,[59] that, in the Augustinian world, keeps us faithful to the insight of humility – that we are timebound in everything here below, that our love is an unceasing search.

In this dimension of the political vision of the *De civitate*, the deep scepticism about a human future and a continuing memory, we see not a further sign of 'Augustinian pessimism', so called, but, more subtly, a corollary of Augustine's pervasive hostility to two things: an elitist concept of human commonalty (immortality as the acquisition of a remembered name) and a nostalgia for some escape from the shapelessness and uncertainty of temporal existence as such (the Manichaean isolation of a pure and inviolate, ahistorical soul in us, the Platonist promise of ecstasy, the Donatist quest for absolute institutional purity, the Pelagian hope to achieve purity of will, unconditioned moral liberty). For Augustine, the problem of the life of the two cities is, like every other question presented to the theologian, inextricably linked with the fundamental issue of what it is to be a creature animated by desire, whose characteristic marks are lack and hunger, who is made to be *this* kind of creature by a central and unforgettable absence, by lack and hunger. On such a basis there is no possibility of building a theory that would allow final security and 'finishedness' to any form of political life. The claims of such a theory would be, ultimately, anti-political because anti-human: denials of death.

There is a long history of modern argument over 'Augustinian politics'.[60] In the first half of the twentieth century, there was a spirited debate in France over the notion of 'political Augustinianism' as a characterization of medieval thinking about Church and state: by means of an over-simplified reading of Augustine's teaching on the sovereignty of grace and the ultimate lack of disjunction between natural and supernatural, medieval writers were able (so the argument went) to claim Augustinian sanction for the subordinating of state to Church. However, many scholars found this itself too unsubtle a characterization of Augustine's influence, let alone of his own thinking: Henri-Irenee Marrou made a major contribution with his argument in the 1950s that Augustine's arguments implied a kind of overlap between the City of God and

---

[60]For a comprehensive survey, see Michael Bruno, SJ, *Political Augustinianism: Modern Interpretations of Augustine's Political Thought* (Minneapolis, MN: Fortress Press), 2014.

the city of this world, an historical space in which the community of faith and the 'routine' communities of human interest were inseparably interwoven in practice, each influencing the other in myriad ways, though remaining ultimately utterly distinct, with the 'real' history of humanity constituted by the hidden stream of the life of the City of God.[61] This characterization of a *saeculum*, an historical space in which not everything was yet spiritually clear or settled, helped in turn to shape Robert Markus' classic study, discussed in the preceding chapter. This argued, in effect, for a very different kind of 'Augustinian' politics, a pluralist concordat in which the Church pursued its own ends, allowing the state a distinct dignity and autonomy and a freedom to define its human goods without direct reference to theological categories – a 'secular' space with which the City of God could engage in various ways but could never seek to dominate.

Markus' argument is intelligible as a clear repudiation of the last vestiges of theocratic nostalgia – very much in tune with the spirit of the Second Vatican Council, and highlighting some crucially significant points at which Augustine stands apart from the uncritical attitudes of many of his own contemporaries to 'Christianized' political power. But for all its excellences, it suffers from exactly the same problem as so many other twentieth-century studies of Augustine, a lack of focus on the consistently Christological and communitarian aspects of Augustine's thought. The risk in accepting a 'pluralist' reading of Augustine is that it ascribes to the saint an anachronistic view of the political arena. Augustine does not presuppose a political space in which 'values' are negotiated; and while this is arguably a necessary component of any modern political theology, it draws attention away from what is most distinctive in his thought about the ethical and spiritual dimension of organized social life and the exercise of power. John Milbank[62] has been very critical of the notion of a delimited 'secular' space, in the name of a strongly

---

[61]Marrou, 'Civitas Dei, civitas terrena, num tertium quid?', *Studia Patristica*, 2, ed. Kurt Aland and F. L.Cross, 1957, pp. 342–50.

[62]See especially *Theology and Social Theory: Beyond Secular Reason* (Oxford: Blackwell, 1990), 2nd edn 2005; and *Beyond Secular Order: The Representation of Being and the Representation of the People* (Chichester: Wiley Blackwell, 2013).

eschatological theology of the Church as the ultimate form of human sociality and a clearly defined metaphysic of participation in the eternal Word as the foundation of all truthful thinking.

There can be little doubt that Milbank's Augustine is more closely connected with the thought of the historical saint than many of the representations offered in the last half-century, at the very least to the extent that the central issue is our relation to or alignment with the infinite action of divine love. Most importantly, we have to bear in mind that Augustine is not seeking to answer questions about 'Church' and 'state', or theorizing about something called 'politics': he is addressing questions about living well, living blessedly; about what the most enduring form is of human well-being; about what virtues are to be cultivated by those who exercise public office. Out of all this, we can indeed extract elements of a political theology or a political/theological ethic:[63] if we assume, for example, that what Augustine says about the proper spiritual formation of the ruler can be adapted to the formation of the *citizen* in the modern context, there is much that is material for a contemporary ethic of public life and public service. And, as the preceding essay argues, there is also much to reflect on in his analysis of the governing myths of societies in regard to those they see as menacing 'others', especially when the cultivation of a sense of being threatened stands in for a consideration of what is positively desired as a social good – a profoundly pertinent theme for North Atlantic politics at the time of writing these words.

Yet it remains true that what Augustine is really interested in is how the Body of Christ lives: not because he is interested in 'the Church' more than 'the state' or because he has any notion of a schism between private and public virtue, but because he would argue that only a theology of reconciliation with God's act and a participation in that act can deliver real justice. Robert Dodaro's superbly comprehensive study, *Christ and the Just Society in the Thought of Augustine*,[64] spells out the connections between Christ-centred justice in society and the habits of penitence and self-scrutiny which are enjoined on us by our life in

---

[63] As Eric Gregory has done in his very learned and creative book, *Politics and the Order of Love: An Augustinian Ethic of Democratic Citizenship* (Chicago, IL: University of Chicago Press, 2008).
[64] Cambridge University Press, 2004.

the Body of Christ. 'In effect, he argues that the just society is penitential. True justice requires believers to seek from God the forgiveness of their sins and the grace to perform good works.'[65] Thus (as the brief comments earlier in this chapter on Augustine's treatment of the emperor Theodosius suggest) there must be a comprehensive reworking of classical ideals of virtue or piety, a new model of the 'statesman';[66] the public man, the ruler or administrator, will exercise the proper kind of virtue in the uniting of personal humility and repentance with a compassionate concern – born from Christianly-educated emotion – to maintain those conditions that will allow others to attain spiritual maturity. We can see here how the themes of proper appeal to feeling, the proper formation of desire and delight, the entire pedagogy of the Church's preaching and liturgy, the focal significance of Christ as the source of justice, because he is the embodiment of truth, of true relation to the Father and of self-forgetting compassion and humble acceptance of the constraints of fleshly life, all come together in the vision of fully reconciled social existence. And this should encourage us to ask not about how boundaries should be drawn between diverse moral schemes or values, let alone institutions, so much as about what kinds of community actively and effectively form the habits of humble self-awareness that create justice in visible shape – peace, security for the vulnerable, the disciplining of greed and pride. Plenty of political agenda; but the heart of the matter is where the source of sanctification is found.

---

[65]Op. cit., p. 112.
[66]Ibid., chapter 6, especially pp. 193–5, 203–12.

7

Augustine on Christ and the Trinity: An Overview

When Augustine wrote his *Confessions*, he described his journey towards orthodox Christianity very much in terms of a developing grasp of the doctrine of the Incarnation. Scholars are not quite of one mind as to how much this represents exactly how he felt and thought during the long period during which he was finding his way back to the Church; but there is no mistaking the central place he gave to this theme when he sat down to make a coherent story of his life. As he recalls it, he was more and more disillusioned with the Manichaean sect and increasingly convinced that its philosophical basis was confused to the point of being nonsensical. He had gradually become familiar with the teaching of Neoplatonist thinkers who had taught him something about the kind of mental focusing that uncovered the reality of an eternal, unconditioned truth, a life that existed in its own right, free and unaffected by anything else; he had begun to find a better answer to the problem of evil which so obsessed him. Instead of the crude Manichaean solution (matter as the source of evil), he had moved towards the belief that evil was simply (or, in practice, not so simply) the varying degrees of changeability and deficiency in freedom that marked out created things from one another. Yet this vision of the ultimate harmony in variety of the universe somehow failed to motivate him to change his way of life. Deeply dissatisfied with how he was living, he still found it impossible to decide to free himself from idle and corrupt habits.

By the time he wrote, he had come to see that the problem lay in what he came to see as the great absence in Neoplatonism. As he put it very trenchantly in Book

VII of the *Confessions*, the Platonist texts talked eloquently of the eternal Reason at the heart of things, in very much the same way as St John's Gospel spoke of the eternal Word; but what they did not say was that the Word had become flesh. The notion that the fullness of the creative intellectual force that held the universe together could occupy the place of a weak and suffering creature made no sense. As he put it, 'I was not yet humble enough to receive the humble Jesus as my God.'

Christian belief, in other words, was for him not first and foremost the acceptance of certain statements as true, but a sort of moral turning inside-out. Instead of climbing up to Heaven to find the eternal Word, you have to grasp that the eternal Word has come down from Heaven to find you. And this happens when you see yourself not as a boldly questing intellectual mystic, but as a sick person in desperate need of healing, someone whose reality cannot be completed by their own work and attainments but only by a relationship offered completely from outside. Left to ourselves, we can fantasize about gaining wisdom by effort, but in fact we shall only be locking ourselves up still further in our illusions, admiring not the eternal wisdom but our own spiritual skills – and so being constantly frustrated in our efforts to become genuinely wise or good. We have to grow, says Augustine, if we are to feed on truth. And the heart of that growth is humility, facing our essential incompleteness at every level, metaphysical, spiritual, cognitive, moral. Where does God actually meet us? In the free action by which he accepts the limits of mortal life so that he can speak directly to us using our own language. When you see God in Jesus, it is as if you see him at your feet, the suffering or dead body laid out before you; throw yourself down on to that level, 'and when He rises, you will rise'.

Orthodox belief about Jesus therefore involves a spiritual discipline – and this is a key to Augustine's understanding of all orthodox belief. We make no progress without knowing ourselves, as he tells us more than once, especially in the *Confessions*. But this self-knowledge is neither quite what philosophers of the time meant by the term, nor what a modern, psychologically oriented person might suppose it meant. A philosopher would have understood by it the knowledge that each person possessed an immortal, immaterial spirit – and indeed Augustine does insist on this as a crucial part of the process of self-discovery. We need to be aware that we are not simply a bundle of physical systems and instincts. But this in itself can leave us stranded in just the way Augustine describes – a great classical building in ruins. Nor must we think of modern patterns of self-awareness, the result of protracted analysis of our emotions and recollection; in fact, once again, Augustine shows remarkable interest in analysing and chronicling these, far more than any of his contemporaries. But the awareness that matters is the knowledge that we are in need, that we are not self-sufficient. Outside of the relationship that God gives, we are condemned to lonely futility, however much we may be able to tell stories about our fascinating inner lives. That, incidentally, is why the *Confessions* is written in the form of a prayer to God – truthful self-examination can only happen in conversation with God.

So Jesus draws us down to earth as the only way to Heaven. But to be effective he must genuinely speak to us in the language of earth. Augustine develops a very distinctive terminology to think this through, saying that in Jesus the eternal Word and Wisdom of God 'takes the part of a human being'. The language is drawn from rhetoric and drama. *Personam agere,* to play a part or speak on someone's behalf, and *personam sustinere,* to carry someone's role, are terms that evoke the sort of analysis that scholars of rhetoric (such as Augustine had once been) might undertake when examining a poetic or dramatic text: who is this speaking? Are they speaking for themselves or someone else, in direct speech or reported speech? Thus, where Jesus is concerned, Augustine can say that this is God speaking for human beings, carrying the role of a human being – except that this is not a temporary episode; for God to speak truly and definitively for human beings, God must speak from actual human experience, a real life. God makes his own the range of what human beings feel, even their anger and fear, even their doubt and alienation from God, and gives voice to this. It is this principle which dominates Augustine's extraordinary sermons on the Psalms, in which he explains how all the Psalms can be heard as Christ speaking – the Head taking on the 'voice' of the Body, the confused, needy, strident, unhappy voices of flesh and blood human beings.

Because the Word has become human and spoken literally with a human voice, and because he has then, through the holy Spirit, brought believers into an unimaginably intimate relation with himself, as members of his Body, he can present before God completely and truthfully what human beings really feel and think. So in his actual human life and then again in the life of the worshipping Church, he speaks for us, acts out the part of a human being with comprehensive compassion. And pastorally this is important in allowing us to face those feelings and thoughts that we are afraid of or ashamed about; if we fear suffering or complain about God's absence, the Psalms tell us that Christ can make even these words his own and, in taking them to God, open them up for repentance and healing.

But this model of 'acting the role' works in more than one direction. Jesus speaks humanly for us to God, but he also acts the part of eternal Wisdom in relation to us. He speaks for God. And just as his speaking for us is not an episode that can be laid aside, so in respect of this further dimension his whole human identity is God communicating with us. He is always one speaker, one person (in the quite technical sense of the Latin word, the grammatical subject of speech and action); but he speaks for two worlds, two 'natures'. The two lives, divine and human, are both lived equally fully in Jesus, yet he is always one voice; what we encounter is *unitas personae*, a unity of person. So that already, half a century before the Church as a whole had settled its definition of one subject and two natures in Christ, Augustine had sketched out the whole scheme by means of this very lucid and fresh analysis in terms of life and voice.

At the heart of it is the same principle: the eternal Word freely accepts the conditions of human life, and so we too must not seek short cuts out of time and the body but humbly learn to let God's grace deal with them. As we look to the Christ who is both *persona hominis* and *persona sapientiae*, both the voice of humanity and the voice of wisdom, we begin to see how we ourselves may grow into *sapientia*, into the wisdom we need in order to see and live with God.

It is this growth in *sapientia* that gives the clue to understanding Augustine's most original and important arguments in the work of his maturity on the Trinity, the *De trinitate*, written over more than a decade. After an opening sequence of books in which he lays out some of the biblical foundations for belief in the Trinity and deals with some of the objections that had been around in theological controversy during the fourth century, he turns to the question of how we can grasp the idea of some reality that is at once single and triple. A long and dense logical discussion in Books V–VII establishes that all analogies drawn from physical reality (including even interpersonal relations) break down. Yet we know that we are made in God's image; so there must be something about our human world that gives us a clue about unity in diversity at the level of non-material reality.

The question has to be approached, Augustine says, bearing in mind the distinction between different sorts of knowing. *Scientia* is practical knowledge, knowing how to do things, how to find your way around a world of objects and negotiate them successfully. It is oriented towards being useful. *Sapientia* is wisdom, directed towards immaterial reality, towards what can only be looked at and delighted in for its own sake, not used. And of course the life of the mind or spirit (I use both words to avoid any impression that Augustine is interested only in what we should call intellectual matters when he talks about *mens*, mind) is the immaterial reality that is most familiar to us. So when the mind is contemplating the mind itself, it is exercising 'wisdom', contemplative knowledge. We shall find the image of God in us as we advance in this exercise.

In fact our mental life does offer an analogy for oneness in threeness. To be engaged at all in anything we could call mental life is to be involved in three interrelated activities. We are aware of ourselves, conscious of having a past; we remember. We engage actively with what is in front of us, making a coherent shape out of it; we understand. And we have an attitude towards what is in front of us, we make decisions in the light of it; we will. None of these can be thought or spoken about without reference to the other two. We could not make sense of memory except as a deposit of acts of understanding and willing; we could not use the language of understanding without assuming our presence to ourselves and our freedom to make a difference in the light of what we grasp. We cannot see will as a properly mental act if it is cut off from intelligence and self-awareness. The three activities are emphatically not the same, none of them can be reduced to a function of either of both the others. Yet we know exactly what we mean when we speak of our mental life as one activity; we are not thinking about a succession of activities or a group of actions somehow performed simultaneously (singing a song while riding a bicycle and juggling a ball).

Here, then, is the most promising place to start if we are looking for something that shows us how to talk about oneness and threeness. But so far it is only a sort of echo, a 'footprint' of God's activity impressed on his creation.

For it really to be an image, we need more. After all, when we observe our minds acting normally, we are in one sense observing something immaterial, the mind, but we are observing a mind that is itself preoccupied with material things. Take away the daily preoccupations, the trivial activities of the mind, and imagine the mind thinking only of its own nature. But that won't work; the mind is simply not there except as acting in relation to something. If we want to find where the image of God really is, we have to think of the mind thinking of itself in relation to the supreme, unique immaterial reality, God.

So the image of God in us is not a structure of correspondence between our minds and God's mind; it is the mind completely caught up in contemplating God – aware of itself before God, opening its intelligence to God (though God can never be captured in a concept), directed in love towards God – held by this infinite 'object' which is endless awareness, intelligence and love. *Sapientia* brings us to this point, the recognition that our mind is not a noble, detachable, immortal power in itself, but a sort of hunger for God (which is why Augustine said at the very beginning of the *Confessions* that the human heart is 'restless' until it rests in God). And to grasp something of the threefold structure of the mind or spirit (Augustine tells us that the word 'heart' would do just as well) in relation to the eternal is to see how we can begin to make some limited sense of the mysteriousness of God's being as Father, Son and Holy Spirit.

But we need to exercise a little caution here. Augustine is careful not to say that in the Trinity there is a divine mind in which the Father is memory, the Son is intelligence and the Spirit is love. All three activities belong to the Trinity as a whole, to the degree that the Trinity can be seen as something akin to mental or spiritual life. And since the divine life is 'simple' – that is, it is not a blend of separable components, acts or modes of life – all that is true of the Father is true of the Son and the Spirit: the divine life is one and indivisible. This also means that Father, Son and Spirit are not three instances of one sort of life, because we should have to find something extra to the one life or essence that made them separate; and the simplicity of the divine life does not admit of the idea that a divine person could be divine essence 'plus' something extra.

What we can say is roughly this. In our own mental life, what distinguishes the three actions of the spirit is not any kind of spatial difference (since we are talking about non-material reality), nor is it the difference between acts with diverse objects or goals. It is one mind relating to itself in diverse ways; the distinction is in the relations. The category of relation does not add anything to the essence, it only specifies a sort of conceptual position. So, *a fortiori*, with the Trinity. The three agencies are distinct in virtue of their relation to each other. The Father is distinct from the Son because he stands in the relation of a source to what flows from it; the Son relates to the Father as a life or agency that is derived, not simply generative; Father and Son relate to Spirit as giving agencies relate to gift. In Father, Son and Spirit, one identical life is lived; but it is lived as generating, as generated, as given. Only in these modes is it real. There is no divine essence prior to the three specific interdependent ways in which it is lived. 'Being God' is 'being Father, Son and Holy Spirit', nothing more and nothing less – just as 'being a spiritual subject, a mind' is 'remembering, understanding and loving', nothing more and nothing less.

Augustine has often been accused of starting from the divine unity and arguing to the three persons; but it should be clear that this is a serious mistake. He never for a moment allows that you can separate divine life from the agents who live it; that life is essentially defined as eternal loving freedom and wisdom generating, generated and given. That loving wisdom cannot exist except in this interrelated threefold life (any more than a mind can exist except as the complex threefold action that constitutes it). It is wrong to say – as is still too often said – that Augustine stresses divine unity where the Greek Fathers stress divine plurality. As most recent research amply spells out, Augustine and the Greek Fathers are working with much the same issues and often come up with related solutions, though their vocabulary is so different. It is helpful to see Augustine as offering a long explanatory and exploratory note to the insight of St Athanasius, half a century earlier, that the unity of God was the unity of one life, one active nature, not the unity either of a quasi-material substance, a sort of stuff, nor the unity of an 'individual' in the sense we use the word for human persons.

It is true that Augustine warns against misunderstanding the terminology we use, and is sensitive to the different resonances of words in Greek and Latin. Certainly his use of *persona* to say what there are three of in God does not mean that he is thinking of anything like three psychological subjects – just as in his Christology *persona* indicates, as it were, a part that is taken, a position within a complex of related points, though it is not, of course, a role adopted only for a time or an external appearance, a mask (one of the possible meanings of *persona*), unrelated to the essential life within. It is the specific way in which this kind of life (divine life) is real – here and here and here, as source, as product, as gift; and what is unique about the Trinity is that each way in which divine life is real is absolutely and necessarily bound up with the two other ways in which it is real. Each 'person' is the divine life in one particular relation to itself – but that word, 'itself', does not indicate some abstract single nature, but the other related realities or agencies that in fact constitute divine life.

It should be clear that all this is not for Augustine an exercise in speculation, a matter of refining conceptual patterns. We can only grasp any of this if we are converted – if we are turned away from our usual preoccupation with limited material things that we can master and exploit towards an attitude that looks with wonder and delight at truth for its own sake; if we move from *scientia* to *sapientia*. But this also involves recognizing that the mind itself is not a thing that can be contemplated as if it existed as a complete or self-contained entity. When we see ourselves clearly, we see a complex process of mental or spiritual action that is at its deepest level open to what it is not – to the infinite active truth that is God. And in this discovery of who and what we are, we also recognize each other in a different way; we perceive the image of God in each other and we acknowledge that there is one good for all human beings, one standard of justice. Our conversion has immediate interpersonal repercussions. Augustine was working on his great masterpiece of social theology, *De civitate Dei*, during the same years he was writing *De Trinitate*, and we should not be surprised if there is a lot of overlap. It is certainly wrong to accuse Augustine of a narrow individualistic approach to salvation or the knowledge of God. What conversion rescues us from is the mindset for which the basic 'default position' in human affairs is the struggle for acquisition and control; *sapientia* cures us of this illusion and exposes to us our fundamental belonging together as humans made in the divine image.

Augustine makes essentially the same points in what he has to say about the doctrine of Christ's divinity and the doctrine of the threefold God. We begin to know what the doctrines are about only when the nature of our self-awareness begins to change. We have to give up a false 'spiritualism', an ego-centred mystical language. We are not pure spirit, and we cannot make ourselves at home with the infinite God by a technique of detaching ourselves from our limitations. We must embrace what God has embraced – the compromising and difficult life of the body and the emotions. Yet this is emphatically not a refusal of ascetic detachment in its proper sense, which is the release of the spirit from being enslaved to limited goals, to the dream of possession and control. Wisdom will teach us – if we allow it – that our deepest desire is never fulfilled by the possession of an object; it is the unfathomable emptiness that opens out on to God. At this level of nakedness, all human beings are one. And when God becomes fully and consciously the object of such desire, the image of God in human beings is realized; we come to share in God's relation to God. Our unlimited, dependent openness to God is a finite sharing in God's eternal openness to God, the divine life aware of itself and understanding itself and loving itself. Our holiness is not a fixed achievement but a journey, without any final limit in this life, into ever-greater dependence and longing, into a love that has no end.

So Augustine makes many contributions to the vocabulary and conceptual repertoire of Christian theology. He settles the Latin usage of 'one person' to describe the unity of Christ, and he distinguishes between the oneness of nature and the threeness of the persons in the Trinity.

He opens the door to a rich tradition of reading the Psalms as spoken by Christ, on behalf of his struggling fellow humans. He provides a psychology, a structure in which to discuss human consciousness, that will last a thousand years, and which still haunts the European mind. But the most significant aspect of his treatment of the central theological mysteries of Christianity is his clear realization that to believe in the Incarnation or the Trinity is a skill of holy living as well as holy thinking; it is inseparable from a revolution in your image of yourself and from learning a loving openness to the infinite love of God. Growing in love is also growing in wisdom, in the freedom from functional and possessive ways of thinking. And growing in wisdom is growing in understanding of the truth that God is three and one, gift and movement in eternal simultaneity – a paradox to the mind that wants to own and control but a natural and joyful perception for the mind that through Christ is caught up into God's life. It is worth remembering that while he was writing on the Trinity he was composing not only the *De civitate Dei*, but his works against the Pelagians. Shorn of the details of controversy, these are all about the radical quality of what happens when Grace enters. We do not have to confront a God who sets before us demands that must be met by our free choices; we have to surrender to sovereign love, so that we become new, and our own activity is opened up to the Spirit who is supremely the gift of love. We understand Augustine the controversialist a great deal better if we begin from the Augustine who recognized that he could not know Christ's humility or the Trinity's interrelation without his natural capacity being wholly overtaken by the gift of the trinitarian life.

8

Wisdom in Person: Augustine's Christology

In his enormously rich monograph *Les conversions de s. Augustin* (1950), J.-M. Le Blond observed that Augustine saw the incarnation as a *révélation de méthode spirituelle*. Augustine's deepest and most significant 'conversion', he suggested, is that from *Gottesmystik* to *Christusmystik*, meaning not that the incarnate Christ somehow replaces the transcendent divine nature for Augustine as an object of contemplation, but that the sense of Christ as the path to and the form of transfiguring and participatory knowledge of the transcendent God becomes ever more pervasive, more obviously an organizing principle.[1] In what follows, I hope to trace some of the ways in which this theme works as such an organizing principle in Augustine's theology.

By the second decade of the fifth century – essentially by the time of the completion of the *De Trinitate (trin.)* and *De civitate Dei (civ.)* – it is possible to see in Augustine a notably coherent christological scheme. The definitive studies of T. van Bavel and, more recently, of H. R. Drobner have established some of the important shifts in Augustine's christological vocabulary; Drobner, in particular, has also made plain the roots of so much of that vocabulary in the conventions of rhetorical analysis.[2] Among the questions raised by this is why Augustine's Christology fits so comfortably with the theology of

---

[1] J.-M. Le Blond, *Les conversions de s. Augustin* (Paris: Aubier, 1950), p. 145.
[2] T. J. van Bavel, *Recherches sur la christologie de saint Augustin* (Fribourg: Éditions Universitaires, 1954), and H. R. Drobner, *Person-Exegese und Christologie bei Augustinus: Zur Herkunft der Formel Una Persona* (Leiden: Brill, 1986).

Cyril of Alexandria in its resonant affirmations of the unity of the incarnate Word, when those in the Eastern Christian world who employed comparable methods from rhetoric ended up with a much more dualist reading of Christ's person. I want to suggest that when we have grasped with Le Blond the logic of seeing Christ as the form of the spiritual path, with all that this involves, we may understand why the 'Cyrilline' structure imposes itself.

Briefly, my argument is simply that the unifying principle of Augustine's mature Christology is the understanding of Christ as *sapientia*. Wisdom, as defined in *De doctrina Christiana* (*doctr. chr.*), in *trin.*, and elsewhere, is the contemplation of the eternal, God's delight in God; as such, it is what we hope to receive by grace, so that we acquire a share in that reflexive contemplative love which is God's very life. But that divine love as bestowing itself on creation is (as may be seen from a close reading of the later books of *trin.*) identical with that divine action which seeks the 'justice' of another's good or joy, and is therefore bound up with the divine identification with us in the incarnation. *Sapienta* is oriented to incarnation, and thus to the rhetorical paradoxes which involve the divine Word speaking not only human words, but also words of spiritual distress or apparent doubt – the constant theme of so many of the *Enarrationes in Psalmos* (*en.Ps.*). And the upshot in practical terms is, as Le Blond asserts, that 'incarnation' becomes the path we must follow, *la soumission de vesprit aux symbols temporels*.[3] The embrace of our creatureliness, and resistance to all that draws us away from the recognition of the centrality of *time* in our learning of holiness – these are the actual consequences of the act of incarnation, making sense of both the individual path of sanctity and the Church's corporate life and discipline.

These themes are announced very straightforwardly in *Confessions* (*conf.*) book VII, where Augustine offers an already very nuanced account of what it is to become wise with the *sapienta* of the divine Word, a wisdom which is not available through the speculations of the Platonists;[4] this world's 'wisdom is overtaken by the humility of the incarnation. While the wisdom of the world seeks truth by escape from the body, by techniques designed to free us from the

---

[3]Le Blond, *Les conversions*, 19, cf. 133–4.
[4]*conf.* VII.ix.13.

distortions imposed by fleshly life, God's wisdom takes root in us only as we accept our bodily limitation and our spiritual frailty as things we cannot cure from within. Wisdom must become milk for infants if it is to enter our minds; it must be encountered in the flesh. The incarnation both requires and makes possible the conditions of its understanding: 'non enim tenebam Dominum meum Iesum humilis humilem'.[5] Grace humbles us so that we may accept the way of humility as the way to truth; only *prostemere* allows us to rise to the heights of God's wisdom. God's love brings the eternal Word into the human world, and that same love allows us to face our creatureliness and our sin in honesty, knowing that God's will is for our good. In so doing, we reflect God's *caritas* and know God's light, the *lux supra mentem* which is accessible only to love.[6] The displacement of our desire to rise by our own strength delivers us from the idolatry of the self which impedes love. Absent this process – as in the Platonic books – and growth becomes impossible. When I know that I am presently imperfect, I know I must grow in order to feed more fully on Christ who is the Truth (*cresce et mandu cabis);* and nothing can be built except on the foundation of humility which is Christ.[7]

Here, as in *doctr. chr.*, the underlying point is that the abandonment required for us to receive the true knowledge of God is not, so to speak, the 'spatial abandonment of the world of material things in order to rise to a higher realm, but the abandonment of attachment to the projects and desires of the unregenerate will. The refusal to identify God with any *res* in the world, the recognition of creation itself as *signum*, with the cross of Christ as the central proof of this, is another means of saying that conversion is the willingness to keep moving in time, putting behind those desires that look for satisfaction within time (as though desire could be brought to an end, and time thus reduced to space). Growing into knowledge of the incarnate Christ means the reconstruction of desire into hope for God, the *exspectatio* which Le Blond sees as the climax of the argument of the *Confessions*. By the incarnation, God both binds us to the temporal world as always and inescapably our starting point and dispossesses

---

[5] *conf.* VII.xviii.24.
[6] *conf.* VII.x.
[7] *conf.* VII.xx20.

us of the illusion that there is a point within that temporal world where we can settle. Every point in the temporal order becomes a point of departure, to borrow a phrase from Michel de Certeau. The leaving behind of our limited material condition is a temporal and not a spatial matter, in that it involves the journey of growth and learning in time. The *peregrinatio*, which is the basic form of discipleship, is the willingness to see every present moment as the place which a desire for God obliges me to leave, yet also as the necessary prompt or stimulus to the journey of desire, not as something simply to be negated. This is Platonism still, we may well say, but given a distinctive turn by the intensification of the particular promptings of history, focused on the crucified Christ.

To imitate the humility of the incarnate Christ is to come to occupy his position vis-à-vis God, so that his humility is indeed the doorway to knowledge of the eternal. This is the force of the language about divine *humilitas* that we find early in the *De trinitate* (and, note, not too far distant in time from the *Confessions*). In *trin.* IV.ii.4, in the course of one of Augustine's most extended treatments of the person and work of Christ, this is spelled out very explicitly. We are unfit for the contemplation of God because of our sin. Wicked and proud as we are, we can be made capable of participating in the divine Word, being illuminated, only by means of *sanguis iusti et humilitas dei*. God stoops to become a righteous human being so that, as human but not sinful, he may intercede for us so that, created though we are, we may still contemplate God. God is what we are not by nature; but by the Word's participation in humanity, we may share the Word's divinity in being enlightened with his light (and thus, by implication, sharing his contemplative relation to the Father). In an image which Augustine goes on to develop at length, the incarnate Word 'adds' to our humanity in *congruentia* or *convenientia, concinentia* or *consonantia*, 'what the Greeks call *harmonia*,' an element which in its 'Simplicity' overcomes the discords or fractures of our 'double' humanity. The merciful will of God forms a human identity in which mortal body and damnable soul are united with the single purpose of divine love so that they are made capable of seeing God and being resurrected. Of this resurrection, Christ's own is given *in sacramento et exemplo*.[8]

---

[8]*trin.* IV.iii.6.

The incarnation here is seen as the act of divine self-offering which, so to speak, gathers up the elements of broken humanity and constitutes thereby a new humanity, integrated in virtue of the divine act which takes and holds the twofold life of human beings, body and soul, bringing them into harmony. Augustine spends a good deal of time in book IV elaborating the mathematical appropriateness of adding a *simplum* to a *duplum*; but the theological heart of the argument is in effect an anticipation of the scholastic notion that the humanity of Christ is distinct not because of an extra element alongside the human soul and body (as if the incarnate Word were part of a threefold complex of equipollent elements) but because the soul–body compound is in this case concretely animated and individuated by a single divine agency. That is a more involved issue than can be discussed here, but, as we shall see later, it illuminates the most distinctive feature of Augustine's deployment of rhetorical idiom in this context.

It also relates to the theme opened up a little later in trin. book 4 and very prominent in Augustine's preaching. In *trin.* IV.ix.12 Augustine reflects upon the prayer of Jesus in John 17, that the disciples will become one as the Father and the Son are one. Jesus, says Augustine, does not simply speak of a unity of nature (*unum*) between himself and his disciples, although the Church may say that it is *unus* with Christ, one subject, in the sense that there is one head of the Body and one Body. The focus is on the total unity between Son and Father, which is to be reflected among the disciples: this is to be not merely the natural unity between members of the human species but a harmonious *will*, a tending toward one and the same blissful heavenly end. The *unum* of the Father and the Son is a unity of substance and will; so for the Church the unity prayed for is *dilectionis societas*. This *societas* is attainable only in Christ, who binds us together in such a way that we are no longer divided by wanting radically different things. The common life becomes an image of the single focus of the trinitarian life upon its own intrinsic joy; as we are corporately directed toward this bliss, we share in God's self-relatedness. Here the major themes of the closing books of *De trinitate* are already sketched, but they are related very directly to the understanding of the Body of Christ as the form of our renewed life under grace.

But one of the most interesting aspects of this passage is the reference to the sense in which the Church and Christ are *unus*. The argument of the passage is thereby connected to the theology of Christ as Head of the Body which pervades the *Enarrationes in Psalmos*, where it is used precisely as a tool of rhetorical criticism. Who speaks in the Psalms? Christ as Head; and as Head, he makes his own words that would otherwise shock or puzzle, words of guilt or suffering. Just as his death (as we are told at *trin.* IV.ii.4) is meritoriously effective because it is voluntarily endured, not received as punishment, so the entire range of what we might call death-directed experience in humanity is voluntarily embraced by the incarnate Word. Augustine's *de agone* offers a classical exposition of the *aproslepton atherapeuton* argument (i.e., 'that which is not assumed is not healed'), and much of the *Enarrationes* can be read as an elaboration of this. In an utterance like 'My God, my God, why have you forsaken me?' (Matt 27:46; Mark 15:35; Ps 22:1), we can identify the speaker not simply as a guilty and suffering human subject, but as the one who freely undertakes to make all human guilt and suffering his own. By incarnation, death and resurrection, the Word creates a relation between himself and the human race that brings all human experience within the scope of healing and restoration. The Word animates the particular soul and body that is Jesus, and in so embracing *this* human nature becomes the animating principle of any and every human identity associated with him by baptismal incorporation and the gift of the Spirit. The speaker in the Psalms is the Christ who tells Saul in Acts 9:4 that he is persecuting *him* (the Acts text is referred to fourteen times in the *en.Ps.* as a hermeneutical principle).[9] *en.Ps.* 88.30 adds a further dimension, connecting the Head and Body theme with the earlier one of divine humility: '[Christ's] love did not allow the Head to separate himself from union with the Body' even in the exalted state following the Ascension. Thus there is no context in which Christ speaks simply as human or simply as God; he speaks as the one who by taking on humanity through his divine will and power has become Head of the Body, speaking uniquely as representative of humanity *in virtue* of his divinity. The 'right' of the exalted Christ to speak for humanity rests upon the divine decision to take flesh – and not only to take the specific flesh of Jesus of Nazareth but to create *by* that flesh the historical Body that is the company of believers, so that their variegated and flawed

---

[9] *en.Ps.* 39.5 and 87 are particularly clear in enunciating this.

human experience may be offered by the eternal Word and touched with his transforming presence.

It is possible, then, to say, as does Augustine in *Enarrat. Ps.* 21, that Christ speaks in *our persona*. The expression *personam sustinere* is used here, as in other places, to mean something like representing, acting in the role of someone. It is more or less the same in sense as another of Augustine's locutions, *agere personam*, and both are used by him in the works of the 390s to express aspects of the incarnation. For a related locution that does not have to do with Christology, but that also suggests a deeper level of significance, we may turn to *trin.* XII.xii.18: Adam and Eve both deserve punishment for sin, as each *personam suam portabat*. The fact, though, that Adam and Eve also represent different dimensions of human subjectivity and decision making should not lead us astray into thinking that somehow different bits of our selfhood are judged independently (as Eve would have been judged even if Adam had not sinned). Each of us is *una persona . . . unus homo* considered as an agent, a subject of desire, thought, and projection; each of us is judged as a single agent. *The persona* here is the terminus of responsibility, what finally speaks for or answers for our thoughts and desires, for the way we are. *Persona* operates on the frontier between legal, rhetorical and what we should call psychological reference.

But we need to be alert to the complexities of this. The Word of God may be said to speak or act in our *persona* in virtue of his assumption of humanity (and there are of course several issues about how that 'assumption' is best characterized, to say nothing of the varied vocabulary for it). *Agere hominem* appears in several early works (*De ordine* and *div. qu.* LXXXIII) as a way of describing the Word's action. But this does not mean that the *persona* of fallen humanity, the *homo* activated by the Word and for which he speaks, is some kind of independent subject associated with the Word of God. The Word's ability to sustain this *persona* is, as we have seen, grounded in the Word's eternal act and determination, the act that assumes or includes humanity in its life. Hence, prior to anything that can be said about the Word speaking our 'person', is the belief that the entire earthly life of the incarnate Son is a speaking or acting in the person of divine Wisdom: *agere personam sapientiae dei*.[10] The core theological conviction emerging more and more strongly in the 390s and early 400s is that the incarnate Word constitutes a *unitas personae* in taking human nature. *trin.* IV.xx.30 speaks of the *homo* who is joined or even 'mixed' with the Word so as to form such a *unitas*, and there are very many examples of this definition of the incarnate *persona* as being the Word in union with the soul and the body (which latter two normally constitute a *persona* of themselves).

It becomes clear that Augustine's *persona* is a flexible, or, better, an analogically complex term. Its basic meaning is fairly plain: identifying a *persona* is identifying who is speaking, whose role is in question in a complex of interchanges, verbal and otherwise. On that basis, *persona* questions about Christ can be answered at several different levels. The words of straightforward human suffering or fear in the Gospels are spoken in the *persona* of a fully vulnerable member of the human race; the words that must be attributed to Christ as the Word speaking in Scripture, especially in the Psalms, are spoken in the *persona* of what we might call the human condition in general, the condition of sinful people cut off from God. But the entire phenomenon that is the Word incarnate invariably speaks for the *persona* of divine Wisdom, since it is the action of divine Wisdom that creates the divine–human grammatical subject we hear speaking in Christ. *Agere hominem* in this sense depends upon *agere sapientiam*, since the utterance of human grief or pain is the result of Christ's being freely engaged, as Wisdom's embodiment, in the world of historical suffering and struggle. Thus the *persona* of Wisdom is the foundational identity with which we have to do; it is present and active in the form of the concrete historical *persona* that is a soul and body united with the divine Word; and as that historical *persona* incorporates human experience beyond its own individual limits, by setting up the relation of Head and Body in the reality of the Church, the person of divine Wisdom is free to take the role of lost humanity, *agere hominem* in the widest sense.

To engage with Augustine's use of *persona*, then, is to encounter a concept providing a fluid and many-faceted connection between exegesis, soteriology and Christology in the stricter sense. We may say that the answer to 'Who

---

[10] *De Agone* 20, 22.

is speaking?' where Christ is concerned is always *sapientia;* yet this does not entail a divine speaker who can be identified alongside a human one. *Sapientia* is indeed and ultimately the contemplation of God by God, but it is also that which prompts and makes possible the presence of God in what is not God, in the order of creation and in the human mind. Van Bavel rightly observes that, from the first, Augustine sees the incarnation as the revelation of divine reason so that our human reason may be awakened; but as his understanding *sapientia* develops, rather more than reason comes to be involved. Wisdom is identical with *caritas*, and so it is oriented always to the other's good. The *persona* of Wisdom cannot therefore be isolated from its action as *caritas;* to say that Christ constantly acts in Wisdom's person is not to assert that he always speaks or acts as divine Word *simpliciter*, as though the humanity were both separate and insignificant. The *persona* is Wisdom-in-action, Wisdom engaging with what is not by nature God (cf. *trin.* IV.ii.4 again) so as to incorporate it into the divine life and make it capable of seeing what Wisdom sees, knowing what it knows, contemplating the absolute otherness of the creator as if it were located where eternal Wisdom is located, in the heart of the divine self-knowledge and self-love.[11]

Hence the truth of Le Blond's observation with which this essay began: Augustine's Christology is about spiritual method. In the first instance, it is the 'method' of God's own life, the method of *sapientia*. In contemplating the divine life with joy and delight, Wisdom realizes itself as love, the radically disinterested love that seeks the fruition of others in the same joy it knows; all that Augustine wrote about creation itself and in *doctr. chr.* about the character of divine and created love must be understood in the background here. The humility of identification with the created other is the fitting expression of this, and the fitting means by which created life may become capable of

---

[11]It is a huge mistake to imagine that the *trin.* and *civ.* are only tangentially related: what the former has to say about common desire and about the character of justice is only one indication of the parallel nature of the two great treatises. We ought to be able to discern that *trin.* is a treatise about politics, just as *civ.* is a treatise about Christology. The formula of *civ.* XI.2 in respect of Christ's work, *quo itur, Deus; qua itur,* homo, reminds us that the book as a whole is a meditation on how desire is judged and reconstructed so as to release us from rivalry and violence; and that this reconstruction is effected only in the Body of Christ which exists because of the sacrifice of Christ.

divine contemplation, since it involves the 'inclusion' of human experience in the life of the divine Word, by incorporation into the Body of Christ. Since our prideful self-assertion is the root of our separation from God, and the multiplicity of selfish goals and private definitions of human delight is the root of our separation from each other, only our humility opens the way to belief in the saving power of Christ and to reconciliation with God and each other.

One Christ

It is possible, then, to see why the use of rhetorical categories leads Augustine to a conclusion very different from those of the Antiochenes who (as Drobner demonstrates) have what are in some ways comparable concerns. The familiar debate in the Eastern christological controversy over whether the sayings of the incarnate Word could be divided according to whether they are spoken by the Word or the human individual Jesus is circumvented by Augustine – not because he has a straightforwardly 'Cyrilline' account of union *kath' hupostasin* (this is not Augustine's mental world), but because of a more carefully integrated sense of the absolute dependence of the human speech of the incarnate one upon the single act of divine Wisdom. The stress in *Trin.* book 4 on the *simplum* that is the Word's presence and activity is significant. As we have seen, it brings to the *duplum* of unredeemed humanity not simply a third element to contribute to a sum total, but an integrating unity which transforms both parts of humanity. The phraseology of *trin.* IV.iii.6 is instructive: here Augustine speaks of how the single death and single resurrection of Christ serve to overcome the twofold death to which we are condemned. The *simplum* of the Word's agency is the principle through which our natural elements are transformed, not a sort of extra subject.

Consequently, the typical Antiochene anxiety about distributing the *dicta* of Jesus cannot really arise. What substantiates or gives active presence to this particular *duplum* of soul and body is the action of the Word, without which no *human* word can be spoken by this individual, Jesus of Nazareth. He exists because the Word has elected to be incarnate, and thus what he says is said because of the eternal Word. The Word is therefore never 'alongside' the human speaker. It is neatly put in *trin.* XIII.xviii.23: in the saints, God 'reigned', *regebat*, while in Christ he 'acted', *gerebat* – a very characteristic Augustinian word–chime.[12] The act that defines the speaker is always the act of *sapientia*, not a divine act engaging with the act of another subject. There is, one could say, no 'drama', no dialogue of resistance and engagement and submission, between Jesus and the Word, as between the Word and other human beings. That is reserved for the relation between the single reality of the Word incarnate and God the Father. Here the natural and eternal self-surrender of the Son is enacted in the circumstances of weak flesh, both displaying and creating the possibility of obedience to the Father in all circumstances; human pride is overturned by divine humility.[13] The divine act of humility in the incarnation itself, as portrayed in *conf.* book VII, becomes the unifying theme of the human life of Jesus. And utterances of the incarnate Word which sound inappropriate to God are thus shown to be entirely fitting to divinity since they are the product of that loving *sapientia* which is the wellspring of the incarnation.

So Augustine avoids the pitfalls of Antiochene exegesis on this question by refusing to consider the human voice of Jesus in abstraction from the divine self-determination which is the coming of the Word in the flesh. How exactly he comes to this position is far from clear, but I suspect that we should read it as very closely connected with his developing concern with exegesis in the 390s, and the resultant nuancing of his understanding of *sapientia*. Increasingly, the pattern of Christ as 'reason' incarnate opens out, as the 'unreasonable' in Scripture has to be systematically interpreted. There has to be a theological way of making sense of the claim that God speaks in the oddities and contingencies, the fragmented and not always edifying words of the Christian Bible; and in *doctr. chr.* and *conf.* a twofold hermeneutical strategy is developed, which has the consequences for Christology that we have already sketched. Scripture is a sign, that is, a communication drawing us beyond itself, requiring change and growth, the acceptance of deferred desire (including deferred comprehension); and the embrace of this unfinished and unfinishable discourse has to be recognized as what is appropriate to temporal

---

[12] *Cf. ep.* 187.
[13] E.g., *trin.* IV.x.13.

subjects who cannot of their own efforts lift themselves out of the contingent world to eternal verities.

Reading the Bible correctly and understanding the character of God's work in the incarnation are clearly inseparable in the major works of the 390s; our humble acceptance of God's accommodation to our condition correlates with the understanding of divine humility as the unifying foundation for all God's revealing work. To paraphrase *conf.* book 7 once again, if we cannot see that God takes our fleshly and temporal condition seriously enough to use it as his medium for communicating, we shall not take it seriously; and vice versa. *trin.* book IV echoes both *conf.* VII and considerable tracts of *civ.* in defining the essence of religious error as the attempt to achieve reconciliation with God by means of strategies, whether ritual or meditative, to engineer a way out of the human condition; in *trin.* IV.xii.15, the three magi are presented as models of those who abandoned magic and human wisdom to adore *humilitatem domini* and learned to return to their *patria* 'by another way', the way of humility taught by Christ. With a curious passing allusion to the imagery of the *Phaedrus*, by this time a trope in philosophical writing, Augustine warns against supposing that the wings of virtue can be nourished by ritual and magic; instead we are weighed down more than ever by our efforts to rise.

So Augustine's concern with humility develops during the 390s towards the mature polemic in *trin.* and *civ.* against pagan theurgy as well as pagan speculative metaphysics; and the incarnation has a focal place in this argument. But there is a further dimension, harder to trace with precision, that has to do with the evolving sense of what *sapientia* means. As the concept becomes more and more evidently connected with absence and dispossession in its human exercise (*doctr. chr.* is significant in this), so when it is applied to God, its divine exercise becomes more and more linked with *caritas* and *justitia*. To enact the person of Wisdom is inevitably bound more closely with the fundamental act of self-humiliation or self-dispossession in the Word's becoming flesh. So to represent Wisdom is precisely to represent an agency that is displaced for the sake of another. The dual idiom of the Word made flesh, the *agere* of *homo* and *sapientia* inseparably, makes complete sense as a resolution of the exegetical issue.

It would be tempting but misleading to say that Augustine provides a rhetorical version of what is for the Cyrilline tradition a more obviously metaphysical schema for understanding Christology. Cyrilline theology is not simply the attempt to isolate and define an under-girding 'something' in Jesus that can be described as divine; it is, no less than Augustine's language, concerned with finding what agency it is that gives unity to the components of Jesus' humanity, and displaying that unity as the act of the second person of the Trinity. Equally, Augustine is not in any sense replacing an account of metaphysical subsistents with a 'functional' union between the Word and human individual (as if this were a transcription of the stale debate in New Testament criticism two generations ago about whether the New Testament ascribed ontological or functional divinity to Jesus). *Sapientia* is for Augustine a real, substantive agent – both the 'locus' from which the Father can be contemplated and the specific, eternal act of loving contemplation, the person of the Word of God. But it would be fair to say that, to the extent that all Augustine's reflection on the nature of being a subject is deeply involved with reflection on language – representation, relation of word and external reality, memory as self-presence, verbal images as both prompting and expressing the complex re-routings of desire – it is not surprising that his theology of the incarnation should be, in effect, an account of how God speaks within the nexus of human relations; and that human salvation or transfiguration should be linked so often with the idea of the Word's speech taking up and taking over the varieties of confused or rebellious human speech, anchoring the tumultuous instability of what we feel and express in a solid and unbroken self-communication, the Word's self-giving to the Father. Most significantly of all, though, and most challengingly, this pattern of christological exposition insists that there can be no accurate discussion of the incarnation that is not itself incarnationally modelled – humble in its awareness of the inescapable context of material history, alert to the question of how *justitia* is realized, open to the dangerous and potentially humiliating solidarity of fallible and sinful human agents, and refusing prideful isolation. *Agere personam sapientiae* is for all believers the task of learning a new speech apt for the city of God, a *méthode spirituelle* that is both political, in the widest sense, and prayerful, continuous with the unbroken, transfiguring enactment of Wisdom that is Jesus Christ.

9

The Paradoxes of Self-Knowledge in Augustine's Trinitarian Thought

I

Augustine's treatment of knowledge and certainty in *De Trinitate* X has frequently been compared with Descartes' *Second Meditation*.[1] The mind's awareness of its own reality is presented as the paradigm of certitude, the decisive refutation of radical scepticism, in a way that, on first reading, unmistakably evokes the *cogito*. What the present essay sets out to show is that we ought not to stop at the first reading: what Augustine has to say about *self*-knowledge here is only intelligible in the light of a fuller reading of *De Trinitate* VIII and IX, and a grasp of where the argument is heading after Book X. Even in his comparable treatments of scepticism and certitude elsewhere, it may be questioned whether anything like the Cartesian agenda is in evidence. Descartes seeks an irreducible assurance that *all* our thoughts and impressions are not deceits; his goal is to establish that the thinking subject's thought of its

---

[1] *The Philosophical Writings of Descartes*, tr. by John Cottingham, Robert Stoothoff and Dugald Murdoch (Cambridge: Cambridge University Press, 1984) vol. II, pp. 16–23. The parallels were noted by Arnauld in his objections to Descartes (ibid., p. 139, referring to *De libero arbitrio* II, iii, 7), and Descartes (ibid., p. 154) acknowledged and welcomed the comparison.

own activity is the single foundational principle of all intellectual operations, the most simple and directly accessible and invulnerable epistemological datum we possess.[2] Augustine's aim is something less radical and programmatic. He wants to refute 'Academic' scepticism, which is based specifically on the fallibility of sense-perception: no impression of the senses carries with it an assurance of its own veracity, and so no such perception can be received as certain. Therefore, we never have unquestionably valid premises on which to base inferences; we can never advance beyond probability. This, it should be clear, is something distinct from Cartesian doubt; and Augustine's various responses accordingly do not set out to establish an infallible touchstone for all knowledge, a single foundation, but rather attempt to show that, since there are things we know quite independent of *inference*, programmatic scepticism cannot in fact be intelligibly stated.

The parallels and the gulfs between Augustine and Descartes would need several more papers to explicate; but the main point for our present purposes is to note that Augustine's discussion of the certitude of self-knowledge is better described as an analysis of the grammar of the 'subject' (not simply the intellect) than as a quest for assurance against the possibility of global error. And this is why the discussion is an integral part of the argument of the final books of *De Trinitate*, not simply a tiresome digression. Ultimately, what these observations contribute towards is the full articulation of that theological anthropology which the *De Trinitate* displays, the analysis of how the structures of being human speak to us of the life of God even in their very difference from the divine life.[3]

Back then to Book VIII, where the trajectory begins that leads to Book X's treatment of self-knowledge. Books V to VII have arrived at an impasse; they have served to clarify something of the *structure* of trinitarian language, but the clarification of formulae is not enough for authentic understanding. We

---

[2] See J. A. Mourant, 'The *Cogitos*: Augustinian and Cartesian', *AS* 10 (1979), pp. 27–42; E. Booth, *Saint Augustine and the Western Tradition of Self-Knowing*, The St. Augustine Lecture 1986 (Villanova: Villanova University Press, 1989); Gerard O'Daly, *Augustine's Philosophy of Mind* (Berkeley and Los Angeles, CA: University of California Press, 1987), pp. 162–71.

[3] Cf. chapters 3 & 10 in the present volume.

must proceed *modo interiore* if we are to arrive at an understanding of the essence or definition of the truth that God is. To know or acknowledge that God is truth is at least to grasp that the divine persons cannot be portions or subdivisions of a primordial substance, and that there can be no inequality as between the way in which the persons possess or manifest or exemplify divinity. But having drawn this anti-materialist conclusion, we cannot go any further positively: the mind cannot form an abiding concept of final truth, being weighed down with particular and material impressions. It can have momentary and unthematizable contact, but no more (VIII, ii).

Thus, at the very beginning of the long and massively complicated argument of these last books, Augustine signals his refusal to concentrate on the mind's capacity for abstraction; and here we encounter a first paradox. The last eight books of *De Trinitate* are usually and rightly seen as a gradual purification of our understanding of the image of God from all that is 'lower,' material and contingent: the mind is only God's image when all trace of worldly impression is absent and it is open wholly to what is immaterial and eternal. Yet here Augustine dismisses – almost casually – the possibility of the mind conceiving eternal truth, *succeeding* in the effort of abstraction. What gradually becomes plain in these books is that the mind cannot contemplate eternal truth as an object in itself: it can encounter it only through a particular kind of self-reflection. And this self-reflection likewise cannot be the perception of mind itself as object; it exists only as an awareness of the mind's working, the mind's movement. This movement in turn is only intelligible as the movement of desire. It is – as we shall see in Book IX – the fact that the mind knows truth in and only in knowing itself as knowing and loving that constitutes the mind as an image of God, so that the understanding of mind at its most radically distinctive opens the door to some understanding of the unity in diverse articulation of the divine life of *sapientia*.[4]

This still lies ahead from the viewpoint of Book VIII, but helps to explain why Augustine so summarily turns away from discussion of truth in isolation, and begins to treat the question of the good (VIII, iii). Our mental life involves

---

[4]Cf. chapter 10, esp. pp. 173–6.

not only the effort for conceptual possession but the element of judgement, the taking of attitudes, positive or negative, to what we perceive. We approve, we love – or we want to avoid. By what inner criterion do we monitor our wanting and our wanting to avoid? The activity of the reasoning self entails that that self is both moving and moving intelligibly or purposefully; it trusts itself to make judgements about negative and positive goals. Therefore, Augustine argues, it presupposes an orientation to what is comprehensively, non-contingently good. We might spell out the argument like this. Human desire can be set out phenomenologically, as Augustine more or less does at the beginning of VIII.iii – here are the sorts of thing people like, enjoy, approve of, *want to experience*. But such an analysis would leave out the rational element in approbation – connecting this desirable thing with that, recognizing this as analogous to that and so as comparably desirable; and, as so often elsewhere in Augustine,[5] this analogical skill or capacity for recognition is held to presuppose a capacity to abstract from this particular and that particular so as to identify what, as desirable, they have in common. Yet, as we have seen, this identification cannot issue in an *object* for the mind: to see the reasoning self advancing through a *history* of affective and attitudinal responses, a series that has some cohesion and consistency to it, *is* to see what the non-contingent Good is. It is that to which the maximally consistent rational self is tending.

The notion of analogical skill, however, is severely tested by certain cases. What does it mean to love justice, to love just persons *as* just? We are not here dealing with objects of perception that we can classify in the ordinary way; we do not learn to recognize justice by recognizing material features in common between objects. The ordinary structure of recognition involves first of all a strategy of classifying perceptions (the capacity to assign to genus and species): we recognize this as being like that, and this is the ground for our ability to say that they are coherently or reasonably desirable – our ability to make the higher order judgement that they both participate in what I treat as good. But when I recognize a person as just and am positively affected towards that person because justice is desirable, what is going on? Justice is not a feature of someone – like brown hair – which can be recognized by

---

[5]E.g. *De libero arbitrio* II, viii, 22–x, 28 and *Conf.* VIII. 17, etc.

the simple identification of learned and agreed material signs: it is not to be understood, in fact, except by a practitioner (just as a tone-deaf person couldn't be expected to recognize, to have affective attitudes towards, the different levels of musical performance; she might know what material acts counted as 'performing music,' but could not operate any specifically musical categories). However, people who are not saints love people who are, and love them for their holiness; and *quis diligit quod ignorat?*[6] Augustine's discussion of how the holy can be loved rightly or intelligently by the not-so-holy is in fact an attempt to find a way into the more far-reaching problem of how the human mind can love God; but we shall return to this in a moment.

If I am not a practitioner of justice, I do not know what the word means; yet I love or desire or approve of just persons precisely because of what distinguishes them as just. I must then have some inbuilt skill at recognizing justice – not like the skill involved in ordinary analogical judgements. I recognize not by comparing one object with another, but by comparing the perceivable pattern of life in another person with my own aspiration. In other words, the love of a righteous person is intelligible because the pattern I perceive is what I want to realize in myself (VIII.vi). I know what I want to be: which is a slightly odd kind of knowledge, undoubtedly, but one which gives us the recognitional skills ordinarily associated with knowing. Augustine's emphasis on the fact that the meaning of *justitia* is not to be learned *nisi apud me ipsum*[7] simply states that our induction into the use of moral concepts depends on the presupposition that what is proposed as a pattern of behaviour is something we can reasonably be expected to find *attractive;* or, in other terms, moral knowledge, skill in moral judgment, cannot properly be ascribed to anyone who has no sense of what it might be to *want* to be thus-and-not-otherwise in their behaviour. Moral knowledge is no more constituted by an ability to classify certain patterns of behaviour as generally the objects of moral people's approbation than musical knowledge is reducible to the ability to classify certain activities as what musical people count as making music. Moral knowledge involves a particular kind of alertness to motivation (desire once again) inaccessible to

---

[6]*trin.* VII.iv. 6:
[7]*trin.* VII.vi. 9:

the person for whom the critique or refinement of motivation is not a problem because they have no moral wants. It might be said in passing that a society unclear about what moral wants it should nurture in its citizens will produce minds largely incapable of understanding moral crisis and moral tragedy: how many good productions of *Macbeth* or *Measure for Measure* have you seen in the last ten or fifteen years?

I have been paraphrasing Augustine fairly freely; but my aim is, I hope, a legitimate one – to query the common assumption that, when Augustine appeals to an 'inner' source or criterion for knowledge, he is appealing simply and rather crudely to innate data, notions that can be uncovered by introspection. As I hope to show further, the introspection of *De Trinitate* (and other works) is not a search for epistemological buried treasure but something more like an invitation to observe what we can't but take for granted in speaking about mental life at all, as distinct from speaking about the process of registering external impressions. And the discussion in *De Trinitate* VIII of loving justice and just persons is a significant example of his method in this respect. We do in fact talk about loving justice, and we admire the saints; by what logic do we suppose that there is a cognitive and rational dimension to this, given the distinctive nature of what counts as 'knowledge' in the moral sphere? And the issue of this discussion is to bring into focus the centrality of *dilectio* or *caritas* in the understanding of God. Once more, we are directed *away* from a solitary knowing ego as the doorway to theological insight. When we have grasped that we have a fundamental orientation towards the good, we are able to see the centrality of wanting in our human constitution. When we see how this wanting helps us make sense of the partial, often muddled, always mobile business of moral knowledge, we see how closely our love of the morally advanced is bound to our own aspiration. We love the saints because they show us the form of life we recognize ourselves as desiring; and that self-recognition is awakened in us by the attractiveness of others. Justice itself *is* loving, since it wills the good of all, not only its own fruition: the righteous person's righteousness is an active will to diffuse the good, to make others loving. Hence, Augustine is able to complete the first cycle of his argumentation in VIII.viii: what our moral longing longs for, loves, is love, in that it is directed to persons who are loving (for just people are loving people). This is why love of God and love of neighbour are not really to be distinguished: love of the neighbour is love of the actual or possible presence of loving generosity in him (either we see it and approve it or don't see it and long for it to be there); but to love loving generosity as the goal and standard of our humanity is to love it as the good, *simpliciter* – which is to love it as God.

So far, then, Augustine has moved from observing the centrality of appetition in human rational activity to an analysis of moral self-recognition in terms of understanding the self's directedness towards *iustitia*, and thence to the conclusion that our moral and intellectual nature is to love loving – and so to love God, who is *caritas*. So far from being directed towards a solipsistic interiority, we are given an account of mental life in which the fundamental category is lack of and quest for an other to love: the moral will is realized only in and as will for another's good. Outside this, it is wholly void.

II

Book IX is the first serious attempt to apply the framework thus elaborated to the divine life as explicated in the trinitarian dogma. Revelation tells us that God is trinity and that we are in God's image; the discussion of Book VIII has elucidated something of what it means to say that God is love, and that we are oriented to loving the reality of love. So how does the structure of our finite loving minds correspond to that of the infinite loving agency of God? What Augustine essentially has to do here is to display the proper differentiation between self-knowing and self-loving. Book VIII has insisted that to know oneself one must see oneself as loving: my subjectivity is thus engaged in a threefold pattern, the self, its 'other' and the action of loving which binds the two. But this is to take the self as related to something external; as Augustine will elaborate in due course, this cannot be a satisfactory image of God. Yet the self as loving itself yields only two, not three terms (IX.ii); so we must go back and refine our model a bit further. I do not love myself without knowing myself as loving, and that self-knowledge is not the same act as my self-love: *mens enim amare se ipsam non potest nisi etiam nouerit se. Nam quomodo amat quod nescit?*[8] The self is other to itself in two ways, as what is known and as what is loved, and because true and rational love is grounded in recognition of love *in* what is loved, it presupposes a knowledge of love's object. Perfect self-awareness would mean wholly to know the self as loving because the self is wholly in love with itself (IX.ii, iv, and v). Self-knowledge and love thus exist in inseparable interconnection: there is no self that is not knowing and loving, no self that can claim to be whole or truthful that is not knowledge of a loving self, no self-loving without the *acknowledgement* or awareness that love is what the self is engaged in.

The trinitarian pattern is slowly coming to light, as is a second and profoundly theological paradox about self-knowledge: it arises out of love, yet it is presupposed by love. The mind generates its inner word, the *verbum* famously discussed in IX.viii, because behind all knowing lies intention and appetition, hopeful wanting directed to what is strange and other.[9] The moral issue for finite minds is whether this appetition is *caritas* or *cupiditas* (the desire simply to possess, to overcome the other's otherness). So for the mind to know itself as a knower, it must know that its cognitive efforts arise out of love, true or false: and in turn, full self-love depends on fully grasping the lack and desire out of which we live; it cannot flourish without knowing. And when the mind is in this way fully attuned to itself, its knowledge is a perfect 'image' of itself. The mind has 'begotten' a *verbum* reflecting its own reality (IX.xi). The paradoxical relation of knowledge and love here sketched should alert us (though it has often been missed by commentators) to the paradoxical character of the relation between Son and Spirit set out in the later sections of *De Trinitate*, where it is by *no* means to be concluded that the Spirit is in some way subordinated to the Son; but that is another and longer story, which would involve teasing out how Augustine suggests something like a mutual dependence of Son and Spirit.[10] Enough for now to note how he so defines self-knowing and self-loving as to make each unintelligible without the other, and how his means of doing this is the reiterated pointing to the radical incompleteness and other-directedness of created selfhood.

---

[8]*trin.* IX.iii, 3:

[9]*trin.* XI.ii and vii; *De musica* VI, etc.

[10]See, e.g. *trin.* XV.xvii, 29: the Spirit is bestowed on the Son by the Father in the act of begetting.

Perhaps we should pause for a moment here, in the hope of a little more clarity – even if it is only the clarity of a further turn of the paradoxical tack. The finite self's perfect self-correspondence is, on Augustine's account, conceptually very odd indeed. It fully knows itself as a reality that is *not* 'full,' not a finished and determinate object: it knows itself as loving, and, the more loving it is, the more perfectly in love with itself it is. But perfect self-love can only exist on the basis of perfect other-directedness. When the self becomes a perfectly adequate and proper object for its own love, it has become perfected in the love of God and neighbour; it is never a true or adequate term of knowledge if preoccupied with its own 'individual' identity. When it stands in the relations it ought to stand in, it displays its knowledge of unchanging truth, its knowledge of what the good is, of what constitutes *justitia*. Simply to display a knowledge of the contents of an individual consciousness is something quite different, a showing of what is essentially changeable and contingent: to show true self-knowledge is to show what can be authoritatively recognized by another, because it works in precisely the same way as the recognition of goodness in others (IX.ix). Thus, on the one hand, true self-knowledge is knowledge of what is timeless – the nature of love and justice; while on the other hand this can only occur within the temporal world in which the love of God and neighbour is learned and exercised.

III

Here, I think, we touch one of the central themes in Augustinian anthropology; and with this in mind, it should become a lot harder to read *De Trinitate* X as a proto-Cartesian essay. Book IX ends with the distinction (IX.xii) between knowledge as 'product,' something that can be spoken of as *partum uel repertum*,[11] a *proles* or 'progeny' of sorts, and love as the quest which precedes or grounds this bringing-forth. Book X explores further the potential strangeness, already noted more than once by Augustine, of saying that we love what we don't yet know. X.ii enumerates the four senses in which we might take a claim to love what is not known, and reduce this claim to intelligible

---

[11] *trin.* IX.xii.18:

form, but Augustine at the end of this section observes that all this fails to give us any real help in the case of *self*-knowledge, which does not fit any of the four interpretations offered, as he proceeds to show in X.iii. We have to face the central paradox of this entire discussion, Books VII to X, at the end of X, iii: if the self loves the idea of knowing itself, even when still in search of and thus in some measure ignorant of itself, it must at least know what knowing is: but that means that it *does* know itself, because it knows itself as, in general, a knowing subject. You cannot imagine anything that could be called a conscious life that failed to register that what it was engaged in was what was commonly called knowing. Thus, in Augustine's own words here:

> How can it [the mind] know that it knows at all without knowing itself? It's not that it knows some other subject than itself as the subject of its knowing; so it *does* know itself. So when it seeks for itself so as to know itself, it already knows itself as seeking – and so it already knows itself. Thus it can't be in complete ignorance of itself, because in knowing its own lack of knowing, it is to that extent aware of itself. If it was *not* aware of its lack of knowing, it wouldn't be seeking to know itself in the first place. So it is in virtue precisely of itself seeking that it can be shown to be more aware of itself than not. While it seeks to know, it knows itself as seeking, it knows itself as not knowing.[12]

What follows in X.iv, is an attempt to block any crude conclusion that the mind as thus characterized could be divided into a knowing part and a known or knowable part. If the mind knows itself, *what* it knows is the activity of seeking and discovering, not a static object; any other conclusion would be nonsensical, as Augustine has no difficulty in showing. If it knows itself, 'it knows itself entire,' *totam se scit*.[13] In this way, Augustine is able to distinguish self-knowledge from the possession of more or less information: the paradox

---

[12]*trin*. X.iii.5: *Quo pacto igitur se aliquid scientem scit quae se ipsam nescit? Neque enim alteram mentem scientem scit sed se ipsam. Scit igitur se ipsam. Deinde cum se quaerit ut nouerit, quaerentem se iam nouit. Iam se ergo nouit. Quapropter non potest omnino nescire se quae dum se nescientem scit se utique scit. Si autem se nescientem nesciat, non se quaeret ut sciat. Quapropter eo ipso quo se quaerit magis se sibi notam quam ignotam esse conuincitur. Nouit enim se quaerentem atque nescientem dum se quaerit ut nouerit.*

[13]*trin*. X.iii.6:

he presses upon us is that a mind intrinsically incomplete, desirous and mobile, intrinsically incapable of possessing a definitive and unrevisable account of its contents and specific workings, can rightly and intelligibly be said to know itself completely. Self-knowledge is being defined, not as cognition of a spiritual substance, but as awareness of the conditions of finitude and the ability to live and act within them. Hence the further point in X.v that to know oneself is to live reflectively according to one's nature, to live in one's proper place in the universe: as a creature (below God), but a reasoning creature (above the animals). So when we say that someone lacks self-knowledge, we don't mean that she lacks information, or even that she is not given to thinking about herself (the well-known and useful Augustinian distinction of *nosse*, being aware of and *cogitare*, reasoning about, is here deployed). Lack of self-knowledge is a failure in moral and spiritual *habit*, a deficiency in the skills of living according to nature. It is inseparable from failure in love, in the sense that mind misconceives its own nature when it loves (and so identifies with) objects that do not correspond to its most true and fundamental aspirations (X.vi–viii). Of this mainstream Augustinian theme, little needs to be said here, except to underline the way in which Augustine holds together the moral skills of truthful, un-self-regarding love with the capacity for authentic self-awareness – a point, once again, not always adequately weighed by commentators.

All of this is the background to the discussion of the certainty or immediacy of self-knowledge in X.viii–x. Asking how or where the mind is to look for itself is a surprising, a baffling (*mirabilis*) question: there is no alien object to seek, nothing at a distance from the mind itself. The 'quest' is rather for the mind's clear discernment of its own activity – which is possible only through the purification of its loving. When it loves something other than its own loving action (towards God and neighbour), when it is so attached to particular objects and their remembered images that it can no longer distinguish itself, its fundamental orientation to love, from the succession of transient impressions, it fails in self-knowledge (X.viii). Part of the process of rediscovering itself is the kind of self-catechesis described in X.ix–x. We understand what 'know yourself' means, to the extent at least that we know how to use the two words intelligibly; press this further, press the notion of *presence* to self, and you move closer to understanding what it is to exercise mental activity. Augustine's argument here could be very broadly paraphrased in this way. 'Do I know what I'm doing?' is a question wholly unlike 'Do I know (recall, have the ability now to bring to mind) Newton's laws of motion, the date of Augustine's ordination, that man's name?' It is not a search for a possibly mislaid item of information. The answer 'No' might be appropriate as a moment of moral reflection, but it is logically incapable of being a denial of cognition. We cannot intelligibly deny that we are alive, capable of remembering (because we are, in posing a question to ourselves, employing concepts we have learned) and of responding to what is given, forming attitudes and policies (asking a question means *wanting* to know). Augustine is not here, I believe, appealing to some luminous intuition of our spiritual essence, though he is quite capable at times of using language that comes close to this: he is attempting to show us what we cannot pretend not to 'know' – in the sense that we cannot articulate its contrary without self-subverting nonsense. Remember that he is spelling out what *nosse* of the self or mind is, the habit of unthematized awareness, rather than fixing a concept in our intellectual sights. The act of articulating questions to myself, even questions of the most radically sceptical kind, should show me what I can't but assume; and since I cannot (again, logically cannot) think of my mind as one of my mind's objects, I can be shown that – whatever I *think* I am saying – I cannot in fact believe that my mind is a piece of stuff. There is no sane way of behaving that would display such a habit.

Seeing Augustine's argument in this way should, I have suggested, make us very wary indeed of a 'Cartesian' reading of these pages. What is at issue is not the search for an indubitable element in cognition, but a clarification of what can and can't be sensibly said about mental activity, of the necessary difference between knowing oneself and knowing some piece of information or receiving the impression of some object. In this respect – if anachronistic philosophical comparisons may be ventured at all – he stands closer to the Wittgenstein of *On Certainty* than to the Cartesian problematic: Wittgenstein's demonstration of the oddity of using 'This is my hand' as a paradigm of a fact that I'm sure of has some striking points of contact with Augustine's *nosse–cogitare* distinction, in that it reminds us that what I cannot help assuming is not to be assimilated to what I *come to know*. The process of justification and explication involved in discussing the latter are inappropriate in respect of the former, not because

'This is my hand', or whatever, is a supremely good example of something I know, but because we cannot begin to talk intelligibly about *learning* or giving reasons for holding it true.[14]

The end of Book X sketches rather briefly how what has so far been discussed can be summarized by saying that the life of mind is equally, simultaneously and irreducibly memory, understanding and will; and a new phase in the argument opens. What has Augustine so far established? He has, above all, laid the foundations for his later conclusion that the *image* of God in us, properly so called, is not 'the mind' in and to itself (whatever that is – he will effectively dismiss such a notion in the final stages of his argument) but the mind of the saint – the awareness of someone reflectively living out the life of justice and charity. Our interest must be not in introspection as such but in what the saint 'knows', takes for granted as the rationale for and ground of the habits of justice. The saint's mind images God because its attitude to its own life has become indistinguishable from its commitment to the eternal good; when it looks at itself, it sees the active presence of unreserved charity. Its action is transparent to its divine source. Augustine arrives here by dismantling the idea that we could *observe* the self or mind in a neutral way: because what we see when we look at ourselves is desire, we cannot look at ourselves without 'owning' (or refusing to own) that desire, we cannot pretend it is something else.

The paradoxes of self-knowledge – loving before we know, yet needing to know before we love, knowing completely that we have no complete knowledge – are meant to reinforce this upon us, to show us the impossibility of stating any theory of the self as determinate object. We are to know and to love ourselves as questing, as seeking to love with something of God's freedom (in the sense of a love not glued to specific objects of satisfaction) and seeking so to grasp this as our nature and our destiny that we continue to grow in the skills of loving relation and away from *cupiditas*, the possessive immobilizing of what is loved.

En route, Augustine has provided a number of tough exercises for our philosophical wits, at least some of which still have philosophical interest: particularly in a context where debates over the 'mental' status of artificial

---

[14]Wittgenstein, *On Certainty*, ed. G. E. M. Anscombe and G. H. von Wright, tr. Denis Paul and G. E. M. Anscombe (Oxford: Basil Blackwell, 1969), paragraphs 36, 44–4, 84, 94, 140, 192, 341–4, 369–75, 476, etc.

intelligence are being pursued. Augustine's challenge as to whether we can intelligibly assimilate our thinking about our thinking to thinking about a material object or process remains a serious one, in that it does not simply appeal to intuitions of immaterial substance but questions what we can and do actually say. His thoughts on learning moral concepts and on the emotion–cognition frontier are also of lasting interest, however impenetrable their idiom may seem at first glance to the twentieth-century philosophical reader.

His focal achievement in the whole treatise is something very like the opposite of what its critics have often read there. It is an affirmation of the need at least to begin with the mind's involvement, in time and in other selves. But this should not surprise us; if we are misled by reading only fragments of *De Trinitate*, extracting passages or even phrases that seem to present an individualist and crudely dualist anthropology, then we must acknowledge that the same distortion can be caused by reading *De Trinitate* in abstraction from the context of Augustine's whole work at the time of writing this particular treatise. He has only lately emerged from the Donatist controversy; and this should remind us that caritas, for him, has a strongly 'public,' even institutional dimension. It is concretely the bond of peace in the Catholic Church, and we should not fall into the trap of unduly individualizing and privatizing it. The discussions of *De Trinitate* VIII to X may not turn explicitly to the work of Christ and the reality of the Church (for which we must look back to IV and VI, and forward to XV), but this does not mean that the love here enjoined is not the fruit of Christ's grace, or that we can break through over habitual untruthfulness merely by a decision to engage in introspection. Again, the *De Trinitate* is reaching completion as the early stages of the Pelagian controversy are nearing the crisis points of 417 and 418; the inability of created spirit to save itself, the fragile interdependence, in sin and grace, of human persons, the reality of penitence and growth, are all in Augustine's mind as he completes the work. Or take the word *iustitia*; the explicit allusion in VIII, vi to Cicero's definition of the word should bring to mind yet another more or less contemporaneous work, the *De civitate Dei*, especially the account of justice and *pax* in Book XIX, in the content of a critique of Cicero.[15] Justice, like

---

[15] XIX.xxi–xxiv, taking up the earlier and inconclusive discussion at II.xxi.

charity, is a public matter. If the *De Trinitate* does not always present us clearly with anything like these conceptual cross-references, that is no excuse for reading the work as if it were sealed off from the rest of Augustine's intellectual labours of the period.

For the treatise is not a belated Cassiciacum dialogue; even where it echoes idioms and arguments of Augustine's most overtly Neoplatonic phase, these allusions are woven into a web of very different texture. As has more than once been remarked Augustine is not the first to conceive the will to know God in strongly affective or erotic terms: Plotinus bequeathed to him the language of *eros* towards the One, and the earlier Augustine had frequently taken this language, as a Neoplatonist well might, to entail the rejection of goods other than the One, and a desire to leave behind time, body and passion. Already in the *Enarrationes*,[16] in *De doctrina Christiana*[17] and most eloquently, in *Confessions* VII,[18] this entailment is (at least implicitly) challenged; but only in *De Trinitate* does the challenge find anything like a full theoretical rationale (although it is important not to forget how strongly the doctrine of the incarnation works in this direction in *De doctrina Christiana* and *Confessions*). In this mature reworking of the whole theme of 'entering into oneself' to find God, the Plotinian *eros* for the One is transformed into an *eros* directed to the understanding of *eros* itself. God cannot be sought without the seeker seeking and finding, wanting and holding to, the creaturely incompleteness, the exigence and expectancy, that *eros* represents. Before we can rightly want God, we must know and want our wanting nature. To desire the creator, we must first desire to be creatures; by recognizing our openness to, dependence upon, and sharing in the *caritas* of God, we present, we 'image' that *caritas*. Because this recognition involves seeing ourselves as complex beings, articulating our own unity in a tightly knit manifold of activities, it brings with it some clue

---

[16]See, e.g., *En.Ps.* 55. 6 and *En.Ps.* 76. 14 (on not seeking to avoid *affectus* or *affectiones*); *En.Ps.*119. 1 (on the need for humble acceptance of the conditions of our present life, in imitation of the incarnate Christ's humility).
[17]I.xiv.13 on the right use of mortality, following Christ's example.
[18]VII.18 and 20, insisting on beginning with the flesh in which the Word is incarnate and walking in a specific path through human history.

about the unity in self-relation that is God, some *vestigium*; but only in the awareness ('self-awareness' if you will, but it is a misleading term for us who identify it as being *interested* in the self) of the saint, the habit of acting in the light of God's charity, do we recognize the image.

If, as has been said, everything Augustine wrote is really a treatise *De beata vita*, we should hardly expect the *De Trinitate* to be a Cartesian meditation. Ultimately, for Augustine, the problem of self-knowledge is the problem of true conversion; which is difficult, but not *conceptually* difficult. The teases and convolutions of his treatment have the (paradoxical) goal of letting us know that what we lack in tackling the problem is not information or clarity but the truthful love of God.

10

Sapientia: *Wisdom and the Trinitarian Relations*

'The West . . . identified the being, the ontological principle, of God with His substance rather than with the person of the Father.'[1] 'The subsequent developments of trinitarian theology, especially in the West with Augustine and the scholastics, have led us to see the term *ousia*, not *hypostasis*, as the expression of the ultimate character and the causal principle (ἀρχή) in God's being'.[2] 'In the West, especially since the time of Augustine, the unity of the divine being served as the starting point of Trinitarian theology.'[3]

Such statements could be multiplied by even the most cursory reading of twentieth-century Eastern Orthodox writers, and a good many contemporary Western theologians have been inclined to take such judgements on trust, and to conclude that we have relatively little to learn from Augustine in the task of constructing a properly 'relational' model of God's trinitarian life. Augustine's concern with the self-relatedness of the divine essence (on the analogy of the self-perception and self-assent of the human subject) is seen as one of the primary sources of that pervasive Western European obsession with the individual's sense of him- or herself which has led, in the wake of Kant, to the fundamental illusion of modernity, the notion that the private self is the arbiter and source of value in the world. Augustine stands accused of collaborating in

---

[1] John Zizioulas, *Being as Communion: Studies in Personhood and the Church* (London: Darton, Longman and Todd, 1985), p. 41.
[2] Ibid., p. 88.
[3] John Meyendorff, *Byzantine Theology: Historical Trends and Doctrinal Themes* (Fordham, NY: Fordham University Press, 1974; London, 1975).

the construction of the modern consciousness that has wrought such havoc in the North Atlantic cultural world, and is busy exporting its sickness to the rest of the globe, while occluding the vision of the whole planet's future in its delusions of technocratic mastery – a hugely inflated self-regard, fed by the history of introspection.[4]

Leaving aside these more global cultural judgements, I believe that the connection made between Augustine and the consciousness of 'modernity' is a serious error, resting on a superficial reading of his work – especially the *De Trinitate*. In what follows, my aim will be to show how, above all in the last two books of that work, Augustine's reflection on the trinitarian being of God opens up theological possibilities very different from the proto-Cartesian or proto-Kantian tendencies with which he has been charged. As always, the reader of Augustine must allow for the difficulties caused by his diffuse exposition and reluctance to settle on a single technical vocabulary, as also for the undeniable fact that his rhetoric remains Platonic and dualistic even when the substance of his thought is moving in quite another direction;[5] but, this being said, it is still possible to follow through in the *De Trinitate* a single many-layered process of exploration that remains tantalizingly suggestive. It is not, of course, possible to present a comprehensive reading of this large and subtle text in the compass of a short essay, but I hope that, if nothing else, these pages may help to draw attention to the striking absence in recent Augustinian scholarship of any sustained hermeneutical treatment of the conclusions of the *De trin.*,[6] and perhaps prompt a fuller and better study.

---

[4]Apart from Zizioulas' book, the recent work of Colin Gunton should be mentioned in this connection; see *Enlightenment and Alienation* (Basingstoke: Marshall, Morgan and Scott, 1985).

[5]For some comments on this, see 4 of Joseph O'Leary, *Questioning Back: The Overcoming of Metaphysics in Christian Tradition* (Minneapolis, MN: Winston Press, 1985). The argument of the present paper accords with O'Leary's in insisting that we see Augustine as *dismantling* a metaphysic of timeless spirit, rather than simply reproducing the 'ontotheology' of a Plotinus or Porphyry.

[6]This is not to overlook the classical monographs on the subject and the many more recent shorter treatments in general surveys of trinitarian theology. Nothing has yet quite replaced M. Schmaus' standard work. *Die psychologische Trinitätslehre des hl. Augustinus* (Münster: Munsterische Beitrage zur Theologie; photographic reprint, Munster, Aschendorff, 1967, 1927); and J. E. Sullivan, *The Image of God: The Doctrine of St Augustine and its Influence* (Dubuque: Priory Press, 1963), remains an important survey. Many recent works tend still to overemphasize Augustine's concern with the divine unity, and to accept the conventional wisdom as to the difference between Augustine and the Greek Fathers. O. Du Roy, *L'intelligence de la foi en la Trinité selon s. Augustin: Génèse de sa théologie trinitaire jusqu'en 391*

There are two major points to be borne in mind as we read the last books of *De Trinitate*, points which are often grasped with insufficient clarity because they emerge into full light only at a rather advanced stage of the argument. Both affect the interpretation of the 'psychological image', the parallel between the threefold structure of the mind's self-relatedness and the threefold pattern of divine life. The first has been lucidly treated by several scholars, notably by Sullivan in his study of 1963.[7] The *image* of God in us (as opposed to the mere *vestigia* of triadic structures in the mind) is realized when the three moments of our mental agency all have God for their object. The image, in other words, is *not* the mind's self-relatedness. It helps us to discover that we do, in fact, think about our own thinking as both united and irreducibly differentiated:[8] we are enabled thereby to overcome to some extent the logical aporiai of Books V to VII of *De trin*. But we are not thereby given any significant access to what the *imago* is: the image is preserved only when it exists *ad ipsum* (following the better reading here, instead of the banal alternative *ab ipso*) *a quo imprimitur* (XII.xi.16). It is perfectly conceivable that the mind may remember, understand and love itself, according to its nature, and yet be without *sapientia*, the knowledge of divine matters (XIV.i.3): it will in fact, in such a case, not know

(Paris: Edition des Etudes Augustiniennes, 1966), is a richly documented argument for treating Augustine's trinitarian thought as monist and essentialist, a scheme in which the economy of salvation plays relatively little part. F. Bourassa has provided a decisive response to this in two articles, 'Théologie trinitaire chez s. Augustin', *Gregorianum*, 58 (1977), pp. 675–725, and 'L'intelligence de la foi', ibid. 59 (1978), pp. 375–432. Bernd Jochen Hilberath, *Der Personbegriff der Trinitätstheologie in Rückfrage von Karl Rahner zu Tertullians 'Adversus Praxean'* (Innsbruck: Tyrolia Verlag, 1988), however, still tends to follow the usual tradition of interpretation; but his discussions of Augustine rely very heavily on secondary literature and do not tackle the concluding books of *De trin*. (see pp. 97–104). Pp. 48–9 offer a useful survey of recent treatments: A. Schindler's article in the *Theologische Realenzyklopädie* (Bd 4, pp. 645–98) has obviously influenced Hilberath's presentation of the issues. Two writers who have not simply accepted the prevailing account are Yves Congar and Bertrand de Margerie. Congar, in *I Believe in the Holy Spirit* (London: Geoffrey Chapman, 1983), does far more justice to the pluralism of Augustine: vol. I, p. 78, sets aside the idea of Augustine taking the divine unity as his starting point, and vol. Ill, pp. 80–95, are full of insights, especially, on the overlap between Augustine and the Eastern tradition. De Margerie, *La Trinité chrétienne dans l'histoire* (Paris: Beauchesne, 1975), pp. 159–72. is also a balanced discussion, which, like Congar's, emphasizes the links between Augustine's trinitarian theology and his ecclesiology.

[7] As referred to in the preceding note.

[8] This, rather than any rigid doctrine of the 'faculties' of the soul, is what is in question in Augustine's argument; which means that criticism of the particular tripartition of the thinking self which Augustine prefers does not necessarily touch the main point at issue. Augustine is not resting his case on an unexamined model of a mind that has three clearly delimitable capacities, but on the problems and paradoxes of a mental activity that can be an object to itself.

or love itself *truthfully* if it is a self-contained object to itself. Augustine's argument, as he summarizes it in the early chapters of *De Trinitate* XIV, has a paradoxical and teasing character. Take away from the mind its awareness of itself as activated by outer sensations or even by inner images, its awareness of itself as acting truthfully or virtuously, all those circumstances in which we can say *cognoscibilia cognitionem gignunt* (XIV.x.13); what is left? Apparently (so we should expect) the mind's awareness of its own 'pure' activity, that which is not *adventicia sibi*; but, having said that this is the *imago quam quaerimus* (ibid.), Augustine almost immediately *denies* that the image is constituted by self-awareness in the usual sense at all (xi.14). We are not able to know or love ourselves 'accurately' unless we know and love ourselves as known and loved by God; so that, for our minds to be re-formed in *sapientia*, their prime object must be God as intelligent and loving, God as creator of beings who are able to share in his wisdom: *colat deum non factum cuius ab eo capax facta est et cuius esse particeps potest* (xii.15). Thus the mind comes to share in the *justitia* and *sapientia* of God – not by having characteristics in common with God, as if God and the mind both shared in righteousness and wisdom, both offered instances of these things, but by receiving the just and wise activity whereby God communicates to creatures (ibid.). For the mind to acquire *sapientia* is for the mind to see itself sustained and embraced by this self-communicating action of God; to see itself as being directly formed by this relation to God's wisdom, not given an identity by its relation to 'lower', transient objects (xiv.20). Its knowing and loving of God in this context is also a knowing of its proper place in creation's hierarchy, its freedom from temporal and material conditioning in its deepest orientation. It is possible for human minds to be free for God, because there is nothing in the order of creation that intrudes between the mind and God's self-communication.

What emerges from this important section of Augustine's argument is that the mind as independent individuality cannot image God; when it reaches the point at which it can apprehend its activity apart from activity in relation to this or that object or stimulus in the world, it either apprehends itself as *acted upon* by God, or it generates the fantasy of being a self-subsistent agent, an abstract individuality beyond all relations. For it to see itself as acted upon by God is to know that it is known and loved by God; and in this knowledge it acquires *sapientia*, the knowledge of what is eternal. And what is eternal is the self-imparting activity of God as creator, as giver of the *justitia* and *sapientia* by which we come to share in divine life, to actualize the divine act in our own temporal and finite context. The image of God, in short, is realised when we come to be in conscious relation to the divine act that establishes the possibility of relation; when we see ourselves as acting out the self-imparting of God by consciously yielding ourselves to be known and loved by God. Since that being known and loved by God is the foundation of our reality in the first place, since we exist because God desires to impart his love, knowing ourselves as loved creatures is the only way of knowing ourselves truthfully. And if we exist because God desires to impart his life, we exist as sharers in knowledge and love, as beings whose self-awareness and self-relatedness is possible in virtue of relatedness to limitless knowledge and love. Even the dimmest human self-awareness, far short of *sapientia*, acts out of a buried and inarticulate connectedness with eternal knowledge and love; the re-formation that grace effects is the activation of this forgotten link which unregenerate consciousness can never uncover of itself (XIV.xv.21). We find our nature as loved creatures through the experience of being redeemed creatures. That we can be saved only by sheer gift is the revelation that gives us access to the unknown but always presupposed ground of all our distinctively human activity, the ground in gift, in the turning of God to what is not God in uncaused love.

Growing into the image of God, then, is not a matter of perfecting our possession of certain qualities held in common with God, nor even simply – as a rapid reading of *De Trinitate* XIV might suggest – coming to have God as the formal object of our mental activity. It is for us to be at home with our created selves (our selves as produced, derived), and so to be at home with the action of a creator. We come to 'image' God by grasping that our reality exists solely within his activity of imparting wisdom and justice, and thus letting that prior gift form our conscious reflection and decision-making – which of course is not done by our effort but by the receiving of the grace of Christ which reconnects us with our vocation to be God's created image. The image of God in us might be said to entail a movement into our createdness, because that is a movement into God's own life as turned 'outwards'. What this practically involves is something to which Augustine returns in *trin.* XV, when he discusses the nature of the life given to us in the *donum* of the Holy Spirit, the life of corporate charity (see XV.xxxii.18 in particular). But it should be clear enough from XIV that Augustine's view of the image is, to say the least, very imperfectly characterized as 'monist' or individualist. Not only does it insist upon the fulfilment of the image being a matter of *relation* to God (and of charity realized in us by the Holy Spirit), it also depends upon the belief that the God who is imaged himself wills relation by imparting his own life. And this latter point throws some light on the complex arguments of Book XV, and on what might be meant by Augustine's denial that the mental trinity in us could in any sense *correspond* to the trinity that is God's life.

Augustine, in XV.iii.5, refers back to earlier discussions in the work (notably VII.iii. 5) where he has cautioned against supposing that, when we call the Son power or wisdom, or the Holy Spirit love, we are identifying the person with the quality in such a way as to imply that the Father has his wisdom only through the Son. What is said of God adjectivally, what is said about the sort of life that must be God's, is said of the whole trinity together and of each of the persons equally: these predicates belong *et universae trinitaii . . . et personis singulis* (XV.v.7). We can, Augustine suggests, reduce these predicates to three, eternity, wisdom, blessedness, three fundamental 'clusters' of rules for the appropriate use of the word 'God'. To be divine, a life must be without limit, possessed of intelligence and order, and content with itself (v.8) – a rather striking echo of the classical Indian definition of the divinity as *saccidananda*, being, consciousness and bliss. This reduction of divine predicates is achieved by recognizing that there is in God no distinction between substance and quality, no set of things *happening* to be true of God as opposed to the things *constituting* God as God. This is why, although the three 'clusters' identified here have a certain usefulness in spelling out the diverse kinds of things we need to say in order to clarify what we mean by 'God', they do not themselves represent a real trinity in God: their reference is one and the same (vi.9). We could quite properly select only one as implying all three – *sapientia*, for instance; and the task would then be to show how this predicate itself entailed a trinitarian life.

We have already had a glimpse of the authentic pattern of this life, says Augustine (vi.10) in the eighth book of the work (VIII.x.14), where mention was first made of the triad of *amans et quod amatur et amor*. At that stage, the notion was too difficult for us to grasp fully; we needed to go through the long purification of our ideas about self-awareness, with its paradoxical climax, that occupies Books IX to XIV. In Book VIII, the idea of an unchangeable Good drawing our minds to itself in love was discussed (VIII.iii.4–5), leading into a consideration of the problem, 'How can we love what we do not know?' (iv.6). Love, Augustine proposes, arises from *recognition*, recognizing in something or someone else a pattern (*forma*) of justice or goodness that we already know within ourselves as the source and norm of our own judgement (vi.9); we begin to understand the trinity as we understand love, love considered as the desire for *justitia* in persons, that desire which can impel us even to self-sacrifice (vii.10). We must be in love with loving, we must desire that there *be* love, in us and in others. This is what it is to want *justitia*, the right and proper relation between things, which is for us human beings right (loving) relation with our maker. It is thus that *caritas* or *dilectio* itself provides a model of the trinity. Love loves love – which means that love characteristically loves the act of love or the condition of being in love with something further. We can only love love when it is actually loving (obviously); the love that is loved cannot be an abstract or objectless state, enclosed in itself: *caritas* therefore implies, in addition to itself as an act and a relation, a loved object and the love that is in that object to make it worthy of love. There is love, there is what is loved and there is the loving that exists in what is loved. This, I think, is how we should read the statement in VIII.x.14, *amor autem alicuius amantis est, et amore aliquid amatur*: 'love is love for a lover [an objective, not a subjective genitive], and something must be the object of that lover's love'. In simpler terms, there is my love for someone, their love for someone or something, and whatever that someone or something is: these three terms constitute the reality of love as we know it. Any act of *caritas* which is authentic (as opposed to the acquisitive compulsion we sometimes stupidly call love – VIII.vii.10) presupposes such a triad. When I see myself as loving, I know why I love the Good: the Good is no stranger to me to the extent that I know how to love, and in the Good I recognize the norms, the *forma*, of my own inner life. My lovingness, to coin a barbarous term, is a condition that assumes the presence of an other – so that my presence to the Good becomes a sign of the loving nature of that Good, enabling me to grasp the continuity between what I am and what the Good is.

Augustine ends Book VIII by warning that we are not yet at the end of the investigation; leading Burnaby to say, rather oddly,[9] that the analogy of love has only a small place in the saint's thought. The reference back to this section in Book XV tells against such a judgement. The point is that, while the triadic structure of *caritas* or *dilectio* shows us where to look for illumination about the trinity, it is, as it stands, an analogy resting on the relations between a subject and an *external* object. *This* is why the enormous digression of IX to XIV is necessary: we must discover whether there is anything we can say about the subject relating to itself without the mediation of anything outside itself if we are to try to say anything about God; and, as we have seen, Book XIV is the culmination of this venture. There is nothing that can be said of the mind's relation to itself without the mediation of the revelation of God as its creator and lover. At the heart of our self-awareness is the awareness of the self-imparting of God, whereby we perceive the eternal fact underlying our existence. Book XIV ought to be moving us back to the fundamental insights of Book VIII: the latter showed us that our recognition of a changeless Good rested upon the possibility of recognizing its continuity with our mental life, and the former showed us that this very recognition is the work of God's *sapientia*, a gift from the creator. What we recognize *in* ourselves and *beyond* ourselves is the eternal Good as turned towards us and sharing itself with us. We are ready now to understand that the *sapientia* of God (which, we have been told in XV.vi.9, is identical with his essence) loves the creation which it freely makes; and, if it loves other realities, it cannot be without love for itself or, consequently, knowledge of itself. If it is *eternal* love, it has no need for an object outside itself, and if it is eternal *love*, it must be the kind of threefold *caritas* we are familiar with in our world.

The later books of *De Trinitate* are so laboured and so diffuse in their structure that it is extremely difficult to see how they form a single argument. Not to see this, however, is to risk disastrous misunderstanding. It may be as

---

[9] John Burnaby, ed. and tr., *Augustine: Later Works* (Library of Christian Classics VIII) (London: SCM Press and Philadelphia, PA: Westminster Press, 1955), p. 54, n. 38.

well, therefore, before going any further to attempt a summary reconstruction of the argument as I have tried to outline it here.

(i) We presuppose in all our judgments an unchanging Good, an end of all our desiring (a familiar Augustinian theme; see, e.g. *Confessiones* VII.xvii);

(ii) If we desire it and utilize it in judgment, we must in some sense 'know' it;

(iii) The form of our judgment about goodness is a recognition that this which we see is akin to what is present in us already;

(iv) Our approbation of the Good is inseparable from wanting the Good to come to be in all;

(v) Thus our presence to or share in the Good is a non-self-directed desire: *caritas*;

(vi) Thus the Good we love in others also has the form of love;

(vii) What we love is what is loving; hence the trinitarian form of love;

(viii) But how can this tell us about God since it presupposes the kind of differences that apply only to the world, not to an eternal and simple and changeless reality?

(ix) We must strip away from the mind its conditioning by 'adventitious' factors to see if we can understand the notion of an unconditioned self-presence and self-love;

(x) We conclude that our own presence to ourselves is never other than conditioned by our being the objects of divine knowing and divine loving;

(xi) Thus the whole process of recognizing the Good in us, which is part of our intellectual and moral self-presence, is the fruit of being loved by God;

(xii) We know (*secundum quid*) what God knows because God loves us and imparts to us a share in his life as *sapientia*;

(xiii) God's *sapientia* is thus identified as itself love – a desire for the Good to be in others;

(xiv) As eternal, it must be unconditioned (cf. the remarks on the grammar of God's eternity early in Book XV);

(xv) God is in love with God, and the God whom God loves is the God who loves God: threefold *caritas* with no extraneous conditioning – which the rest of Book XV endeavours to clarify further.

What should be particularly noted is that Augustine, so far from separating the divine substance from the life of the divine persons, defines that substance in such a way that God cannot be other than relational, trinitarian. Because the divine life in its coming forth to creation can only be grasped as self-imparting, *sapientia* and *caritas* are inseparable; and *caritas* is inconceivable without relatedness. If God is eternal wisdom, he is eternal love. The divine essence is not an abstract principle of unity, nor a 'causal' factor over and above the hypostases: to be God at all is to be desirous of and active in *giving* the divine life. That is the essence, the definition of God for our purposes; there is no 'divinity' not constituted by the act of *caritas*, and thus no divinity that can adequately be conceived apart from the trinity of persons.

This in turn throws some light on what Book XV clearly implies is the nature of the *imago* in the human mind: because the terms of human mental activity do not correspond, except in a rather loose way (xxiii.43), to the persons of the trinity, the mind images, in its ensemble of characteristically mental operations, the trinity *in toto*. It is a trinitarian life appropriate to the created order, as against the trinitarian life appropriate to eternity. As we have seen, the eternity of God involves absolute self-identity. In God there is 'nothing pertaining to the nature of God that does not pertain to this trinitarian life' (vii.ll), and nothing that is true of one person which is not true of all – so that (as Book VII had already stated) we should be wrong to say that the Father is wise through the wisdom he begets or loving through the love he sends forth as Spirit (vii.12). Because all are divine in virtue of the one *sapientia* which is theirs, and because that *sapientia* involves all we mean by memory, understanding and love, no one person performs a specialized mental act on behalf of all: the Spirit would not be wisdom *si alius ei meminisset eique alius intellegeret ac tantummodo sibi ipse diligeret* (ibid. and cf. xvii.28). Human beings, on the other hand, are not human in virtue *only* of being capable of a 'sapiential' life: our humanness is not *constituted* by memory, understanding and love, but by other things as well – mortality and animality (vii.ll). We only possess what God immutably *is*. Thus we cannot understand the simultaneity and totality of divine *sapientia*: our mental operations are irreducibly time-bound (vii.13). We know partly through self-perception, partly through sense-perception (xii.22); although (xi.20–xii.22) our own production of a *verbum* and the relation of that *verbum* to action has some serious analogy to the life of God, this dual character of our knowing, self-related and other-related, means that there is an abiding unlikeness (xiii.22). Our knowledge is not like God's – nor will it ever be: it will always and necessarily be a *sapientia* learned or acquired (xv.26), even when it is assured (as it now is not) of a truthful basis (xv.24–6).

The image of God, created *sapientia* in us, has therefore a rather paradoxical character. Our ordinary mental activity is radically unlike God's activity; nothing will actually assimilate us to the absolute self-identity of God's nature as loving wisdom. We image the divine wisdom to the extent that our self-perception is a perception of our own absolute dependence on the self-giving of that wisdom: to the extent that what we see when we look at ourselves is freely generative grace. And this means that we must perceive ourselves as time-bound, limited and vulnerable, as being in need of grace, not as self-generating. Our *sapientia* does not terminate in a vision of ourselves as timeless spirit but in the recognition of our created distance from God: only so do we become wise, because only so is God's creative wisdom made the object of our self-knowing. Thus the temporal successiveness, the fragmentary and rather insecure life of memory, understanding and will in us is appropriately the vehicle of the divine image, in its very *difference* from God: self-understanding as a creature (in the fullest sense, involving awareness of a loving creator) is the reflection of God's love, and so of God's sapiential being. It is to become aware of the all-pervasiveness in a human mind, a human life, of the divine *caritas*. The purification of the mind from temporal conditioning described in Books IX to XIV is not designed to lead us away from our knowledge of ourselves in the world, but to show how the most abstract form of self-awareness we can attain confronts us with the love of God irreducibly there beyond or before us. To recall what was said earlier, the image is a 'movement into our createdness'.

If we are ontologically incapable of being *sapientia* as God is, our task is to let the process of our mortal existence be transformed by the self-knowledge of grace which is our proper wisdom. It is thus very much in order when Book XV turns to a consideration of the Holy Spirit as agent of our transformation and of our participation in the life of God. The Spirit is called *caritas* or *dilectio*, not because the Spirit alone *is* love, but because the effect of the Spirit's work is the effect of love, as far as we are concerned – i.e. the Spirit *facit nos in deo manere et ipsum in nobis* (xvii.31; cf. xix.37). Likewise, the Spirit is *donum* (xviii.32– xix.38) as the agency making love present in us to be the formal cause of our salvation. It does not matter that *dona* may also be used of the Spirit, since the way in which the one saving *dilectio* is appropriated to the needs and callings of diverse human beings in the one Body of Christ involves a plurality of relations between the Spirit and us (xix.34). The title of *donum* does not mean that the Spirit's divine status depends on the relation of God to the world; the Spirit is God eternally. Nor does it mean that the Spirit is, as gift, inferior to the Father and the Son as givers; God gives God, having nothing else to give: *se ipsum det sicut deus* (xix.36). The Spirit, as God, cannot be passive, an object to be passed on by the agency of Father and Son: *non est illic conditio dati et dominatio dantium sed concordia dati et dantium* (ibid.). In other words, the Spirit's godhead is precisely that of Father and Son: the loving wisdom of self-giving. But we may say of the Spirit in particular what is true of divinity in general (*dilectio, donum*) because it is through the Spirit that the life of love and gift which is God is lovingly given in the specific history of our salvation and to concrete and diverse individuals. It is because of the Spirit that we have access as redeemed creatures to *sapientia*, because of the Spirit that we may be taken up into the life of self-impartation which we recognize as the ground of our very relation to ourselves.

The Spirit is 'common' to Father and Son (xix.37, xxvi.47, xxvii.27) not as a quality characterizing them equally, an impersonal attribute, but as that active divine giving, not simply identical with the person of the Father, which the Father communicates to the Son to give in his turn (xxvi.47–xxvii.48). This is perhaps the most difficult aspect of Augustine's thought in Book XV. The Spirit's 'identity' in the eternal life of God has to be defined mostly by negations. As we have seen, the Spirit is not passive or impersonal, but a subject who gives (that is what it means to be divine): the Father, in eternally giving (divine) life to the Son, gives that life as itself a 'giving' agency, for there is no abstract, pre-personal or sub-personal divinity; he gives the Son the capacity to give that same giving life –

which, in our history, is the giver to us of the relation of gift that exists between Father and Son. *Se ipsum det sicut deus*: the Spirit as God gives God, gives the reality of self-sharing *sapientia* that exists eternally as the Father's generation of the Word. The Spirit's act of giving is not that of the Father begetting the Son, nor is it that of the Son 'releasing' the Spirit into the world by his gift of himself to the Father; but it is the act of God giving, and so is no less a 'person' than Father and Son. The Spirit proceeds *principaliter* from the Father (xvii.29, cf. xxvi.47–xxvii.48 – a perfectly clear indication that Augustine did not teach a procession of the Spirit *tanquam ab uno principio* in the scholastic sense): but the context makes it plain that we are not therefore to conceive of the Father as a primary 'self-positing subject' out of whose indeterminate plenitude flow the Son and the Spirit.[10] Augustine insists in precisely these passages (xxvi.47–xxvii.48) on the absolute simultaneity of the trinitarian relations, in a way which makes it impossible to accept any crude account of the Father's priority, or even any model of the trinity in which the Father as prime 'possessor' of the divine essence distributes it to others (we have noted that the divine persons do not 'possess' the divine essence, but are what it is).[11] *Sapientia* exists *by* generating an other, it has its being as lover by being actively for another: the Father is Father, and so is concretely and actively God, by being *for* the Son. *Sapientia* exists by being eternally loved, eternally contemplated, it has its being as what receives and responds to such everlasting love: the Son is Son, and so is concretely and actually God, by being *from* the Father. And *sapientia* exists by being, quite simply, love in search of an object, it has its being as the act of everlasting love which is given form but not exhausted by the mutual gift of Father and Son: the Spirit is concretely and actually God by being *from* or *through* the Father and the Son, in the sense of being the agency that constitutes their relation itself active or productive. In eternity, that productive love is – we must suppose – 'satisfied' in turning everlastingly to the exchange of generating and generated wisdom as its perfect object. In the economy of salvation, the contemplative

---

[10] See John Milbank, 'The Second Difference: For a Trinitarianism without Reserve', *Modern Theology*, 2.3 (1986) pp. 213–34, esp. pp. 220–25.
[11] Note, in XV.xiv.23 and xxi.40, the language of the Father 'speaking', 'uttering', what he is in the Word, rather than *giving* what he *has* to another.

vision of Father and Son that is the work and the identity of Spirit (God's love loving the love of God) is worked, realized, in creatures, as they are drawn out of their distance from divine love to share the relation between Father and Son, and so themselves to live in the bond of *caritas* with each other – the bond of love which is the life of the Church, the *communio sancti spiritus* (Augustine's favourite theme in his anti-Donatist writings).[12]

The notion of the Spirit as love in search of an object may seem a slightly odd one; but xxi.40–1, though densely and obscurely expressed, casts a little light. Here Augustine, while granting the inadequacy of the created analogy of mind in his usual way, invites the reader to reflect, nonetheless, on the role of love in understanding, of understanding in love, and of memory in both, so as to discover an inadequate but quite authentic intuition of the inseparability and mutual conditionedness of the divine persons. *Nisi reminiscendo non redit ad aliquid, et nisi amando redire non curat nostrae cogitationis intuitus;* thought involves 'interest', a desirous intent, a kind of *eros*, which sends us into the memory in search of the image, the *visio*, which we need in order to complete our thinking, in order for our thinking to be recognition, i.e. to be continuous and coherent. This love, this *eros* of thinking and interpreting, unites the history of our perceiving with the present experience of perceiving, establishing the former as 'parent' of the latter. *Ita dilectio quae visionem in memoria constitutam et visionem cogitationis inde formatam quasi parentem prolemque coniungit* (xxi.41). The *dilectio* of thought is what makes thinking a coherent activity, an act from which we can rationally *go on*. Thus, turning from image to archetype, we can say that it is in the love of the Spirit that the entire process (to use a hopelessly inept temporal term) of the sapiential love which is God finds its completeness, its inner 'conjoinedness', and so exists as a reality capable of action *ad extra*, even though it is in need of nothing *ab extra*.

So far, then, from Augustine's trinitarian theology dealing inadequately with the Holy Spirit, it succeeds, for the first time in the history of Christian doctrine, in giving some account of how and why the Spirit is intrinsic to the trinitarian life – a task which not even the most sophisticated pages of Gregory of Nyssa

---

[12]Especially *De baptismo* III–V. and *Ep.* 185.X.43.

manage with any great clarity.[13] Like the Cappadocians, Augustine remains unsure how best to distinguish the generation of the Son from the 'breathing-out' of the Spirit in any but these highly metaphorical terms (xxvii.48); but he is not unduly worried by this, and I believe he is right not to be worried. He has established a way of talking about the pattern of divine relation, complex but not at all incoherent, which can manage perfectly well without anything but provisional and heuristic terms to draw a distinction whose significance is made plain in the whole analysis of the movement of eternal loving wisdom. Is the price of all this an insupportably 'monist' picture of God? As Burnaby points out,[14] Augustine is absolutely clear that 'the Persons [of the trinity] are not faculties or functions of a divine Ego': there is no self of which the movement of *sapientia* is a part, as mental life is a part of human life, and the conscious life of mind a part of mental life overall, and the sapiential life of grace a part (until we get to heaven) of conscious life. There can therefore be no question of any subordination of trinitarian plurality to a unity of essence. Thus there is no simple answer to the question of whether Augustine thought in terms of one divine 'consciousness' or three. The persons of the trinity are not three phases of one ego, but neither are they three quasi-independent agents in serial conjunction. The one life of *sapientia* which is God's life is by definition a conscious, intelligent, knowing life; it is also, as we have observed, a life that is (again by definition, once we are clear what *sapientia* really means) a life that generates relations of love and so generates otherness, difference. The divine wisdom exists only *as* something like a relation between subjects. Yet the 'content' of what these subjects are conscious of is formally identical, differentiated only by the locus of this or that subject within the overall pattern

---

[13]David Brown, *The Divine Trinity* (London: Duckworth, 1985) (esp. ch. 7), believes that the Cappadocian theology of the trinity is preferable to Augustine's in its greater fundamental clarity about the distinctness of the persons; but Brown is not able to show how a Cappadocian analysis manages the question of the eternal distinctness of the Spirit in any more than a superficial way. Brown's subsequent remarks on the question in his defence of his book, 'Wittgenstein against the "Wittgensteinians": A Reply to Kenneth Surin on *The Divine Trinity*', *Modern Theology*, 2.3 (1986), pp. 257–76, repeat a number of points about Augustine's supposed interest in the unity of the divine essence which I think to be unsustainable, but also hint at a trinitarian model not in fact all that far from that of the later books of *trin*. I am grateful to Dr Brown not only for discussion of these questions, but for the opportunity of reading his unpublished paper on 'Trinitarian Personhood and Individuality', which seems to me to be still closer to an Augustinian perspective.
[14]Op. cit., p. 31.

of relation or interdependence. Hence, in XV.xiv.23, Augustine's observations on the knowledge of Father and Son: the Father knows all things both 'in himself' and 'in the Son' – that is, he knows himself as ultimate initiator of all, and he knows *in* this act of knowing how this initiating act is realized in, 'uttered' in and as the Word. The Father knows the Son because he knows himself as (and only as) the Son's begetter; the Son knows the Father because he knows himself as (and only as) the one generated by the Father (*ille gignendo, ille nascendo*). They do not know different things, nor do they know themselves as independent individuals: they are not independent objects to themselves. We are left with little to say but that *sapientia* is a conscious life whose consciousness of itself exists only in a manifold interrelation of loving acts – or rather, a differentiation and self-reflexivity within one loving movement, which is also more than 'self-reflexivity' in the ordinary sense because it is, though complete in itself, also indeterminately in search of an object to love, and thus both sufficient to itself *and* productive.

I have been arguing that Augustine cannot be held responsible for a move towards individualism in anthropology and abstract theism in theology. The introspective method of *trin.* is designed to 'demythologize' the solitary human ego by establishing the life of the mind firmly in relation to God – and, what is more, to God understood as self-gift, as movement into otherness and distance in self-imparting love. As the work moves to its conclusion, it turns more and more into a meditation on the imparting of divine *caritas* through the Holy Spirit, and thus a meditation on the human self within the communion of believers. Likewise, the more and more elaborate discussion of the themes of love and gift in Book XV, against the background of earlier and more sketchy remarks, makes it quite plain that the clichés about 'beginning from the divine unity' as determining Augustine's theology are of no use whatever in understanding what is going on in his greatest theological treatise. He is no less concerned than any Greek theologian to secure the unity and simplicity of the divine nature, but, as a *polemical* concern, this appears very rarely in *De trin.* There is certainly no trace at all of a Neoplatonist interest in the One at work here[15]. What Augustine *does* achieve is the transformation of a concept of

---

[15]*Pace* Brown, 'Wittgenstein against the "Wittgensteinians"', p. 269, and others notably Du Roy.

the one divine nature as the content of the three divine subsistents (a concept which can suggest a rather static picture of that nature) into the vision of the divine nature as an activity (sapiential love) that cannot but exist in trinitarian relation. This is hardly monism or 'abstract theism'. Contemporary theology is increasingly taken up with forms of trinitarian pluralism that threaten to become mythological – the divine life as interactive drama – and such trends need to be balanced by serious attention to Augustine's account. Modern trinitarian pluralism is often a wholly intelligible reaction to the unhelpfully formal versions of trinitarian orthodoxy current in scholastic textbooks or to the abstract unitarianism to which liberal Protestantism tended. But it is not the only possible way of retrieving this central element in the Christian grammar of God; and if it is content with a highly anthropomorphic plurality of agencies, it will miss the central element in Augustine's analysis – the understanding of the divine *nature* as loving wisdom, as relational, and thus the integration of the doctrine of the trinity with discourse about God *tout court*. A trinitarian theology prepared to stick close to the fundamental Christian perception of being given a share in the unlimited gift and exchange that is the joy of God will have much to learn from *trin.*, with its exceptionally nuanced fusion of theology and anthropology. In his work on Augustine, Tarsicius van Bavel has consistently drawn students of the *doctor caritatis* more deeply into this rich interaction between God and the *humanum* in the whole corpus of Augustine's thought. It is therefore appropriate to end this grateful tribute to Fr van Bavel with some words of his on Augustine's anthropology, which might well be taken to summarize what I have here argued to be the main thrust of the *De trin.*:

> This vision involves an immense responsibility for those who are believers. We become responsible as a group for the presence of God's love in the world. For our love of man, in the end, is the love of God himself: God loves the world through us.[16]

Unsurprisingly, in view of so much that has already been said, the area of Augustine's theology of Christ and the Trinity has been revisited with intense interest in the last two decades; so much of what has been rethought in

---

[16]Tarsicius J. van Bavel. 'The Anthropology of Augustine', *Milltown Studies* (Dublin), 19/20, Spring and Autumn 1987, p. 37.

Augustinian studies has its roots in the reconsideration of these themes. We still lack a single authoritative study of Augustine's Christology in English,[17] but Lewis Ayres's long-awaited *Augustine and the Trinity*[18] has more than adequately filled the gap where his Trinitarian thought is concerned, building as it does both on close research in Augustine's own text and an outstanding expertise in the wider field of patristic theology. The connections between Christology and Trinitarian thought are summarized helpfully by Basil Studer in a chapter of his overview of early Christian doctrine,[19] and he published a comprehensive introduction to the *de trinitate* in 2005,[20] particularly helpful in tracing the history of its reception throughout the medieval period and the course of modern research. In Germany, the encyclopaedic study of Roland Kany, *Augustins Trinitätsdenken*[21] is not likely to be surpassed for a generation or more; it examines every aspect of the work, including the complex question of the dating of its various parts, its intellectual and biographical background, and every serious modern treatment of its arguments. And most recently, the proceedings of a conference in Bordeaux in 2010 on the *De Trinitate* have offered still further perspectives on both the exegetical and the philosophical arguments of the work.[22]

In short, scholarship on these central areas of Augustine's thought has been exceptionally fertile in recent years. And while we cannot speak of a uniformity of view, it is fair to say that certain perspectives on Augustine's philosophy and theology are now a lot harder to defend than they used to be. The supposed polarity of Eastern and Western trinitarian thinking is a theme still to be heard in some inter-church polemics, but, while there is unmistakably a difference in idiom and emphasis between Augustine and many Greek theologians, few

---

[17]Goulven Madec's article in the *Augustinus-Lexikon*, vol. l, fasc.5/6, ed. C. Mayer (Basel: Schwabe, 1992), cols 845–908, and his book on *La Patrie et la voie: Le Christ dans la vie et la pensée de saint Augustin* (Paris: Desclée, 1989), indicate the scope of what is involved in such a project. The *Augustinus-Lexikon* article has a particularly clear summary of the 'whole Christ' (*totus Christus*) theology so prominent in the sermons on the Psalms, cols 879–82.

[18]Cambridge University Press, 2010.

[19]*Trinity and Incarnation: The Faith of the Early Church*, ed. Andrew Louth (Edinburgh: T.&T. Clark, 1993), pp. 167–85, with a helpful bibliography.

[20]*Augustinus* De Trinitate. *Eine Einfuhrung* (Paderborn/Munich/Vienna/Zurich: Ferdinand Schöningh), 2005.

[21]Tübingen: Mohr Siebeck, 2007.

[22]*Le* De Trinitate *de saint Augustin: exégesè, logique et noétique*, ed. Emmanuel Bermon and Gerard O'Daly (Paris: Institut d'Etudes Augustiniennes, 2012).

would want to oppose them in the once conventional way – Augustine as privileging unity of substance over diversity of persons. And scholars such as Reinhard Flogaus have shown how much use was made of Augustine by so prominent a Byzantine theologian as Gregory Palamas.[23] John Behr's interrogation from an Eastern Orthodox standpoint of how Augustine uses the language of divine fatherhood[24] is a reminder that not all questions or doubts have been resolved; he argues that Augustine cannot be entirely absolved of at least a tendency to treat the divine persons as one 'subject' for certain purposes. But this sympathetic and carefully argued essay still rather sidelines the deeply Christocentric logic of so much of Augustine's argument; Orthodox reservations may yet be capable of further reassessment in this light.

Similarly, the 'Cartesian' reading of Augustine's thought on self-knowledge has continued to be challenged, despite some robust counter-attacks.[25] Kany notes that the majority of scholars would deny that the Augustinian analysis of self-knowing plays anything like a key role in his thought in the way that the *cogito* does for Descartes, but he also provides a very interesting discussion of the various scholarly analyses that have seen Augustine's influence in Descartes' modification of his earlier theories about the *cogito* in the direction of a more 'performative' or interactive account of knowledge and truth (i.e. seeing the issue not as one of how we attain certainty but as a question of how we clarify the conditions for any kind of intelligible communication; the practice of Augustinian self-questioning establishes the self as a *communicative* self, a speaking agent). But his final judgement on the numerous philosophical readings of the *De Trinitate* – in relation to both ancient and early modern or modern philosophy – that have been developed in recent decades is that they leave the reader with

---

[23] See Flogaus's paper, 'Inspiration – Exploitation – Distortion: The Use of St Augustine in the Hesychast Controversy' in *Orthodox Readings of Augustine*, pp. 63–80.

[24] "Calling on God as Father: Augustine and the Legacy of Nicaea", ibid., pp. 153–65. Behr quotes a passage from *De Trinitate* V.xi/12 in which Augustine allows that the whole Trinity can be called 'Father' in certain contexts. The wording is certainly unhappy and the implications as troubling as Behr says. But some of Augustine's credit can be saved if we note that he is arguing that the act of regenerating us as children of the Father is (like all divine acts) the act of the entire Trinity, so that the Trinity *might* metaphorically be thought of as 'fathering' us, even if the result is a specific participation in the Son's relation to the Father (as Augustine takes completely for granted and spells out eloquently throughout the work and elsewhere). But this is admittedly stretching things; Behr has a point.

[25] See above, pp. 23–4.

a severely abridged version of the work: 'any interpretation which attempts to exclude the theological element from the *De Trinitate* is going to be deficient for that reason'.[26] This is not to say (as scholars like Wayne Hankey have tended to assume) that a certain caution about making Augustine a Cartesian leads straight to an unhelpful merging of reason and revelation, a denial that Augustine is trying to construct rationally credible arguments. Augustine is very plainly labouring at a kind of conceptual clarification that is not in itself resolved by revelation. But the theological *context* remains crucial: Augustine gives a coherent account of the complex activity of self-apprehension in memory, intellect and will or love; but he could not be faithful to his own presuppositions and still maintain that this mental life could be accurately known if it were thought of as capable of existing or functioning independently of its relation to the triune God.

Which also means that it could not be thought of independently of the love that is intrinsic to the divine act by which eternal wisdom becomes the inner life and energy of a finite world, in creation and redemption; the act in which we finite redeemed agents find our renewal, the act which is the unifying reality in the community of belief. Locating Augustinian love in this context, in its fully Christological and Trinitarian meaning, helps us see what is amiss in readings that seek – yet again – to turn Augustine into an apologist for private or individual spiritual fulfilment at the expense of a true sense of the claims of the specific, historical human other. And the last chapter of this book attempts to restore to the understanding of Augustinian love something of this concreteness in relation both to the incarnate God and the human other that has been obscured by selective readings.

---

[26]Kany, op. cit., pp. 289–94; quotation p. 294. On the Descartes question, and in relation to Chapter 9 of the present volume, see also the two detailed studies of self-knowledge in the *De Trinitate* (by Christoph Horn and Charles Brittain) in Bermon and O'Daly, op. cit. The second of these in particular illuminates the way in which Augustine is moving towards a theory of intellect as essentially *the thinking of itself* – a thinking which is obviously 'empty' if it seeks to identify a determinate object apart from its current active knowing of specific things. I have tentatively suggested – in a foreword to the Bordeaux collection – that Augustine anticipates not so much Descartes here as Hegel in directing us to the idea of 'absolute' knowledge, knowledge as such (see Kany, op. cit., pp. 279–80 on earlier suggestions about their relationship). As we noted much earlier, we can agree that, for Augustine, the intellect knows itself completely; but it knows itself as always *being activated*, not as a self-contained substance in which certain kinds of knowledge are stored. On this whole are, see also Luigi Gioia, *The Theological Epistemology of Augustine's* De Trinitate (Oxford: Oxford University Press, 2008), especially chs 8 and 9.

11

Augustinian Love

Werner G. Jeanrond's wide-ranging *A Theology of Love* includes a chapter on Augustine's concept of love, divine and human, dealing not only with the Saint's understanding of sexuality and marriage, but with far wider issues around 'subjectivity, agency and community' to borrow the subtitle of one section.[1] Following Hannah Arendt's well-known discussion of Augustine's doctrine of love in her doctoral thesis,[2] Jeanrond concludes that this is a 'theology of love [that] does not help us to form human community'.[3] Augustine's understanding of the optimal form of community, the Church, depends on the idea that ecclesial solidarity is necessary primarily because of the fact of sinful solidarity, not as a form of transfigured mutuality, which is surely what the New Testament requires us to believe. We are primitively linked with each other by original sin, by a shared inheritance; grace binds us together so that we are better able to resist the pull of a world in which human solidarity means only death. And because no human person can be loved in and for himself or herself, as *De doctrina Christiana* famously says, but only for the sake of God, no real content can be given to the mutual love of believers. Grace *dissolves* the solidarity of sin so as to connect us directly with God; from this point on, our relations with one another are indirect or even abstract, never relations of true interdependence, and what unites believers

---

[1] Werner G. Jeanrond, *A Theology of Love* (London: Continuum/T.&T. Clark, 2010), pp. 57–61.
[2] Cf. Hannah Arendt, *Der Liebesbegriff bei Augustin: Versuch einer philosophischen Interpretation* (Berlin: Springer, 1929). The thesis was written in 1927–8 and published in 1929. For the English translation cf. *Love and Saint Augustine*, ed. Joanna Vecchiarelli Scott and Judith Chelius Stark (Chicago: Chicago University Press, 1996).
[3] Werner G. Jeanrond, A *Theology of Love*, p. 61.

is faith rather than love. Put more sharply, love ceases to be 'constitutive' for the Church, except in the sense that *God's* love is the sole creative agency at work, drawing individuals out of the toxic community of original sin. Love as something undertaken by human subjects is not ultimately of value here.

Now this is, to put it mildly, an odd reading.[4] Jeanrond very properly points out the problematic character of most Augustinian teaching about sex and the body (though even here there is more to be said: as usual, what is interesting about Augustine is not the attitudes he shares with his contemporaries but what is unique to him;[5]) but the broader analysis is puzzling. I want to invite him to a re-reading of Augustine without the distorting medium of Arendt's interpretation, which I believe is eccentric to the point of perversity, in the hope of showing that what is most central in Augustine's understanding of love is by no means so alien to Jeanrond's own concerns. To do this in full detail would need a far longer exposition than can be offered here so what I shall do is to take three related aspects of the mature Augustine's theology which unambiguously tell against Arendt's version.

But one general observation may be in order at the outset. Arendt's focal argument is that the effect of Augustine's teaching is to withdraw the human subject from the public and political sphere; love as he understands it is 'worldless', to use her terminology,[6] and functions as an alternative to the *agon* of political labour, the construction of actual communities of law and human nurture. She is, of course, writing in the middle of a cultural crisis about the moral possibility of politics, the Germany of the 1920s, and Augustine has become for her the symbol of a 'beautiful-souled' diversion from the political imperative. But a less constrained reading would be able to show how Augustine is arguing in effect that the very notion of the 'public' and the 'political' depends on a Christian anthropology, in the sense that only a rectified love, delivered from crippling self-referentiality, can prevent us from spinning apart into

---

[4]For a thorough critical examination of Arendt's Augustine, cf. Thomas E. Breidenthal's 1991 Oxford D.Phil thesis 'The Concept of Freedom in Hannah Arendt: A Christian Assessment' (Unpublished Diss. University of Oxford, 1991), and idem, 'Arendt, Augustine and the Politics of Incarnation', *Modern Theology*, 14.4 (1998), pp. 489–503.

[5]Cf. Margaret Miles, *Augustine on the Body* (Missoula, MT: Scholars Press, 1979).

[6]Cf. Hannah Arendt, *The Human Condition* (Chicago, IL: University of Chicago Press, 1958), p. 53.

unmanageable rivalry. Augustine is constantly beginning his analysis not simply from a generalized conviction about 'original sin' but from a highly specific diagnosis of how self-defence, self-deceit and self-aggrandizement combine to poison interrelation in human affairs. Augustine, far from dissolving solidarity in favour of a community held together by the implicitly violent imperative of holding a single faith,[7] is seeking to identify the ways in which sin's solidarity is – paradoxically – what dissolves any *actual* human communality, so that grace becomes the means of releasing the possibility of concrete and truthful social existence. The themes we are going to look at here should all be thought through in the light of this fundamental point.

The first of these is to do with Augustine's account in the *Confessions* of his own early experience of love – and more particularly of *loss*. In *Confessions* IV.4–9, Augustine describes what he went through when an intimate friend of his teenage years died (having been baptized in his last illness). This account is the earliest we have in Western literature of the complex processes of bereavement – anger, self-doubt and 'survivor's guilt', the pain of seeing familiar, once shared, sights now organized around an absence, wanting to be dead, fearing death, and so on. A pivotal moment in this account is the poignant and pregnant phrase in IV.7: 'What mindlessness it is not to know how to love human beings humanly [*humaniter*]! And what a foolish human I was then, so impatient in coping with the human condition!' What he portrays is thus in some way an 'inhuman' love: by investing his very identity in the relation with his friend.

Augustine has involved himself in a deeply ambiguous mode of subjectivity, in which, in the absence of the loved one, what is 'there' to be loved is the emotion of grief itself. The actual and independent reality of my mortal friend is swallowed up in an absorption with my state of mind and heart, including my memories and images of what I have lost. My love is incapable of letting the loved one be free of my subjectivity, even though death is the most dramatic possible reminder that what I love is not under my control. The logic is that to

---

[7] Arendt argues this from the first of Augustine's *Homilies on the First Epistle of John*. Her interpretation is cited in Werner G. Jeanrond, *A Theology of Love*, p. 60: a seriously eccentric reading of a text in which faith in the Risen Christ is treated as the doorway to that mutual communion which is the earthly form of our salvation.

love 'humanly' would be to love in the awareness that the one I love exists in a context other than my needs or projects. Extreme grief of the kind Augustine describes, with its detachment from the reality of the object of love, implies that I have made the other carry too much in my imagination. Dealing with grief of this sort is learning to return to the fact of shared mortality, to the *humana*, the human affairs or human condition from which Augustine sees himself as shrinking.

This is not an attitude indifferent to the specificity of the object of love, seeing such an object as simply a 'reminder' to love God. There is indeed a sense of solidarity in the mortal condition; and we have to keep a watchful eye on our friendships and loves if we are to avoid using such relationships to assure ourselves that we are not really mortal. In IV.8, Augustine memorably evokes the joys of friendship, including the joys shared in what we would call 'body language', the expressive communication of eyes and faces as well as speech, only to insist that this is *in itself* potentially an escape from a starker reality – so that if interrupted by a death, we feel we have lost ourselves as well as the one we love. Loving humanly, it seems, must be a love that refuses to ignore the mortality and limitedness of what or whom we love. Forget this, and we are left with an intensity of felt intimacy that ultimately and subtly refuses to 'release' the person loved from the bonds of that intimacy.[8] And to love the friend as mortal is to love him or her 'in God': that is to love them as they relate to God. This will sound like a form of Arendt's 'indirect' relatedness unless we recall that for Augustine any attempt to love or indeed to know anything except as related to God is illusory. And this brings us to our second Augustinian theme.

As has been argued at length by several recent interpreters of Augustine,[9] the discussion in *De Trinitate* of the image of God in humanity turns, *not* on the idea that our inner ecology of memory, intelligence and will reflects the inner

---

[8] We might compare this with C. S. Lewis's expressed concern in his celebrated *A Grief Observed* (London: Faber and Faber, 1961), pp. 18–20, that he should not turn his dead wife's memory into a self-serving image under his control.

[9] See especially Michael Hanby, *Augustine and Modernity* (London: Routledge, 2003), pp. 27–46; Luigi Gioia, *The Theological Epistemology of Augustine's* De Trinitate (Oxford: Oxford University Press, 2006); Lewis Ayres, *Augustine and the Trinity* (Cambridge: Cambridge University Press, 2010), pp. 273–318. For a thorough overview of the recent debate, see Roland Kany, *Augustins Trinitätsdenken* (Tübingen: Mohr Siebeck, 2007), pp. 393–404.

relations of the Trinity, but on the belief that when we look inwards, we see, ultimately, a threefold inner life whose *constitutive object* is God; that is, our remembering, our understanding, and our willing are what they are because they are created so as to have God as their proper object.[10] Being related thus to God is what it is to be a spiritual subject, whether or not we acknowledge this. When under the leading of grace, we consciously align ourselves with this innate God-directedness, the image of God in us comes to light – a remembering which is primitively the remembrance of God, an intelligence which is primitively the understanding of God and a will which is primitively the loving of God. As God in God's own being has God's own self as object, so do we in finite measure. Grace both uncovers and satisfies the 'drawn-ness' towards God that is inbuilt in the structure of mind and sentience. The image of God in human beings is thus the human being turned towards God, having God as object. This implies that if we seek either to know or to love another human subject as if they subsisted independently of this directedness or drawnness, we are pursuing a phantom. Just as Augustine's concern in the *Confessions* is to identify and warn against a love that de-realizes its object, so here he is pulling us away from any picture of human actuality that forgets the central and constitutive fact about human subjectivity – that it is oriented towards the endlessness of God.

If that is the case with us as humans, we need to revisit and rethink slightly the difficult language in Augustine's *De doctrina Christiana* about loving other human beings 'for the sake of God', *propter Deum*.[11] This has an undeniably grudging ring to it: if I say that I love a friend of my spouse 'for the sake of' my spouse, or perhaps that I keep on the shelf a hideous Victorian china dog 'for the sake of' my grandmother who loved it and bequeathed it to me, the implication is clearly that – independently of spouse or grandmother – I would have no particular reason to feel any warmth at all for these objects as such. They have nothing in themselves that is lovable as far as I am concerned, and what makes them appropriate objects of love on my part is their association with another object. But this is not at all the model Augustine is describing. The question which prompts his formulation is whether a human being is

---

[10]Cf. especially Augustine, *trin*, XV.
[11]Cf. Augustine, *doctr. chr.* I.xxii.20.

appropriately loved in the mode of 'enjoyment', that is, as an end in itself; and his answer, with appropriate qualification, is that this would be to treat another human individual as independently promising final bliss to me, signalling nothing beyond itself.[12] This would be to make the other human being something different from – indeed, something *less* than – what it in fact is. Each human subject is both *res* and *signum*, both a true subsistent reality and a sign of its maker. If I refuse to treat it as a sign of its maker, I take something from its actual ontological complexity and dignity, while at the same time effectively inflating that complexity and dignity to a level it cannot sustain. Only God is to be enjoyed without qualification; only God is *a sign of nothing else*.

To say, as Augustine does in *De doctrina Christiana*, that we therefore 'use' rather than 'enjoy' other human subjects in our love for them is obviously problematic because of the apparent implication that human love is only ever instrumental to something else; and this is clearly what Arendt and, following her, Jeanrond find difficult and unacceptable.[13] The phraseology is indeed rebarbative to anyone who is attuned to the moral problem of 'using' another individual. Immanuel Kant's exhortation to treat others as ends not means is deeply ingrained in the modern reader. But before we completely discard what Augustine argues in *De Doctrina*, we need at least to do justice to the argument, and to recognize that it is an argument which runs through a significant part of his mature work.

The fundamental point could be expressed as the concern that *we should not pretend that any human other is God*: that is to say, we should not treat them as if relation with them could secure our eternal bliss, *beata vita*, or as if they could be seen, responded to, known, loved as if they were not images of God – signs of more than they contain or embody. Augustine's terminology of using and enjoying does not do quite what he wants it to do here, and in arguing that God is to be 'preferred to' or, perhaps, 'given priority over' created objects of love, including human others, he comes uncomfortably close to

---

[12] Ibid., I.iii.3–v.5, xxii.20–xxiii.22.

[13] Cf. Werner G. Jeanrond, *A Theology of Love*, pp. 52–8.

assuming something he is in fact seeking to avoid – the notion that God and human others are in competition for our love.[14]

If relation to God as God's image is intrinsic to every human identity, if every human subject knowing and loving himself or herself is in some sense and in some limited measure loving God, whether they are aware of it or not, God *cannot* simply be a rival for our love. It is impossible to love the human other, just as it is impossible for me to love myself, without God being involved as the animating presence to which my subjectivity and the other's subjectivity are always present. And this secures in our love a sense that the other is at some level free of my needs and preoccupations, turned towards God before they are turned towards me and turning back constantly into that light – a theme given definitive expression in Dante Alighieri's parting from Beatrice in the *Commedia*.

For Augustine, loving human beings *humaniter* is loving them with regard to what if they are signs of – infinite love; and so far from this being a way of rendering others instrumental to my own spiritual advance, contingent occasions for me to learn the love of another (God), this is intended both to liberate the other from my agenda or my fulfilment and to undergird the conviction that the love of the contingent mortal neighbour in her or his contingency and mortality is the vehicle for loving God, not something which, in straightforwardly instrumental fashion, we discard when the separate and higher purpose is attained.

In keeping with Jeanrond's discussion,[15] my aim is to ask what is to be learned from Augustine, not simply to argue that his account is without flaw or ambiguity; and it seems to me that perhaps the most important insight is precisely this insistence on loving the human neighbour truthfully – as mortal not divine, yet also as irreducibly a sign of God, a subject whose subjectivity means or 'intends' God. The other I encounter is always already engaged with and by God, and any love directed towards them is illusory to the degree it forgets or ignores this. And this is why – to move on to our third theme – the Christian community for Augustine is emphatically not *first* a body united as

---

[14]Augustine, *De Doctrina Christiana*, I.ix.9.
[15]Cf. Werner G. Jeanrond, *A Theology of Love*, pp. 61–5.

it were externally, through common expressions or experiences of faith, but a body in which mutual love and service, delight in each other and support for one another in need, do indeed *constitute* the ecclesial identity.

A full-scale account of Augustine's ecclesiology would be out of place, but a glance at the *Homilies on the First Epistle of John* will make the point economically enough. In the fifth homily,[16] Augustine speaks about the imperative to be ready to give your life for the sake of a fellow member of Christ's Body, and goes on to describe our willingness to give up what we do not need in order to meet the material needs of our neighbour as the first step towards 'dying' for the neighbour.[17] It is clear that the love between believers is very much a matter of what is both imperative and possible here and now, in attention to the specific reality of the other.

The interplay of love between members of the Body is not some sort of shadow of a more real or fundamental love of God to which the specifics of the human world are irrelevant. In the sixth homily,[18] we have an echo of the argument in Augustine's anti-Donatist polemic about the difference between receiving the outward sign of the Spirit's coming in the sacrament of baptism without receiving the bond of *caritas* in the continuing common life of the community.[19] And in the tenth homily,[20] we find both (again) a clear distinction between faith with and without *caritas* and an argument to establish that the mutual love of Christians is in fact 'the one Christ, loving himself': believers love Christ in loving each other, but it is throughout the act of Christ both loving himself and loving the Father. To imagine that we can love Christ without loving his Body on earth is as much nonsense as to think you can love the Son without loving the Father. Augustine puts it pithily: 'Love can't be divided into parts. Choose for yourself what you'll love and you get the others too.'[21]

---

[16] Augustine, *Tractatus in Epistolam Ioannis ad Parthos*, V.4.
[17] Ibid., V.12.
[18] Ibid., VI.10.
[19] Ibid., *Ep.* 185.X.43, also cf. Augustine, *De unitate* IV.7 and *De baptismo* IV.
[20] Augustine, *Tractatus in Epistolam Ioannis ad Parthos*, X.3.
[21] The translation is from John Leinenweber, *Love One Another, My Friends: St Augustine's Homilies on the First Letter of John* (San Francisco, CA: Harper Row, 1989), p. 102. This is a particularly readable version.

The connection of this with the pervasive importance to Augustine of the unity of Head and members, grounded in one of his most frequently cited New Testament texts, Christ's words to Saul, 'Why are you persecuting me?'[22] surely means that whatever is said about *caritas*, *amor* or *dilectio* in Augustine's work needs to be read in the light of this basic ecclesiological principle. It is not only that, in the most general terms, it is impossible to abstract human individuals from their ontologically given relatedness to God as the natural (even if hidden) direction of their intelligence, memory and will; it is also essential to recognize that loving the human other within the body of Christ entails an even more intimate connectedness between God and the object of love. The other in the Church is a place where Christ's love is active; and the love that is Christ's acting in me moves out to the love acting in the other which simultaneously moves towards me. Whether or not I am actually aware of the full range of human others to whom I am bound in this way (after all, he says, one eye cannot see the other in our own bodies), I am in fact united with them, seeing from the same perspective and moving in the same direction.[23]

This is why Arendt's judgement on Augustine's ecclesiology seems perverse: she contrasts the 'interdependence' of natural solidarity with the mutual love at work in the Church, concluding that 'one individual's relationship to another ... ceases to be a matter of course, as it was in interdependence', because the love of the believer is always marked by 'specific indirectness'.[24] Jeanrond summarizes this as implying that 'the community of believers is not built on love, but on a biologically mediated common destiny into which God sends his revelation of grace'.[25]

---

[22]Constantly cited in Augustine, *Enarrationes in Psalmos*; cf. idem, *Tractatus in Epistolam Ioannis ad Parthos*, X.3.
[23]Ibid., VI.10.
[24]Hannah Arendt, *Love and Saint Augustine*, p. 108, quoted in Werner G. Jeanrond, *A Theology of Love*, p. 61. Cf. Elisabeth Young-Bruehl in her excellent biography of Arendt, *Hannah Arendt: For Love of the World* (New Haven, CT: Yale University Press, 1982). See the notes on pp. 74–5 that Arendt's reviewers objected to the fact that she had presented the 'thinker' not the bishop, and that she herself did not see Augustine as essentially a theologian. This is illuminating, but she is not the only reader of Augustine to suffer from the attempt to interpret him as a philosopher in abstraction from the exegetical and theological writings in which we see his concepts actually at work in what he would have thought their proper environment.
[25]Werner G. Jeanrond, *A Theology of Love*, p. 61.

But this is an unsustainable reading of Augustine. Whether Augustine's model is adequate for a contemporary theology of love or not (and I believe it is more adequate than most), it needs to be recognized that it depends radically on the assumption that the human subject is by nature oriented towards God, communicating divine meaning by the bare fact of its intellectual awareness and volitional reaching out; and by grace embodying the specific act of Christ whose saving work has released this basic intentionality to exercise its proper scope. Our temptation is constantly to project on to the things and persons around us expectations they are unable to fulfil, and so to shrink both them and ourselves. We reduce the fathomless meaning of the other (fathomless because of its opening out on to God) to the dimensions of our own need; we enslave ourselves to objects of desire that pretend to a finality and all-embracingness they cannot have. If we try to love human beings independently of loving God, we ignore what they are; we do indeed 'use' them, in the contemporary sense of the word, we make them serve our purposes, and in so doing make ourselves *their* servants in a sense quite opposed to the mutual serving of the members of Christ's Body.

That this is embedded in what is often an uncomfortable vocabulary and argued with a good deal of ambivalence towards the flesh and its emotions is undeniable (though we should not lose sight of the fact that love of one's own body is repeatedly used by Augustine as a paradigm of what proper self-love entails). Yet the question Augustine poses is whether we can shape a viable theology of human love without acknowledging that the dignity of the human object of love is bound up with its character as pointing Godwards.

If you begin with an ontology that either sees God as another item in the list of possible objects of love or insists on a radical and near-total discontinuity between the act of God and every finite agency, this 'pointing Godwards' is going to sound uncomfortably like 'pointing *away* from itself'. Augustine challenges us to think again: for him, pointing Godwards is also pointing inwards, pointing to what is most real in the finite object of love – its relation to the infinite act, which is the source of both its being and its meaning. To return to the language of *De Doctrina*, the human subject is indeed a *res*, a subsistent reality, but is equally, like all finite subsistents, a *signum*. It is not exhausted by what it finitely is at any one moment in time. For any finite subsistent, a human or angelic agent above all, to act positively, 'creatively' if you will, is to exercise to the full the capacity to be a sign and thus to prompt and nourish the awareness in other subjects of the infinity of love that is God.[26]

'The human subject is created, recreated and thus ultimately constituted by God's love alone. There can be no talk about any form of co-constituting creativity in human love.'[27] The first sentence is a perfectly accurate summary of not only Augustine's teaching on love and the human subject but, arguably, any serious theological account (any account which assumes the dependence of all things on the free love of the creator). The second suggests that the word 'ultimately' in the first sentence has been tacitly disregarded. Augustine does not maintain that we have no role in shaping one another's human journey in faith and love; the Johannine homilies alone ought to persuade us that he is not advancing some doctrine of the total irrelevance of specific human agency and human relation to the operation of God's action in the Church (a slightly different issue to the question of grace and freedom as Augustine treats it in the anti-Pelagian works)[28].

But he would certainly have argued that the only creativity we could exercise through human love was the mediation of God's love – for the simple reason that the root of love is not in us, any more than the root of our being is in us. It is possible by God's grace for us to be in some measure creative creatures. But unless we remember that we and those we love are alike creatures, we shall cut ourselves off from the only possible source of creativity; we shall be ascribing meanings to the human other that are both more and less than is proper.

Augustine is not, I believe, trying to persuade us that loving my neighbour is 'a mere instantiation of my love of God' – the position which Jeanrond rightly

---

[26]See Michael Hanby, *Augustine and Modernity*, pp. 31–41 for an exemplary discussion of the sign's participation in what it signifies, and of how the signified gives form to the concrete singularity which constitutes the sign.

[27]Werner G. Jeanrond, *A Theology of Love*, p. 61.

[28]The point here is not what grounds or merits divine salvific action but the *form* in which that action is mediated, made intelligible, and embodied in practice.

sees Karl Rahner as contesting.[29] But the Rahnerian idea that the 'basic human act of attention to the neighbour is always already related to the God of eternal life, even though we may not be aware of this relationship' is, if the reading of Augustine I have been arguing is correct, a version of 'Augustinian love'. Which is why I conclude that Jeanrond's proper and significant concerns for a robustly transformative, politically meaningful, participatory model of what constitutes the Church are served rather than subverted by an Augustinian understanding.[30]

'Acknowledgement of conditionality is the only unconditionality of human love,' wrote Gillian Rose.[31] To recognize the boundedness, the difficulty, the failure-haunted character of love, she argues, is essential if we are not to condemn ourselves to the terrors of endless possibility and so endless guilt at our failure to achieve. Augustine would have appreciated this particular version of what it means to love *humaniter*.

The influence of Hannah Arendt's reading of Augustine on love has already been noted in Chapter 6, above, and this final chapter discusses how it has shaped one particular recent reading. But we shall find a similar reading with some similar critical questions in the work of Martha Nussbaum:[32] in the wake of a characteristically sensitive and imaginative summary of Augustine's teaching, fully recognizing that he 'renounces the wish to depart from our human condition',[33] she identifies three major problems which she believes Augustine leaves worryingly unresolved and, significantly, Arendt is cited several times in this discussion.[34]

The issues are, first, the question of whether Augustine's scheme really allows for the love of individuals; second, whether it has any place for human reciprocity, for genuinely mutual engagement with the neighbour; and third,

---

[29] Werner G. Jeanrond, *A Theology of Love*, p. 146.
[30] Ibid., p. 247.
[31] Gillian Rose, *Love's Work* (London: Chatto and Windus, 1995), p. 98.
[32] *Upheavals of Thought: The Intelligence of Emotions* (Cambridge: Cambridge University Press, 2001), pp. 527–56, especially pp. 547–56). Some of this material can also be found – though without the more marked critical discussion – in 'Augustine and Dante on the Ascent of Love' in Gareth B. Matthews, ed., *The Augustinian Tradition*, pp. 61–90, especially pp. 61–74.
[33] *Upheavals of Thought*, p. 547.
[34] Ibid., pp. 550–3.

whether the motivation for compassion in Augustine is the same as that which Nussbaum argues we need for a contemporary ethic, a genuine care for the material and social suffering of others. Nussbaum suggests that it is not the same, that Augustine's compassion is stirred by the fact of human solidarity in sin and error, not by 'each earthly instance of injustice and wrongful death'.[35] Her general conclusion is that Augustine is at best ambivalent about the love of individuals, that he does not provide any satisfactory notion of shared moral agency as a basis for the common (political) life, and that his stress on obedience as the heart of all ethical integrity and virtue, combined with an 'insistent otherworldly direction' for human longing,[36] produces a 'soporific' self, passive and compliant in the face of specific worldly injustices. Despite what Augustine does to reinstate the place of the emotions in the moral life and the way in which he counters the idea that we should be ashamed of need or imperfection, he still reintroduces shame in a manner that has deeply dangerous consequences for a viable public ethic. Unfallen humanity was beyond longing and striving, and restored humanity looks to that as an ideal: thus the erotic, in the most general sense, is something tied to our fallen condition, a shameful loss of *control*. We universally fail in obedience and so need to be directed from above. 'The politics of Eden is this: be ashamed of your longing for objects, your curiosity to know them, and your very wish to originate independent actions. Be so ashamed that you see this as radical evil, and yield your will before the authority of the church.'[37]

This is a strong indictment, even stronger than Jeanrond's. Some of its points, especially about Augustine's alleged indifference to compassion for specific earthly suffering in the neighbour, can be met with reference to the texts about the relief of the neighbour's material needs which have already been cited. And Augustine's warnings about the risks of investing the wrong kind of intensity in human friendship are warnings less about particular affections as such than about an ultimately depersonalizing and instrumentalizing attitude to others that makes ordinary human friendship impossible. No one

---

[35] Ibid., p. 553.
[36] Ibid., p. 552.
[37] Ibid., p. 555.

could read Augustine *in extenso* and conclude that he allowed no place for the love of individuals. But the underlying point is to do with the nature of human solidarity; and both Nussbaum and Arendt agree in seeing Augustine's understanding of this as fundamentally to do with solidarity in sin and helplessness, so that intelligent and purposive *action* in solidarity is of little or no interest in an Augustinian world.

What this leaves out of account, however, is that Augustine takes it for granted that the positive solidarity of mutual care and nourishment is built into the created order in a variety of ways;[38] and that the ultimate destiny of human beings is communion with the Trinitarian God through the medium of the fellowship of believers. As so often in these discussion, we have to be careful not to ignore the entire theological context of what Augustine says about our nature and goal. And this is also why (compare Chapter 1 above) it is potentially misleading to say that Augustine subordinates individual will to the authority of the Church.

As the foregoing chapters will have indicated, Augustine believes that our fundamental problem is not that we are too active and need to be discouraged from 'originating independent actions'; it is that sin makes us *incapable* of real action. If we allow our desire and delight to be fixed upon finite goods, we cease to long for truth or life itself; without the critique of finite desire advanced by Augustine, we allow ourselves to be too easily satisfied and so become 'anerotic', closed in on what we understand to be our well-being. By binding our desire to finite objects, specific and temporal goods, we confine or reduce our humanity and allow these finite goods to define us, so that we end up *reacting* rather than acting, shaping our desires and projects to the limits of what is achievable. When we are released into the full desire of God's goodness, we are more not less active.

Nussbaum's complaint that Augustine seeks to silence the 'independent will' holds only if we ignore Augustine's basic conviction that the one thing we

---

[38]*civ.* XII.xxi, for example, speaks of the 'natural sense of kinship' between human beings as part of God's purpose in ordaining that all human beings should be descended from one individual. Cf. *ep.*155.14 on the natural affinity of humans and their instinctive feeling of neighbourliness. For a recent overview of Augustine's social teaching, see Claude Lepelley, 'Facing Wealth and Poverty: Defining Augustine's Social Doctrine', *Augustinian Studies*, 38.1 (2007), pp. 1–17.

do not have in our own right or resource is an independent will. The fallen will is dependent in all the wrong ways, formed by the pressure of objects without and passions within, by the pressures of honour and public expectation, by the unpredictable world of apparently arbitrary craving. The work of grace is to make us dependent in the right way, dissatisfied with anything less than the horizon of God's own selflessness and seeking to remain open to that selfless agency as it transforms our relation with the world and each other. This is not to remove all the ambiguities from the Augustinian pattern or vocabulary; but it is important not to think of his spiritual and ethical world as one in which alien authority takes over the independent individual: the authority of the City of God, variously experienced and exercised (we should not think anachronistically of Augustine as managing a full-blown system of comprehensive ecclesiastical jurisdiction, let alone some kind of inquisition)[39], exists in order to save us from the passivity in which our natural desire for finite goods become the entire climate of our desiring.

This final chapter has brought us back to many of the considerations sketched in the first chapter, and in several other places in this book. A recurrent concern has been that Augustine has been read with insufficient attention to the theological scheme in which he works, in whose perspective many local puzzles appear in a fresh light. As noted already, saying this does not commit us to ascribing to Augustine a denial of the possibilities of thinking philosophically or a methodological prohibition against beginning from anywhere except Christian doctrine. But it does mean acknowledging that, at least in the works of his maturity, he thinks about the human condition, about epistemology, about self-awareness and so on, within the framework of a metaphysic whose structuring principles are grounded in beliefs about the threefold life of God and the events of Jesus' life and death and resurrection. If he did no more than meditate on these events as preacher and teacher, he would still be an outstanding figure for the Christian tradition; but he would not have the compelling interest he evidently does for those outside

---

[39]For some more nuanced (and not uncritical) discussion of Augustine on authority, see E. A. Clark, 'Distinguishing "Distinction": Considering Peter Brown's Reconsiderations', *Augustinian Studies*, 36.1 (2005), pp. 251–64, and Robin Lane Fox's response in the same issue, pp. 265–76.

that tradition. But if he were only an analyst or a phenomenologist of human consciousness, what is most distinctive about his overall achievement would be obscured.

Essentially, what Augustine is doing is to demonstrate (as one critic said of one of Marilynne Robinson's novels) that Christianity is something that can be *thought with*: not a hermetically sealed set of 'doctrines', nor a faintly religiously inflected philosophy, but a coherent narrative of human growth into divine communion in which issues about time, responsibility, reciprocity, self-deceit, self-awareness, public virtue and personal integrity can be illuminated. For the contemporary reader, this is perhaps Augustine's greatest importance: what he has to say specifically on exegesis or Christology is significant and intellectually serious; but what is most engaging and challenging is the sense of being in the company of a thinker whose doctrinal convictions open unexpected vistas on questions that are not narrowly theological. In other words, he shows theology at work in the shaping of *wisdom* – both in its broader meaning of discerning, patient assimilation of our environment, and in his own more specialized sense of attunement to the eternal life of the Trinity. If these chapters have conveyed something of how Augustine sustains such a vision, they will have served their purpose.

God in Search: A Sermon

*For this my son was dead, and is alive again;
he was lost, and is found.*
(LUKE 15:24)

A Sermon preached for the 1600th anniversary of Augustine's conversion in St John's Dublin, 1987

The gospel reading shows us a God who goes in search of his own; a God urgent to find and bring home what is lost. A great Welsh Calvinist preacher of two generations ago was fond of saying that the Bible said little or nothing about the human search for God and a great deal about God's search for us: the first question in the Bible, he would remind his listeners, was, 'Adam, where are you?' And in that other, Easter garden, Mary Magdalene turns to ask a stranger where her Lord is, only to discover that he has come and found *her*, come back from death and hell to find and call her and draw her with him to his Father and her Father.

If there was one aspect of the gospel that Augustine understood and pondered more than all others, it was this. We can, if we like, read his *Confessions* as if it were the story of a man in search of God – and so it is, at one level. But more deeply it is a story of God in search of his lost child. Augustine asks again and again, as he recalls this or that incident, 'Where were *you*, my God?' He knows that, invisibly, God has been seeking him, urging him homewards, at every turn, waiting disguised in each person and circumstance Augustine meets, and finally, one hot afternoon in Milan, calling to Augustine in the voice of a child singing to itself in a garden and once and for all breaking open the hard shell of fear and self-distrust. 'You cried aloud and broke through my deafness . . . you touched me and set me on fire with longing for your peace.' God knew what he was looking for long before Augustine did; and that has always been at the heart of Augustinian Christianity.

This may sound strange to some readers of Augustine. Is he not also the great celebrator of human desire for God, the restless search of the heart? Of course; but until God has come in search of us, our quest is doomed: we are frustrated and disappointed in what we try to satisfy ourselves with, and we create idols and fantasies to save ourselves from emptiness and so deepen our bondage and anger and misery (it is like drinking sea water to quench our thirst). So it is unless and until God meets our longing out of his own love for us, setting us free to love and desire what is real, what is true. We do not cease to be restless ('we shall not cease from exploration', as one modern lover of Augustine has put it), yet our restlessness is now grateful expectancy, a ceaseless openness to the hidden God who now as always waits for us, speaking in the beauty and terror of things, in the endless disclosures and concealments and deeper disclosures of the hearts of those we love.

Open-eyed expectancy: that is how our desire, our search for God, works *when he has already found us*. As our reading from the *Discourse on Ps* 148 makes clear, God is served and sought *in*, not away from, our involvement in the search for right living with each other: he is to be sought and 'expected' in the face of the stranger, the critic, the outsider, the enemy. God is allowed to come to us where and as he wills. The trouble with putting the human search for God at the heart of things is that it can lead to a self-important, individualistic religiosity that talks glibly about 'my spiritual journey' as a thing in itself, a fascinating exercise in a specialist activity, a very elevated hobby; it can present the Religious Quest as something only rather tangentially related to that comprehensive, clear-eyed expectancy of God in *all* our experiences and encounters that Augustine at his best points to. We *need to know* God has found us, God has taken the initiative: or (like Augustine before his conversion) we shall toy endlessly with interesting systems and techniques for self-improvement while failing to grow in love and attention and compassion.

When we know that God *wants* us – as we are and where we are – we shall be able to go through the alarming and sometimes terrible waste of experiences before us in the hope of meeting the same timeless welcome ('our home does not fall down if we are out of doors', he wrote).

So the conviction that God's search for us comes first is something that has a sharply practical focus. Let yourself trust in that assurance – from scripture and Church, from the lives of the converted – and you are set free to give the world the right sort of attention: a listening for God in patience and openness, a liberty to step forward and risk action and involvement because God waits to be gracious; at every moment he will accept what we are, where we are. We shall be free too from the search of a religious system tailored to our fears, needs or fancies. The truth has come to us – not in a system, but in a call, God's call to Adam, and the Risen Christ's to Mary, and the little child in the next door garden. Truth has come, and is known and received by love because love shows it. *O aeterna veritas et vera caritas et cara aeternitas* – O everlasting truth and truthful love and lovely everlastingness!

But what does it mean to say that God *wants* us? Does the eternal God need us? No, Augustine would firmly say: the miracle is that, although God does *not* look to us for the fulfilment of his being, nor use us to attain his goals, yet he pours himself out to us in causeless mercy. God is not like us, moving through time to fulfilment, realizing purposes through change and growth. He cannot need us; he has no aims as we have. So, says Augustine, we must think of him as 'using' us not for his good but for ours: God's is the only love that is utterly without self-regard (there is nothing in it for him), utterly directed to the other. He seeks us, urgently, relentlessly, passionately, out of the changeless movement of a love that seeks the joy and fulfilment of everything in its createdness and limitation. God 'needs' only to be himself, the radiant diffusion of a love that, in the Trinity, is enough to itself, yet overflows always into the life of what is not God.

Again this is a practical doctrine. We learn that the very nature of love, in its source in God, is a gift and a care that has nothing to do with profit and individual gratification; nothing to do with the warm feeling we have for people *like us*, people who don't threaten or challenge us. It is bound up with that clear-eyed openness of hope towards the stranger, the enemy, that we have seen to be the fruit of God's finding of us. God loves us for no purpose but our life and flourishing: we do not first have to become acceptable. By that love we are set free for trust and risk; and our love begins to reflect God's. The person who has by God's own charity come to live in charity to those who are strangers, who seem to threaten and oppose, such a person has become the living image of God he or she was made to be: a sign to all that there is at the centre of things a power that overcomes our terror and guilt and resentment towards each other. Only on this ground is true reconciliation possible – between black and white, or capitalist and socialist, or Catholic and Protestant: not that we have suddenly become agreeable to each other, become *like* each other; but that the self-forgetting love of God sets us free to be vulnerable to those who are still strange and dangerous. There is no change without that risk. Just as God himself risks rejection from us, so we have no guarantee that our love will prevail; but just as God is never overcome by this rejection, but waits unchanged, so his love in us remains. The way of reconciliation is, for us, a way of pain and uncertainty, not of suddenly finding our enemies our friends: it is only possible for those who have truly opened their hearts to expect to find the God they know waits eagerly for them in every moment.

> Christ beneath me, Christ above me,
> Christ in triumph, Christ in danger,
> Christ in hearts of all that love me,
> Christ in mouth of friend and stranger.

And when Augustine says, in a much-misunderstood passage, that we must 'use' those we love for the sake of God, not love them as ends in themselves, he is *not* saying that all our special human loves are just instruments to be left behind. He is warning us against two distortions of love. We can love another person because they serve our private purposes, we can 'use' them for our own gratification; or we can make them an idol, we can tie ourselves up in them completely, invest all our expectations and fantasies in them. Both are destructive. I must learn to love in freedom: to love the other person without struggling to swallow them up or longing to *be* swallowed up in them. And only the love of God makes this possible. Each man and woman is defined by relation to God, finally; I can't lay down for you your everlasting destiny, nor you lay down mine – that is the sense in which no human being can be an 'end' for another human being. So we must love each other as creatures on the way to God: I must love you as one who is being called and shaped by God, I must leave you free for God. If I can do this, I shall be growing in Godlike love, a love that loves what is really *other* than itself and has no thought of absorbing everything into its own needs. This is how we 'use' the love of others to grow in the love of God – language that Augustine himself was unhappy with and later abandoned; but the insight is sound. The love of God alone sets us free from the terrible urge to possess or be possessed by others – from suffocating jealousy, manipulation or self-abasement. The love of God makes friendship possible – the relation of persons who are happy in each other's difference, in each other's freedom.

So if we can hear what Augustine says to us about the initiative of God in everything, God's untiring search for us and his completely unself-regarding love, we hear the good news of Jesus Christ. Controversy, stress, haste and bitterness could lead Augustine into strange paths, distorting his own insights in the doctrine of the predestination of only a tiny number of the human race; but that must not blind us to the Christian sanity of the vision underlying even these caricatures of the truth. The gospel still sounds through: at the heart of everything is a love that can bridge all difference and enmity, whatever the cost, however long the waiting, however hard and bloody the search for the lost. This is what is poured out for us and in us in Jesus; and we are set free by the assurance that nothing can deflect or weaken such a giving. As free men and women, we may shed some of that light in our relations, as persons, as church communities, as nations: we can make each other free by the risky promise of friendship, the friendship of those who can live with the alarming gulfs of uncertainty that separate us (as Augustine knew so well). Once allow those gulfs to dominate your vision and dictate your action, and you will never know truly creative love. In the world we know, the world of widening gulfs, hardening enmity, violence and suspicion, this is good news we must never cease to proclaim. From over the wall which traps us in our various social paranoias we must hear the voice that cries, 'Pick it up and read! Pick it up and read!' Read the record of God's mercy in Scripture and in the stories of the triumphs of his grace in the saints; read and be moved to trust and action and growth. 'You know what hour it is, how it is full time now for you to wake from sleep.'

Index

absence 13, 18, 83, 91, 126, 152
   of God 5, 9, 28
   language and 2, 6, 8, 55
anthropology 111, 156, 163, 168, 187, 192
Arendt, Hannah 102, 103, 104, 119, 196, 204
   Augustinian love 191–2, 199
   public realm 107–10, 124, 125
atomistic personalism 110–11
autobiography 3, 15–18
   and truth 16, 17–18
   see also selfhood
Ayres, Lewis 188

Balthasar, Hans Urs von 28
Bathory, Peter 110, 123, 125
beauty 57, 62, 64, 66, 75, 93
   and creation 70, 72, 91
Behr, John 189
biblical references
   Acts of the Apostles 146
   Colossians 29
   Genesis 59
   Luke 207
   Mark 146

   Matthew 27, 146
   Song of Songs 47
   Wisdom, Book of 62–3
   see also Psalms
Brown, David 185n13
Burnaby, John 178, 185

Cameron, Michael 38
Cappadocian theology of trinity 185n13
caritas 11, 13–14, 16, 109, 143, 198–9
   Christ and 11, 49, 52, 54–5
   and Christian formation 47–8, 49, 51–3, 54, 125
   sapientia and 149, 152, 177–9, 180
   and trinity 160, 161, 162, 168, 169, 177–9, 180, 182, 184
Cavadini, John 21–2
Charry, Ellen 74
Christ 75–6, 128–9, 198–9, 200
   and *caritas* 11, 49, 52, 54–5
   and death 45, 49, 50, 55, 146, 150
   in Psalms 25–40, 133–4
   and *sapientia* 11, 142–3

as *signum* 49, 52
unity with Church 145–6
see also incarnation; trinity
Christology 14–15, 40, 137–8,
    141–53
  of humility 29–31
  and trinitarian thought 187–8
Church 30, 38, 47, 49, 52, 77, 98–9,
    122, 204
  and coercion 118
  as community 108, 191
  life of 31–2, 184
  and love 192, 199
  and self-knowledge 12, 13–14
  and state 126–8
  unity with Christ 145–6
Cicero (Marcus Tullius Cicero) 111,
    115, 121, 122
citizenship 109–10
Clement of Alexandria 72
cogito 155–6, 189
commonwealth 30, 111–14, 120–1,
    122, 123
communities 126–7
  Church as community 108, 191
  households 108–9, 117, 119–20,
    121
  political 119–20
Confessions 34, 35, 36, 37, 49–50,
    151, 152
  confession of God 3–4
  context of 4, 23–4
  creation 60–2, 65, 68–9, 70–1
  evil 82, 92

incarnation 45
love and loss 192
nature of 3–5
Neoplatonism 131–2
sapientia 142–3
time and self-awareness in 1–24
consciousness 2–3, 7
creation 58, 59–78
  beauty and 70, 72, 91
  desire and 73, 74
cross 49, 54
Cyrilline theology 142–3, 153

Dante Alighieri 197
De civitate Dei 30, 65, 79, 94,
    149n11, 168–9
  evil 92
  politics and the soul 107–29
De doctrina Christiana 27, 35,
    39–40, 151
  language 41–58
  use of creatures 83–4
De Genesi ad litteram 63–4, 92,
    118n39
De Genesi adversus Manichaeos
    62–3
De magistro 40, 56–7
De natura boni 92
De re publica (Cicero) 111
De trinitate 14, 23, 35, 67, 134–5,
    149n11, 150–1, 152, 168–9
  divine *humilitas* 144
  justice 160
  sapientia (wisdom) 171–90

self-knowledge 155–7
summary reconstruction of
    argument of later books
    179–80
unity 145–6
death 5, 55–6, 94, 107, 121–2, 193–4
    of Christ 45, 49, 50, 55, 146, 150
Descartes, René 60n4, 155–6, 189
desire 7–10, 33, 77, 86, 105, 126,
        143, 149n11, 157–8, 167
    deferred 151
    and doctrine of creation 73, 74
    and evil 83, 88, 90, 104
    and existence 81
    for glory 115–16
    longing for God 41–58, 65–7,
        96–7, 112, 139, 144
    persona and 147
    and self-knowledge 101
    sexual desire 7–8
    unfulfilled desire 32
distension 1–2
divine commonwealth 30
divine truth 56
Dodaro, Robert 128–9
Donatism 98
Drobner, H. R. 141
dualism 8, 60, 72
    and evil 95–7

Enarrationes in Psalmos 26–30,
    31–2, 142, 146, 147, 208
equality 108, 117: *see also* inequality
eros 5, 169, 184

evil 65, 69, 77–8, 79–105, 131
    desire and 83, 88, 90, 104
    and dualism 95–7
    existence and goodness 80–7
    moral personality 87–91
    nature of 10
    plenitude, principle of 91–5
    and rationalism 95–7
    tragic, possibility of 95–101
existence 32, 61, 75, 76, 110–11, 178,
        181–2
    and goodness 80–7
    social existence 102–3, 129, 193

Fedrowicz, Michael 38
Figgis, J. N. 110, 118n39, 121
Flogaus, Reinhard 189

glory: desire for 115–16
God
    absence of 5, 9, 28
    confession of 3–4, 18–19
    difference of 49, 51, 53
    and giving 182–3
    image of 136, 173–6, 180–1,
        195
    and language 132, 133
    longing for 41–58, 65–7, 96–7,
        112, 139, 144
    and mind 86–7
    reality of 7, 8–11
    search for us 207–11
    union with 58n29
    see also trinity

goodness 98–100
  existence and 80–7
grace 26, 29, 37, 75, 99, 143, 191, 195, 201, 205
  and community 77, 104–5, 193, 199
  and *sapientia* 175, 181–2, 185
Gregory of Nyssa 184–5
Gregory Palamas 189

Hanby, Michael 75–7
Hankey, Wayne 23n32, 58n29, 190
harmony 62, 64, 144–5
Harrison, Carol 56–7
Hartle, Ann 17
Hartman, Geoffrey 51, 53
Hick, John 80–2, 91–2, 93
hierarchy 59–60, 72, 74, 85, 92–4, 96–7, 114, 115, 117–19, 122–3
holiness 33–4, 138, 139, 159
Holy Spirit 175–6, 182–4, 186: *see also* trinity
Homilies on the First Epistle of John 198
human heart, depths of 32, 35
human identity 144, 146
humility 33, 35, 49, 151, 152
  and *caritas* 48
  Christology of 29–31
  divine *humilitas* 144

imperialism 121
incarnation 12, 13, 20, 27, 30, 31, 34, 45–6, 105, 131–2, 141–53

  and humility 35
  sapientia and 142–3
inequality 92–3, 108, 117, 157
injustice 114, 117
interpretation 54–5, 56
introspection 35

Jeanrond, Werner G. 191–2, 196, 199, 201–2
Jesus, *see* Christ
justice (*justitia*) 93, 113, 114, 116–17, 121, 122, 128–9, 158–60, 168–9, 174–5, 177

Kant, Immanuel 196
Kany, Roland 188, 189–90
koinonia 72–4

language 18, 30, 41–58, 139
  and absence 2, 6, 8, 55
  about divine *humilitas* 144
  God and 132, 133
  religious 34, 39–40, 41
  res and *signum* 41–58
  and understanding 135
Le Blond, J.-M. 141, 142, 143, 149
liberation theology 74
libido dominandi 115, 117, 118, 119, 123
loss 13
  love and 192–4
  self and 5–6
  and virtue 100

Louth, Andrew 39
love 44, 56, 57, 72–6, 139–40, 149,
    160–4, 165, 175, 177–80,
    191–206, 208–11
  Church and 192, 199
  Holy Spirit and 182–4, 186
  knowledge and 54
  and loss 192–4
  sapientia and 183–4

McFague, Sallie 59–60
Margerie, Bertrand de 28n5
Markus, Robert 110, 112n18,
    113n22, 118, 120n11, 123, 127
Marrou, Henri-Irénée 126–7
Mathewes, Charles 4, 5, 102–4
matter 59, 61–2, 67–9
memory 2, 17–18, 36, 135, 153,
    194–5
Merton, Thomas 48
Milbank, John 127–8
mind 4, 9, 10, 35, 85, 138, 139–40,
    186
  and body 8
  God and 86–7
  mental activity 157–8, 165–6,
    180–1
  nature of 136
  and trinity 136–7
moral knowledge 159–60
moral personality: evil and 87–91
Morgan, Edward 57
mortality 55
mourning 5–6

natural theology 53–4
Nazianzen, Gregory 15–16
Neoplatonism 10, 58n29, 131–2
Niebuhr, Reinhold 102, 103–4
Nussbaum, Martha 21, 96, 202–4

O'Connell, R. J. 57n23
O'Donovan, Oliver 44n7

Paul the Apostle, saint 72
peace 90, 119, 121
Pelagianism 75–6, 98, 168
peregrinatio 144
Persius (Aulus Persius Flaccus) 114
persona 38, 137–8, 147–9
  unitas personae 134
personam agere 133, 147
personam sustinere 133, 147
Phillips, D. Z. 105n48
Platonism 50–1
pleasure 7, 8, 9
plenitude, principle of 91–5
Plotinus 63, 69, 169
politics and the soul 107–29
pride 11, 50, 112, 115
Primavesi, Anne 59–60
private realm 107–8
Psalms 146
  Psalm 22: 28
  Psalm 100: 39
  Psalm 140: 27
  Augustine as interpreter of
    25–40
  Christ in 25–40, 133–4

unification of divine/human
voices 26–9
see also *Enarrationes in Psalmos*
public realm 107–17, 124, 125
definitions of 111–14

Rahner, Karl 201–2
rationalism: and evil 95–7
relatedness 13
res and *signum* 41–58, 143, 196,
200–1
resurrection 45, 52, 54, 55, 144, 146,
150
Rose, Gillian 202
Rousseau, Jean-Jacques 17–18

salvation 29, 76, 138, 153
Sands, Kathleen 80, 95, 97–8, 99,
100–1
sapientia (wisdom) 11–12, 134–5,
136, 138
and *caritas* 149, 152, 179–80
Christ and 11, 142–3
and incarnation 142–3
and love 183–4
and trinitarian theology 171–90
scientia (practical knowledge) 135,
138
self: and loss 5–6
self-alienation 10
self-awareness: time and 1–24
self-knowledge 10, 12–14, 22–3,
132–3, 181–2
Church and 12, 13–14

and *cogito* 155–6
desire and 101
paradoxes of 155–70
self-relatedness 13
selfhood 5–7, 14–15, 18, 20–2
sexuality 7–8
signs 40
res and *signum* 41–58, 143, 196,
200–1
souls as 34–7
sin 65n12, 93–4, 97, 99
slavery 117–18
souls
history of 25, 27
nature of 10
politics and 107–29
as signs 34–7
soul–body dyad 145, 150
Stock, Brian 25
Studer, Basil 188
subordination 59, 86, 117–18
suffering 27–8, 29

Taylor, Charles 22
Theodosius I, Roman emperor 120
Thérèse of Lisieux 48
thinking 2, 85, 168, 190n26
time 68
definition of 1–2
future 1–2, 17, 33, 55
and goodness 98
past 1–2, 17–18
present 1–3, 12, 18, 33
and self-awareness 1–24

Tractatus Logico-Philosophicus
    (Wittgenstein) 66
tragic, possibility of 95–101
transfiguration 34, 55, 101, 141, 153
trinitarian pluralism 186–7
trinity 13, 75, 134–40
    and *caritas* 160, 161, 162, 168,
        169, 177–9, 180, 182, 184
    and *sapientia* 171–90
    see also *De trinitate*
truth 8–9, 10, 13, 17–19, 22, 40, 50
    autobiography and 16, 17–18
    divine 56

understanding 40, 105, 135, 194–5
    definition of 2, 17
    language and 135
    of self 18, 20

unity 148, 150, 153
    De trinitate 145–6
    unitas personae 134

van Bavel, Tarsicius 141, 149, 187
virtue 63, 100, 110–12, 115

war 121–2
Wetzel, James 20, 21
willing/will 135, 194–5, 204–5
wisdom 55, 58n29, 63, 132, 134, 141–53
    and *caritas* 149
    and virtue 63
Wittgenstein, Ludwig 66, 166

Young, Frances 15, 16

About the Author

Dr Rowan Williams was Professor of Divinity at Oxford before becoming Bishop of Monmouth in 1992. After ten years as Archbishop of Canterbury, he became Master of Magdalene College, Cambridge in 2013, and is internationally well-known as a theologian, poet and commentator on current affairs.

Rowan Williams's previous books include:

Choose Life: Christmas and Easter Sermons in Canterbury Cathedral
Dostoevsky: Language, Faith and Fiction
Faith in the Public Square
Lost Icons: Reflections on Cultural Bereavement
Teresa of Avila

The Edge of Words: God and the Habits of Language